JOURNALS FROM A WARRIOR'S MOTHER

THE FIGHT

Chrissy L. Whitten

Copyright © 2021 by Chrissy L. Whitten

All rights reserved. No part of this publication may be reproduced, distributed or transmitted in any form or by any means, without prior written permission.

Chrissy L. Whitten
www.chrissylwhitten.com

Publisher's Note: This is a narrative nonfiction memoir. The events and conversations contained in this book have been documented to the best of the author's ability.

All scripture quotations, unless otherwise indicated, are taken from the Holy Bible, New International Version®, NIV®. Copyright © 1973, 1978, 1984, 2011 by Biblica, Inc.™ Used by permission of Zondervan. All rights reserved worldwide. www.zondervan.com. The "NIV" and "New International Version" are trademarks registered in the United States Patent and Trademark office by Biblica, Inc.™

Scripture quotations marked (ESV) are from The Holy Bible, English Standard Version® (ESV®), copyright © 2001 by Crossway, a publishing ministry of Good News Publishers. Used by permission. All rights reserved.

Cover design by Tammy S. Edwards & Chrissy L. Whitten
Illustrations copyright © 2021 by Tammy S. Edwards
Photographs on pages 46, 47, 49, 50, 245, 267, 268, 319, 320, and 323 by Kelli Marone, NILMDTS Affiliated Photographer
Monthly birthday graphics on pages 78, 162, and 216 by Darla Baker-Hurst
Author portrait on page 349 by Casey Linde Photography
Remaining photographs by Chrissy L. Whitten
Edited by Staci D. Mauney, prestigeprose.com
Interior formatting by Danelle G. Young, danelleyoung.com
Book Layout © 2016 BookDesignTemplates.com

The Fight/ Chrissy L. Whitten. -- 1st ed.
ISBN 978-1-7365322-0-1 (paperback)
ISBN 978-1-7365322-1-8 (e-book)

DEDICATION

God,
  I would be nothing without You! Thank You for never giving up on me, continuously reminding me to work on this book project, and for providing everything I needed along the way.

Michael, Lilian Grace, Piper Allegra, and Daphne Mae,
  I love living life out loud with each of you. I love you to the moon and back and for all eternity!

Family, friends, and divine appointments,
  Keep moving forward and trusting Him no matter what!

Nelle Swindell,
  Promise kept!

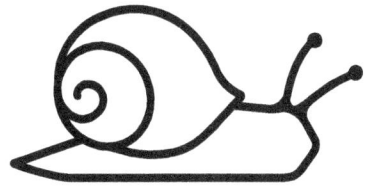

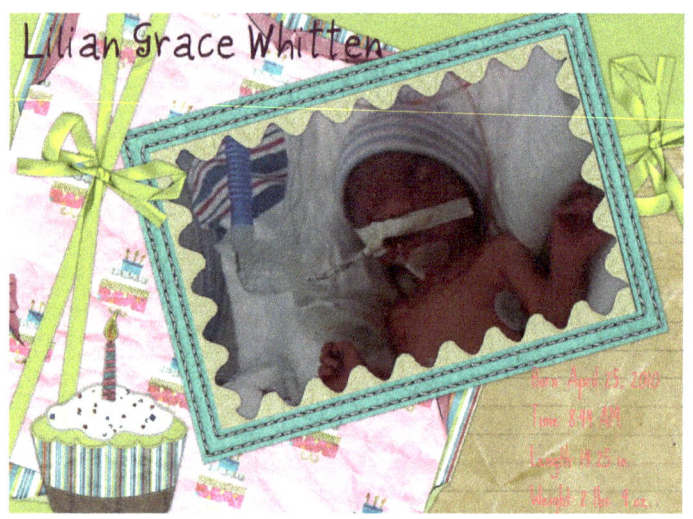

A Warrior Princess is born.

INTRODUCTION

First things first—pray! Pray that God will use this book to help guide, protect, and direct you through your journey no matter if you are high on the mountain viewing the whole world or in the deepest valley looking up and longing for the mountaintop view. Either place takes energy, renewal, balance, learning lessons, and processing as you face what comes your way on the daily walk in life.

This book is not meant for everyone. God knows exactly who needs to read this book to meet their needs. I think that's where people get off on the wrong foot sometimes. We have expectations that someone or something will fulfill what we each need. When those needs are not met, disappointment and frustrations come into play. Keep this in mind when you read this book!

If this book does not meet your needs right now, I pray God will bring you another tool to help meet those needs. Now, that being said, I would like to invite you on a ride I took years ago. Along the way, I wrote whatever was on my heart. I've included titles of songs that spoke to me at the time. I created a playlist of those songs, and you can find them at the following link:

https://open.spotify.com/playlist/0m5jszKtvcesvGL5n2y81m?si=aab622828c544a19

May you find useful information from a mother who is on a journey that involved surviving ginormous storms, climbing mountains of various sizes, withstanding the flames of fires, and walking through valleys below. May you see God woven in every step of my journey. See His light always. I am human. You are human. Buckle up, keep tissues close, and let God work on and through you. Let go and let God! Love from a Warrior's Mother, Chrissy

CARINGBRIDGE

Lilian Grace's story began on the CaringBridge website. We created it to keep friends and family updated about our little miracle, Lilian Grace Whitten. We encouraged friends to visit the site often to read the latest journal entries, look at the photo gallery, and write notes in our guest book. This journal gives you a glimpse into her life and her impact on us all. Get started by reading the following introduction to our CaringBridge website, *My Story*.

MY STORY

After over five-and-a-half years of trying for a little baby, we thought we'd never conceive a child. We endured the heartbreak of two miscarriages and four treatments at a fertility clinic. We were told we had a 0.45 percent chance. That's not even a one-half percent chance of making a child together! We were devastated, but God had a plan.

In September 2009, Lily began her journey into our family. We had planned to adopt a baby girl that October, but the mother took the baby home from the hospital herself. Confused, I still believed God had a plan. Little did I know that on that very same day, I'd find out I was pregnant. Praise God! It was a miracle!

I was very sick throughout the entire pregnancy. In November 2009, I was lucky enough to go to Greece to walk/run the original marathon path with Lily—her first marathon safely protected inside the womb. Every smell, boat ride, and mile didn't help with the normal pregnancy symptoms. By Christmas, I had grown so large I thought I might be having twins. Lo and behold, the doctors discovered I had a large cyst in my right ovary. In mid-January 2010, Lily and I went through emergency surgery, where I had a nineteen-centimeter cyst, my right ovary, and my right fallopian tube removed.

After staying in the hospital for eight days, I contracted C. diff (Clostridium difficile) and lost twenty-five pounds. The surgery and subsequent illness devastated my body. I struggled to gain back the weight and my strength knowing the baby inside was depending on me. Again, God provided. We survived! Not too long after that, we received more devastating news: we found out Lily had six defects with her itty-bitty heart.

And to top it all off, we had to be on modified bed rest for two weeks due to my placenta and membranes separating. My OB/GYN specialist said we had two to three weeks before my water would break. Well, guess what? My water didn't break, but Lily was born two weeks and two days from when she predicted.

Now, we have a two-month preemie, and we know we're in for a long road. Yet God is providing amazing staff and guidance through their attention to detail in her care no matter her diagnosis and their patience with our endless questions. I praise Him for giving us this fabulous little miracle, who is teaching me each day to be bigger and better in life. She's actually doing circles around me!

UPDATE: As Lilian Grace's mommy, I've decided to keep posting journal entries whenever I feel moved. Lilian Grace earned her wings on Thursday, August 5, 2010, at 6:19 p.m. I hope this will give insight into our grieving process after being touched by such an amazing angel here on earth—my Warrior Princess, Lilian Grace Whitten.

CONTENTS

DEDICATION _____ 3
INTRODUCTION _____ 5
1 › Balance _____ 13
2 › Drawing Close _____ 17
3 › Letting Go _____ 19
4 › Steady On _____ 21
5 › His Leading Hand _____ 23
6 › Little Moments _____ 27
7 › Bigger Picture _____ 29
8 › Overwhelmed _____ 31
9 › To Be a Mother _____ 35
10 › God's Love _____ 37
11 › Purpose _____ 39
12 › Peace _____ 43
13 › Holding On _____ 45
14 › Dedication _____ 47
15 › Beyond the Motions _____ 51
16 › Generational Love _____ 55
17 › Roller Coaster Riding _____ 57
18 › Embrace the Storms _____ 59
19 › Basics to Grow _____ 63
20 › Imprints _____ 65
21 › Step Aside _____ 69
22 › Heart Stops _____ 71
23 › Leaning On Friends _____ 75
24 › One-Month Birthday _____ 79
25 › Checks and Balances _____ 83
26 › Grace and Humility _____ 87
27 › Surviving and Thriving _____ 91
28 › Perspective _____ 93
29 › Freedom _____ 97

30 › Breathe	99
31 › Held	101
32 › Ripples	103
33 › Heart Surgery	105
34 › Walking Around the Chair	109
35 › Reality Check	113
36 › Refinement Through Fire	115
37 › Enduring	117
38 › Release and Relief	119
39 › Prayer Request Granted	123
40 › Unwavering Praise	125
41 › Leap of Faith	127
42 › Noise and Light	131
43 › Imperfect Empathy	133
44 › He Is for Me	135
45 › Still Standing	137
46 › Home	143
47 › Sweet Moments While Resting	145
48 › Survival Mode	147
49 › Slowing Down	151
50 › Gratitude on Father's Day	153
51 › Teamwork	155
52 › Cartoons	157
53 › Proud Parents	159
54 › Two-Month Birthday	163
55 › Faith and a Fundraiser	165
56 › Learn and Grow	167
57 › Triumphant at Church & Home	169
58 › Settling into a Schedule	171
59 › Obstacle/Opportunity	173
60 › Shine Bright	177
61 › Another Round	179
62 › Our Little Firecracker	181
63 › A Mother's Intuition	183
64 › Back to the Hospital	185

65 › Deeper Waters	187
66 › God's Strength	189
67 › Tears and Comfort	191
68 › Five-Pounder Club	193
69 › Dreams, Nightmares, and Grace	195
70 › Central Line Surgery	199
71 › A Date with My Mate	203
72 › Strides and Support	205
73 › Strong Women	207
74 › Worn	211
75 › Three-Month Birthday at Home	217
76 › Powerful Name	223
77 › Momma's Surgery	225
78 › Serenity	227
79 › Blood Transfusion	229
80 › Separation Anxiety	231
81 › Battling Toward True Rest	233
82 › Quarantine Season	235
83 › The Silversmith	239
84 › Calm Before the Storm	241
85 › Rest in Peace	245
86 › Celebration of Life	247
87 › An Angel Earns Her Wings	265
88 › Grief Begins	269
89 › Positive Perception	271
90 › Phantom Feelings in Healing	275
91 › Triggers	279
92 › Proof She Existed	281
93 › A Letter to My Younger Self	283
94 › Divine Direction to Houston	285
95 › A Prayer for Trishtan	293
96 › Compassion for Parents	295
97 › Lily's Platform	297
98 › Between the Bumpers	299
99 › Tears Fall in New York City	303

100 › Reflecting on Balance	307
101 › Crown of Beauty	309
102 › Missing My Cowgirl	315
103 › Dust Off and Rise	321
A NOTE FROM THE AUTHOR	325
BOOK COVER LEGEND	327
MEMORY VERSES	337
PLAYLIST	343
ACKNOWLEDGEMENTS	345
ABOUT THE AUTHOR	349
MORE FROM CHRISSY L. WHITTEN	351
REVIEW REQUEST	354
MORE TO COME	354
CONNECT	354

APRIL 30, 2010

1 › Balance

Today was an intense battle. The major thing was temperature. Lily got so hot, and her poor little heart rate was 220 beats per minute (bpm). All around her, lights flashed and bells clanged constantly, making my heart sink. Needing a break, I went to eat lunch. When I came back, the equipment was quiet, and Lily's heart rate was normal.

A team of doctors and specialists held a cath conference, a meeting of professional minds to review our case, to decide what needs to happen to give Lily the best chance at life. We did not get the results or any feedback yet but are hoping to on Monday or Tuesday. I will post an update when we get that back.

Tonight, she was the opposite—too cold. We gathered up lots of tiny blankets to put on her to get her temp up. Talk about life being one way or the other. Too bad balance is so tough to achieve.

I want to encourage you all to look at your lives and see how you are doing on balance. This is something I've struggled with my whole life. I'm all or nothing. So yet again, my sweet kitty cat, a.k.a. Squeaker, is teaching us how to be better parents and people. Thanks, God, for sending in a relief pitcher—my daughter—to get me in shape!

By the way, her nicknames come from her little cries that sound like a squeak and a kitten. It's precious. Michael took me to eat tonight at the Amish Kitchen, and what did I keep hearing but that beautiful little squeak. Have a good night. Lots of love and prayers for you all.

14   Chrissy L. Whitten

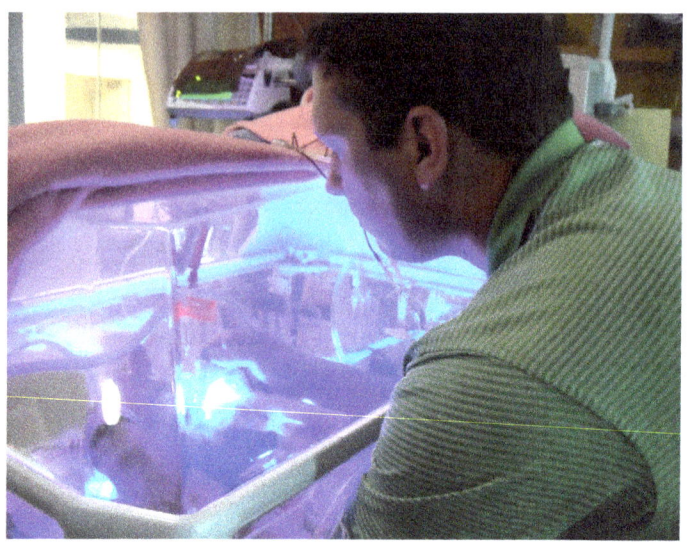

A daddy's comforting touch–Lilian and Michael

♡ *LILY'S VITALS*
They are good tonight.

We read our first devotional tonight from her *One-Minute Devotionals for Girls* covering "Listen and Constant Praise." (I would include the whole devotional, but it's copyrighted.) You are welcome to buy the book and do a daily devotion with us. We will be reading around nine-thirty or ten every night.

The book's author has included a theme for each month. April is "OBEY, OBEY, and OBEY!" Verses include the following: "Listen" (April 25), Deuteronomy 30:20, and "Constant Praise" (April 30), Deuteronomy 32:3–4.

"Listen" covered the fact that we should slow down and listen to God. He speaks to us throughout the day and helps guide us in the direction He has for us. Stop and listen . . . He wants to communicate! Our prayer led us to ask God for help in being still and listening more to Him. What a vital part these two actions can play in our journey with forward movement!

"Constant Praise" covered taking the focus off yourself and your problems and praising Him even for the little things. In our case, this means praising him for Squeaker's size. Even though she is so tiny, there are two other babies smaller than she is. I can't even imagine anything smaller. Remember that God takes care of us always!

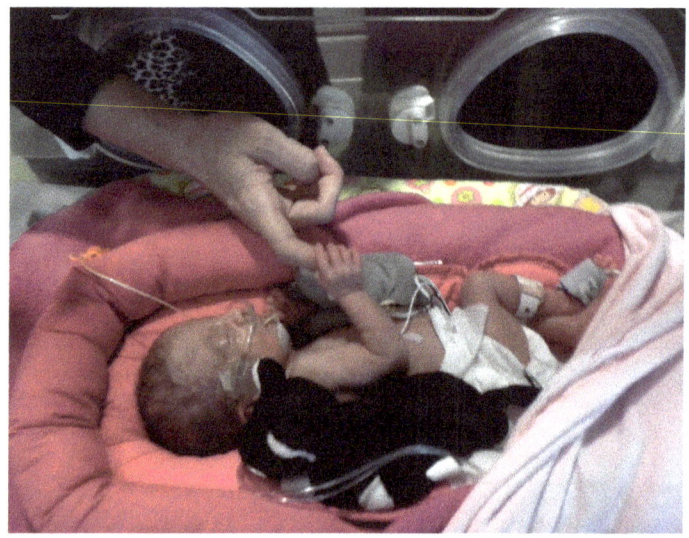

Holding on and drawing closer to what's important

MAY 1, 2010

2 › Drawing Close

♡ LILY'S VITALS
They were great for the most part today. The doctor removed Lily's umbilical arterial line, plus he stopped the phototherapy, a.k.a. blue light, that made her look like an avatar baby. They increased her to 11 mL of mom's milk every three hours. She squeaked to let me know when she was hungry today, and this made my heart happy.

In addition to her good vital signs, we had the most magical moment thus far in our adventure. Michael and I both held our baby girl for the first time using the kangaroo care method. Praise God! My heart was so full I thought I was gonna bust right out of my skin. I can't even describe the euphoric moment. I loved and cherished every minute of holding God's precious little miracle. She squeaked when it was time to switch or be put back in her little homemade womb. The realness has set in. God has brought Michael, Lily, and me so close. Life finally feels complete!

God must get the biggest kick out of creating us and holding us in His arms. He lavishly loves us and helps us through life. I'm blessed to have Him as my heavenly Father. I praise Him for allowing me to experience a small piece of His joy when I hold my own tiny baby.

Another praise for God at the end of the day: Lily digested my milk and gave us two poopy diapers! Yippee!

Tonight's devotional with Lily, "Been There," touched on how Jesus came to earth to walk through life. He is the only human to be perfect. I want to be more like Him.

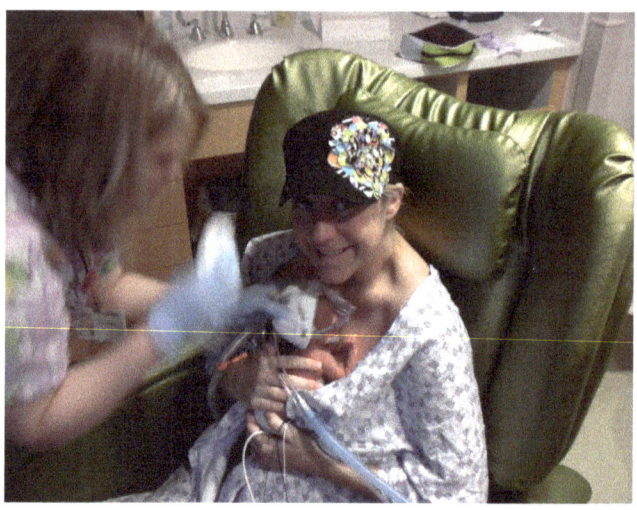

Mommy, overjoyed, holding God's miracle for the first time!

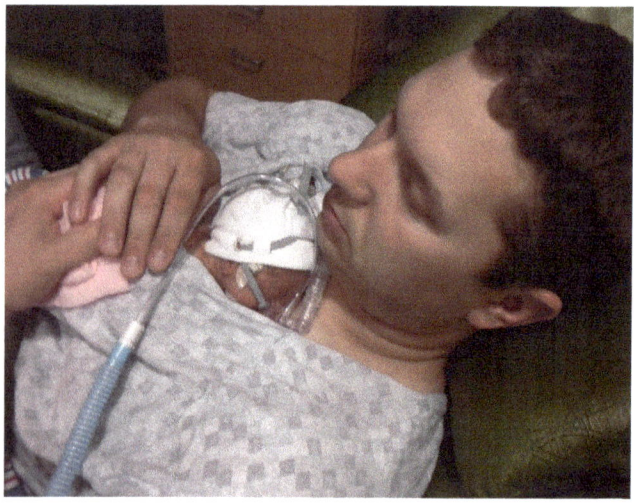

Daddy embracing his baby girl for the first time!

MAY 2, 2010

3 › Letting Go

I left the hospital yesterday for time with my hubby, which kept me busy and distracted from posting. Praise God, I avoided a meltdown like the one last Thursday when Michael tried to bring me home. My chest felt like a load of bricks was on it, and I could barely breathe. I couldn't leave Lily's side. This time, I succeeded in leaving by listening to one of the nurses, who is a godsend. She stressed the importance of getting away every now and then to save my sanity. It wasn't bad. I survived.

So what did I do with my time away? Because I'm healing from surgery, I resisted the urge to deep clean and instead performed some light cleaning to satisfy my clean freak tendencies. Afterwards, I enjoyed going to the baby shower of my dear friend, Sheryl Klenovich.

Enough about us. Here's...

♡ *LILY'S VITALS*
The doctors increased her to 15 mL of mom's milk every three hours. She's made lots of little poopy diapers, which means her digestive system is continuing to work. Yay! She now is on a six-hour rotation with her CPAP machine and nasal cannula, which is incredible and gives her a much-needed break from the machine. She does not like the CPAP machine, and she lets us know by arching her back and flailing her arms. She reminds me of her daddy when he doesn't like something. Drumroll, please! Lily has grown from 14 1/4 to 15 inches. Yippee! And she only lost one ounce, which is amazing. They had told us she might lose 10 percent of her weight. Thank You, Lord, for

> *powerful breast milk! She weighs 2 lbs., 8 oz. We will weigh and measure every Sunday.*

Chest-to-chest, we continued with kangaroo care, which is good for her vitals, and I could seriously do this 24/7. When we use this method, I forget about everything else. All I know is how Lily's heartbeat feels next to mine. I've tried multiple times with no luck to upload pics on Facebook, so I'll keep trying.

I hope you all enjoyed your weekend. I stayed the night at home with Michael and called our nurse only a few times. God is showing me to be patient and trust Him more. It's not easy, but it is worth it. I will post an update tonight after we spend some time with our daughter. Wow, that is like the coolest thing to say...daughter. I may be repeating myself over and over but saying "daughter" makes my belly flutter. Praise God!

MAY 3, 2010

4 › Steady On

Though Michael and I got a lot done today at home, we didn't accomplish as much as Lily did at the hospital. Mondays are big days for checking the progress of her care. Here are some things the doctors did with her today:

> *LILY'S VITALS*
> *Blood gas testing, which shows how her oxygen/carbon dioxide exchange is doing and how stable her respiratory system is.*
>
> *Hemogram to check her hemoglobin levels for her blood count. When they did the last hemogram, she had to have two blood transfusions.*
>
> *Neonatal profile to check electrolytes and such. This gives them an idea of her potassium, sodium, etc., levels. As a result, they are going to add potassium to her milk.*
>
> *Caffeine levels to see if she still needs this treatment for her central apnea challenges.*
>
> *Follow up chest X-ray.*

Her heart rate was really high—over 200—because of so many tests. I placed Lily on my chest in the kangaroo care position because we thought it would lower her heart rate. After starting kangaroo care, her heart rate came down just a little but not as much as usual. Not discouraged, I understood the severity of her day caused her body to react this way. The doctors decided to continue with no visitations for this week. We will re-evaluate next Monday.

Michael and I both got to read to Lily this afternoon. Reading calms both of us, and she really seems to like it. She can sense when we are emotional and stressed, so getting to hear our more calm and relaxed voices is a bonus. Her stats on breathing and heart rate verify her systems' reactions. When her daddy stopped reading, she squeaked, perhaps for more. Almost an hour later, he read Scripture cards by Beth Moore and homemade ones by my girlfriend, Amy Hartling. Watching them, I felt happy and whole.

Helping Michael balance our home and finances kept me away from the hospital again tonight. After almost a month of neglect, our house needed some TLC. Sometimes we take two steps back in order to make any forward movement. God is a wonderful teacher in this kind of dance. We move around the dance floor stumbling, yet God helps us finish each number.

I just got off the phone with Lily's nurse. Her heart rate is still up, but she's doing well. Lily told the nurse through her squeaks that she needs her eight o'clock milk. I guess they got a little behind, but leave it to my daughter to let them know what's up.

Until tomorrow. Good night. Love you all!

MAY 4, 2010

5 › His Leading Hand

My Aunt Sheila sends me uplifting devotionals that speak to what we're going through. One of those devotionals reminded me that obstacles are a way of God getting me to where I need to be with His leading hand.

Dr. Gomez is very happy with Lily's progress. When he strolled into the room for an update, he seemed shocked, impressed, and hopeful with her response to their plan of action. We still have moments that aren't so great, but the overall picture is wonderful! Can I get a praise God? Praise God!

> ♡ *LILY'S VITALS*
> *She is up to 21 mL of mom's milk every three hours with an added nutrient of human milk fortifier (HMF). This is now a full feeding for her. Yay for momma's milk! To know all this pumping madness is paying off makes the pain and inconvenience worth it. They have added potassium to her diet.*

We got to remove her PICC line. Hooray! She hated it and has been trying to rip it out since she got it. She's now getting oral meds. Praise God!

The doctors want to reduce her CPAP therapy time. I know this will make her happy because she really does not like this. Every time they put it back on, she throws a Michael fit!

Lily's heart rate climbed again today, but it's better—and I am gonna believe this for as long as I live—because of some much-needed family time with us. Her heart rate dropped even more after we had girl time consisting of praying, reading, singing/praising, and dancing together. I pray it gets to where they would really like it and extend her time off the CPAP machine. For now, we are six hours on and six hours off the CPAP machine.

Reading takes us to magical places beyond the hospital walls.

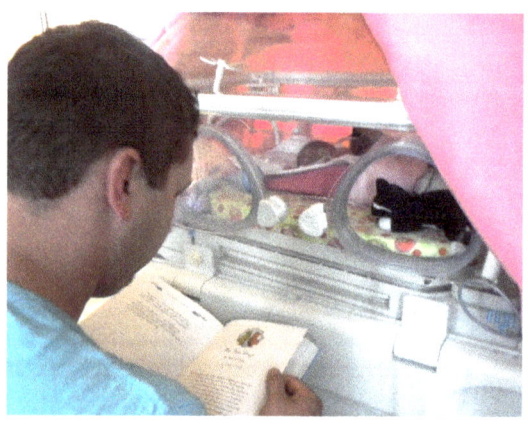

A daddy's voice brings calm when stories are told!

Michael and I took some time away to rest, and while my chest ached from being away from Lily, I'm seeing how important a break is for us. Thank you all for the prayers. I know people are dropping to their knees because of Lily. I hope your faith continues to grow like ours has every day. I could not do this without Michael, Lily, God, family, and friends. We are blessed more than we deserve.

I hope you have a wonderful night's rest. Michael did kangaroo care early, and now I get to after I send this. Praise God for slowing me down so I can enjoy His greatness.

MAY 5, 2010

6 › Little Moments

When Lily's daddy showed up for his breakfast visit, he was surprised to see I had her dressed up in the cutest oversized preemie clothes for the first time. She got too hot, and most were quickly removed. Dr. Gomez increased her to 23 mL of mommy's milk every hour. She did have some reflux today. It wasn't fun cleaning up the mess, and it caused more worry for her overall health. She lost a little weight, weighing in at 2 lbs., 7 oz. We're hoping she gains with the increase in food intake. Pray her system will adjust well. For such a small package, she's producing big diapers.

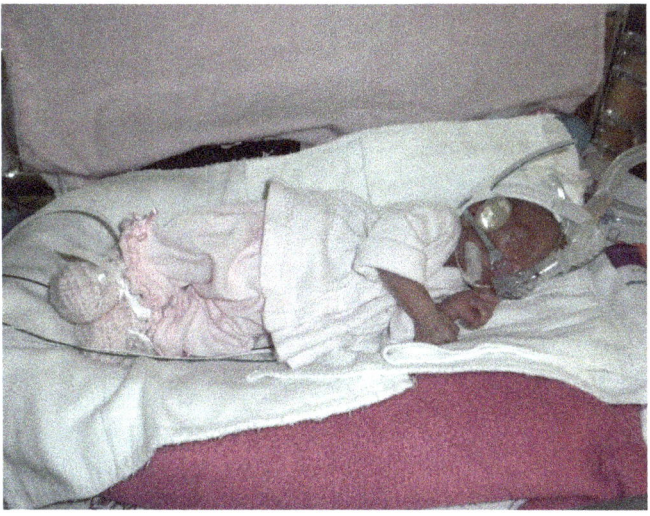

Another first—Lily relaxing in her oversized preemie clothes!

Michael and I each provided kangaroo care for an hour and a half. My session was in the afternoon, and Lily and I both took a much-needed nap. Michael did his session this evening. I think he wanted to sleep, but I was a chatterbox.

They decided to try the CPAP machine twelve hours on and twelve hours off. The increased occurrences of bells and whistles from her CPAP machine make me nervous, but I'll adapt. God has surrounded us with a strong support system, and it's been a nice treat having people from our past want to help.

Lily has another echo scheduled for tomorrow. Hopefully, it will go well. Love you all! Happy Cinco De Mayo!

MAY 6, 2010

7 › Bigger Picture

Talk about having one of those days. It definitely has been one. Lily's tiny heart decided to stay around 200 bpm all day. I'm not sure why it is so high, but it gets to me thinking about how hard she's having to work to be here. I don't want her working so hard she loses more weight. They may not weigh her tonight after all.

She had another echo today. Dr. Gomez left a little bit ago before the results came in. So I'm doing what I do best these days—waiting! This echo checked her whole heart. I pray there's change for the better. How awesome would it be for her not to have heart surgery? Fabulous!

Today, I felt as if I were in an episode of *Grey's Anatomy* or *Private Practice*, minus any doctors in sight or sexy drama. A group of nurses walked down the hallway toward me this morning, making me think of those shows. Come to think of it, it looked more like a scene from *Monsters, Inc.*, when the monsters went to work in slow motion, ready to act. It was entertaining to say the least. They looked hard core and ready for the day. Now, at the end of the day, they have worked their butts off.

Lily and I passed out during kangaroo care for about an hour and a half today. Amazingly, the nurse didn't want to wake us. I love taking a relaxing nap with Lily on my chest.

Good news—she is not going to have to wear the CPAP machine for now. Praise God! Please continue to pray that it stays off because she dislikes it with great passion. Plus, she's becoming quite the piglet. I was pumping and thought they hadn't fed her by the sounds of her squeaks. Surprisingly, only thirty minutes had passed since her five o'clock feeding. She wanted more. That's my girl!

God is reminding me to concentrate on the big picture instead of the little things. I hate dwelling on little things that take up too much time and distract me. I should concentrate on more important issues. So if you find yourself dwelling on petty things, take a step back and glance at the big picture. I'm trying. Love you all!

P.S. Here are two verses from Lily's and my devotional time today: "Try, Try Again," Psalm 73:26, and "Try God," 1 Samuel 17:47. We will fail, but God will not. I'm reminded we are all human and nothing is too large for Him!

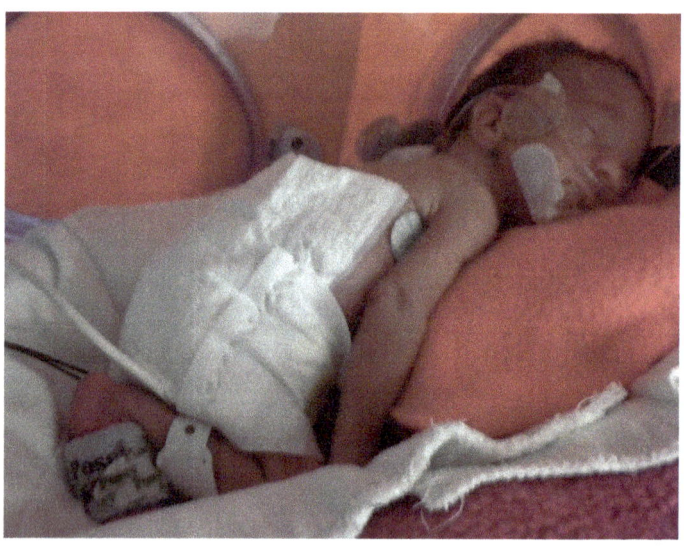

A small part of His big picture

MAY 8, 2010

8 › Overwhelmed

Please do not be alarmed if I miss days updating you. It takes all my strength to type at times. Yesterday, I received the news that Lilian Grace would have her first heart surgery to fix the patent ductus arteriosus (PDA) this next week. So soon! Upon hearing the news, I stepped away for a moment to gather my thoughts. She's so little! Since her poor little heart has been overworking itself this week, we hope the repair will alleviate the problem. For more information about the procedure, visit http://www.nhlbi.nih.gov/health/dci/Diseases/pda/pda_what.html.

Also, the doctors ran tests last night for kidney failure. They started with an ultrasound, and that went well. At midnight, they inserted a catheter, which royally sucked. Through multiple failed attempts, Lily cried and squeezed my fingers in her tiny hands until the nurses finished the procedure. My momma's heart broke watching her, knowing what one of those crummy things feels like as an adult.

More tests are needed, and the date of the surgery is unknown. I left the specific information on a note pad elsewhere. I will update you all for prayers when I know more. Pray God helps her feel no pain while they do all the daily testing and probing.

I've had a couple of bad days. You know those blown-up punching bag clowns that get hit over and over? I feel like one of those, and I keep popping back up for another hit. The last two days, I've felt as if the weight of a 350-pound man was pressing on top of me, trying to bust me. Today, the weight has lifted, and I'm feeling much better.

The girls at my church threw a wonderful baby shower for me. Thanks, girls, for making it so special. Sheryl is going to send me pics, and I'll post on Facebook as soon as possible. We received some fabulous stuff that Lily will love. I can't wait until we can play dress up with the frilly bows and cute outfits.

Michael and I finished our visit with Lily and headed across the street for a free night's stay at the Doubletree. Thank God we won it back in December. We splurged and ordered room service for the first time, taking advantage of some pampering. We enjoyed a free breakfast at the Warren Duck Club. I love hanging out with my superman, especially somewhere this fancy!

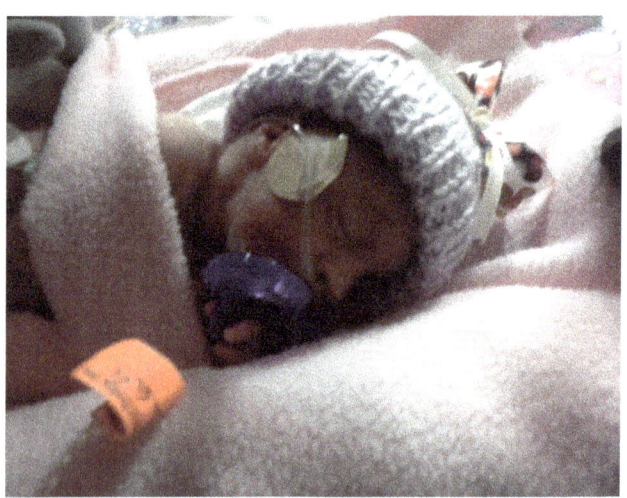

Our Warrior Princess rests peacefully.

I hope you all have a wonderful night. One more thing...I'll never forget the Mother's Day after I miscarried, and my niece went to the front of the church to grab one of the gifts meant for mommies with children. Amazingly, she decided to get a gift for me even though my baby couldn't. This gesture is etched in my heart forever! I have been truly blessed by the outpouring of love from everyone.

Please be patient when we're not quite put together. Staying positive all the time is tough. We are overloaded with information daily. May you experience God's grace and freely give it.

FYI—My sister is designing a shirt to raise funds. The "Pray for a Miracle" shirts for Karen Baker are amazing, and we've been encouraged to do our own. They will have "God Be Big" on them with Lily's name and a verse. I'll post details as soon as we know more. Love you all!

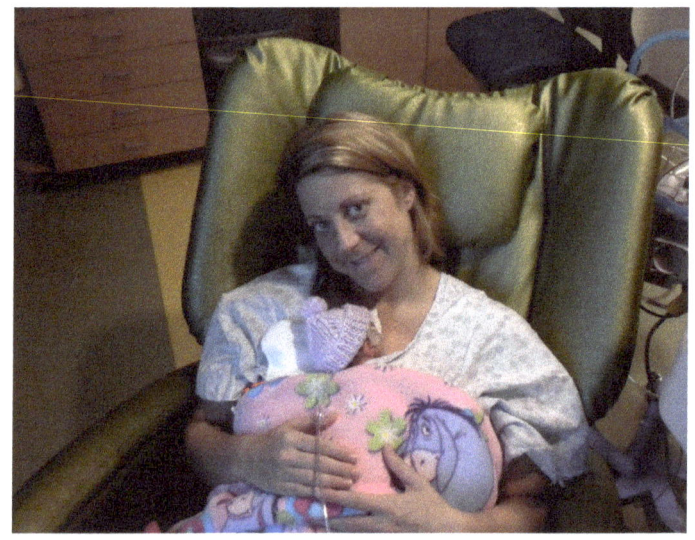

Motherhood feels so good.

MAY 9, 2010

9 › To Be a Mother

God placed the desire to be a mother in my heart at a young age. This led me to work with kids at church and 4-H, where God allowed me to become part of their lives. I was told too many times how wonderful a mother I would be, yet years went by without any children of my own. Seeing those sweet kids every day didn't extinguish my desire, but in fact, heightened it. After Michael and I married, I drove him crazy talking non-stop about my desperate need to become a mother. I brought it up at all hours of the day and night, and I shed countless tears. Many times, I shut myself away in my closet, crying out to God with tears rolling down my face.

All those sorrowful tears from the past have been replaced by joyous ones. To be a mother is the coolest job a woman can have. Even though I've been a mother for only fourteen days and the ride is just getting started, I think I can safely stand behind that statement.

Though our situation is rare, having Lily join our family feels so right, even during the not-so-fun times. I love her so much and would do anything for her, even trade my life. I praise God for giving me the amazing gift of my daughter. I appreciate our Father more for the sacrifice He made in sending His Son to die for our sins. The sacrifice He made was incredible.

♡ LILY'S VITALS

She is doing really well. She gained quite a bit of weight back. Drumroll, please! She weighs 2 lbs., 10 oz. Hooray! She has grown in length as well to 15 ¾ inches. Praise God! My heart soars with this report. She's a rock star and even survived getting blood drawn tonight. She really is a Warrior Princess. (Thanks, Rachel Foley, for that nickname.)

We are waiting for her cardiac doctor to sign off on a date for heart surgery. I will post as soon as we know. Please pray for the prep, surgery, and post-surgery recovery. Her little heart needs to survive each one of these surgeries she faces. Love you all! Thanks for all the awesome words in our CaringBridge guest book. We appreciate it all!

MAY 10, 2010

10 › God's Love

Memory Verse 1

⚔ *"And I pray that you, being rooted and established in love, may have power, together with all the Lord's holy people, to grasp how wide and long and high and deep is the love of Christ, and to know this love that surpasses knowledge—that you may be filled to the measure of all the fullness of God" (Ephesians 3:17–19).*

These verses were on back of a card I bought for Sheryl Klenovich's graduation. We cherish the experience of how wide and long and high and deep is His love. I looked in my Bible for a side note and found a perfect explanation of our journey. We are getting to testify by living out our deeper appreciation for His love that the above verses pour out.

I'd like to challenge you to put Ephesians 3:17–19 on a card. Put it in your car, on your fridge, or anywhere else where you will see it. Memorize it and know God is showing all of us through our experiences and Lilian's just how much He loves us and the magnificence of what He does for us.

> ♡ **LILY'S VITALS**
> *Lily's heart continues to have episodes where it beats too slowly (a.k.a. bradycardia or bradys). I learned the procedure to return her heartbeat and breathing to normal, but I continue to stress. It seems trivial to get your baby's attention through a gentle touch on the shoulder or stimulating them with the sound of your voice, reminding*

them to breathe. Yet these small suggestions create big responses for survival. Praising God to the fullest, she gained another ounce to reach 2 lbs., 11 oz.. Pray she continues to gain weight while I keep pumping that milk! Currently, she is down to one Lasix every twenty-four hours for her heart. She purposefully bradys for the sole purpose of sleeping on her tummy, because she is very much like her daddy in this way. They both love and need their tummy time when sleeping.

We meet with the doctors tomorrow morning at nine to discuss her status and heart surgery. They've been waiting on her genetic test results and consultation from one more doctor. Another baby with worse heart problems is ahead of her. Please pray for this baby boy and his team—for knowledge and the ability to help make him well again. Good night!

MAY 12, 2010

11 › Purpose

Memory Verse 2

⚔ *"And the God of all grace, who called you to his eternal glory in Christ, after you have suffered a little while, will himself restore you and make you strong, firm and steadfast" (1 Peter 5:10).*

Our hearts are full of grief and sorrow because we got sucker punched with news about Lily's genetics yesterday. She has an extra eighteenth chromosome, called Edwards Syndrome. Usually, babies with this syndrome don't survive birth, or if they do survive birth, they don't live more than fifteen days past their birth date. Lily, our Warrior Princess, is completing day seventeen from birth.

Since her life expectancy is unknown, we are choosing to go out in style. I told Michael that we are like rock stars on a world tour. I'm on the drums knocking them out, and he's on the acoustic guitar showing some love. Even knowing the outcome, we see this experience as a blessing and would do it over again. Our parents visited with Lily today, and we are so glad we could share this special time together.

Please do not prolong your sadness. Lily has been a great witness in her short time. She continues to fight the good fight. Michael and I are living out God's glorious will to teach, stretch, grow, and change people for the good through all this. We've seen more people drop to their knees and trust God. We hope her story continues to touch all who hear it.

Does this bring tears to our eyes? Yes, both sad tears and joyful tears. I couldn't ask for anything more than God's blessings throughout. We get to be parents. I've longed to be a mother to my own child for my whole life. How lucky am I to have a Warrior Princess rocking out God's purpose in furthering His kingdom? Wow is all I can say right now because I am in awe of her influence. We even have nurses who come to see her when they aren't working our shift. It's refreshing to know they want to check in and say hi even when they are assigned to different patients or floors of the hospital.

We appreciate the love and support of our family, church, and friends. We couldn't do this without you. Knowing you care and want to help is huge. We are dealing and making our way, so we may not call or ask for something. Remember, we love you very much!

Michael and I have discovered that our past experiences prepared us for this current journey. Praise God that we can finally see a bigger picture for our life. I thank God for all our experiences, good or bad, that have equipped us to be who Lily needs us to be. To learn more about her syndrome, go to http://www.trisomy.org/.

My devotional with Lily from the *One-Minute Devotions for Girls* was about the power of words. His words are powerful, and nothing is bigger. When He speaks things into existence, they exist. His plans will always be bigger and better than our plans. Trust the process and remember His power. He makes all things possible.

I began typing this post earlier this evening. I thought I was doing well until I wasn't. I owe my parents, sister, mother-in-law, brother-in-law, and sister-in-law an apology for my actions and reactions a little bit ago. Something was said, and I cracked. I yelled and threw a little chair, which hit the corner of the wall in the lobby and created a hole in the wall.

I snapped! I tried to remain strong, but I couldn't take any more. I don't want to go down like that. I want to soar and rock this out. Sometimes our emotions can get the best of us. May God help me not to snap like that again. Holding in our emotions is dangerous and can lead to hurt, chaos, and destruction. Remember to breathe, own your emotions, and process them daily.

MAY 13, 2010

12 › Peace

Picture yourself stargazing on a worn bench under a Texas night sky. A cool summer breeze flows over you while the beautiful song "Peace" by Watermark serenades your heart. A great peace overwhelms your spirit and flows into the depths where disappointment, turmoil, frustration, bitterness, brokenness, and sadness slowly get washed away. His peace never runs dry, even during life's uncertainties and the unexpected turns in the journey.

In summer 1999, my life turned upside down in an avalanche of change. It was more than I could take in. Several close family members died that summer, and I faced an internal battle of whether to stay in college or change degrees. I wanted to quit, to give up. In that moment, sitting on an old, worn bench in Marble Falls, Texas, at Camp Champions, I heard this song and surrendered my plans to God, realizing He would take care of me. I didn't quit, even though my heart was broken then just as it is now. God mends the heart that has been ripped, stretched, or crumbled.

We feel peace right now just as I did on that worn bench years ago. It's comforting to have the greatest parent ever believe in us and trust us with Lily. He lets us go through the hard things in order to get us to another level. He equips us!

♡ *LILY'S VITALS*
Despite the intensity of yesterday, we had a beautiful morning together, and she's doing better. I praise God for kangaroo care time and cherish each session because it might be the last. Lily weighs 2 lbs., 13 oz. She lost an ounce from the previous day's weight. She's had some bradys and apnea episodes, although these episodes have been fewer.

Lily and I decided to give her daddy his Father's Day gift early to make it extra special. I love that he's an amazing daddy already and shouldn't have to miss his first Father's Day. He doesn't even realize his own strengths and how special God has made him. He's destined for great things, and he's playing one of his roles today. I'm so lucky to have a godly man leading our household.

I love watching Lily sleep. It's breathtaking. Can I get a "praise God" as loud as you can? Yes, right now! Because He is giving Michael and me more days with Lily than we ever thought possible. I love watching Michael kangaroo care. Daddy-daughter bonding is spectacular. Okay, one more shout out loud...Praise God!

People have asked what they can do for us. One thing you can do is love on your kiddos that are here right now. Enjoy every minute with them. Give them a huge kiss on the cheek and bear hug from Michael, Lily, and me. If you don't have kids, love your life. If you don't like what you see, change it for the better. Knowing we have right now is more precious to me than ever before. We all take things for granted, so start doing the opposite. Appreciate everything, and look for God in it all because He is here waiting to enjoy the ride with you. Good night!

MAY 14, 2010

13 › Holding On

Lily and her grandparents spent some quality time together the past few days. I wish I could give them more time together, but Lily's breathing problems tonight made that difficult. She's been well, but she is limited.

The bells on the machines keep clanging. This leads to overstimulation and more problems. Pray she recovers quickly and has a wonderful day with Pastor Matt Blair, who is performing her baby dedication. We wish we could have a big one, but we will record it and try to figure out how to share with you all. I'm overjoyed we get to do something real and special with her.

> *LILY'S VITALS*
> *She is still on caffeine, which I'm hoping will help with the breathing problems tonight. She had a few bradys earlier today. We didn't weigh her because the nurses decided she should not be touched except for changing her diaper. We will have to wait to weigh her for an update.*

Some fun for today—Lily discovered her tongue and stuck it out to tease us. Plus, though I'm not sure how fun it is for us, she thinks it's funny to hold her breath. She sticks her legs and arms out, stares up at the ceiling, and holds her breath until we rush over. Then she looks at us and starts breathing. Her first attempt at doing this had the nurses, filled with fear and urgency, dropping everything and rushing past me to get to her like a valuable antique was about to crash into a million pieces. I stood frozen trying to figure out my place in all of it. It's annoying with all her breathing problems, yet we joked about her newfound discoveries and ability. With everything happening, the normal parenting things we experience keep us grounded.

Our Warrior Princess keeps moving forward. Continue to pray with us that the Father's will be done, no matter how long it takes or what it looks like.

God is Big, and nothing is too small or too large. I love His understanding and peace. A few people have sent emails or messages stating they are not where we are, and that's okay. We all take different roads, speeds, and processes. Just because I get it now doesn't mean I'll have it together later. All I know is that I've jumped into His arms. My arms are wrapped tightly around His neck, and I'm holding on for dear life. I know that once her last breath is done, I will melt, cry, and lose it, but I pray I'll keep trusting Him and hold on to the peace He's given me. We are strongest on our knees, so drop, talk, stop, and listen to Him. It's fabulous when I do this! Good night!

Let His light shine, Warrior Princess.

MAY 15, 2010

14 › Dedication

Oh, what a day, sweet Jesus! Lilian Grace's baby dedication was more extravagant than I could have envisioned. Thank You, Lord, for giving us this special moment with our baby. Her vitals were remarkable during the ceremony thanks to answered prayers, and she looked like the most amazing Warrior Princess who ever lived.

A beautiful promise and dedication

A professional photographer from Now I Lay Me Down to Sleep (NILMDTS), an organization of volunteers who help families facing situations such as ours, blessed us by catching all the moments of Lily's dedication. Lily experienced the movie star life with paparazzi! She has had her picture taken more than most people I know.

Thanks to Pastor Matt Blair, Jennifer Blair, and our family for being here to cherish such an incredibly rare moment. We even sang "I'm in the Lord's Army" and "Jesus Loves Me" (I always have to give it an added touch ever since hearing Whitney Houston's version from the movie *The Bodyguard*). God is here! We recorded the event and will figure out how to share it with you all soon.

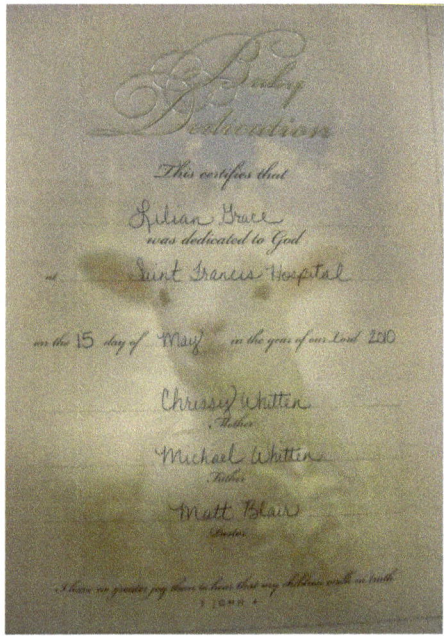

Keepsake for life

Lily and I enjoyed a very fitting, wonderful devotional today about holding on tight and remembering to find constant renewal in Him for our spirits to persevere. When we put our hope and trust in Him, His strength and power will guide us through whatever we face daily. Lily is soaring high and victorious through this life, unaware of her limited time.

I need to cover something before I close. Many have apologized for crying and not keeping it together in front of us, but guess what? Letting your emotions go is good for us. It shows us you care and love us. We all are going through this process together. I know we will be on different cycles, so please feel all your emotions when you feel them. That's God's way of releasing tension from the heart and soul. Michael and I cry at different times. Today was a day of rejoicing for us. I cried later by myself because I was on such a high when I was around everyone. So please show your emotions and love without feeling sorry about what you are feeling and when you are feeling it.

It makes my heart and soul happy to see just how God is changing people through Lily. She lights up the world and is a beacon in the darkness. She rocks! Good night!

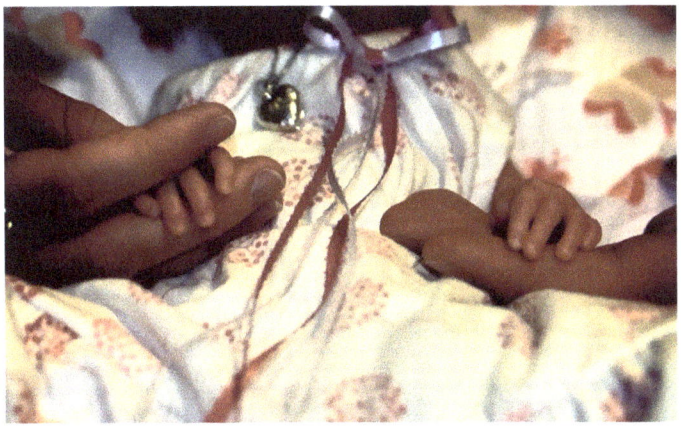

Hand in Hand = Together

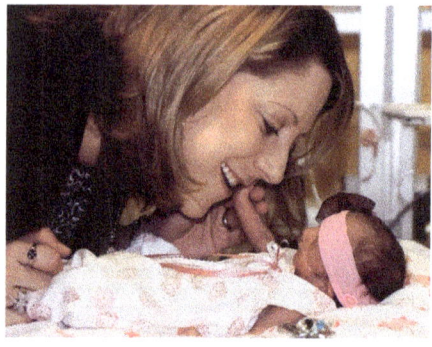

A mother's adoration and care

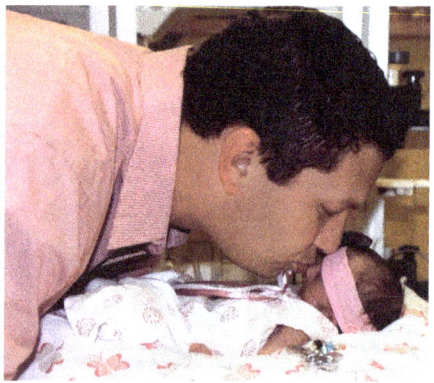

A father's love and protection

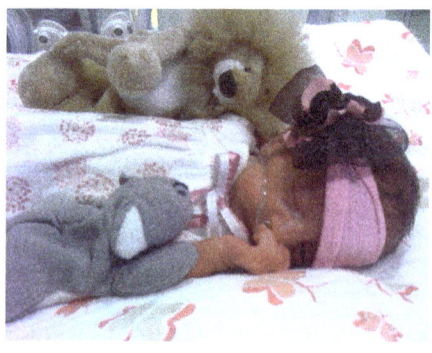

Let her sleep, for when she wakes, she will move mountains.

MAY 16, 2010

15 › Beyond the Motions

I love dearly the strong, emotional song "The Motions" by Matthew West and want to live life to the fullest by facing my fears and feeling all the raw emotions. To live life going through the motions is the opposite of how I want to proceed. Life will always bring heavy, hard things that can weigh us down and deter our purpose. I don't want to back down when it gets hard. I have hope for God's will to be done, whatever that looks like. Even so, I have to admit my heart is breaking tonight.

Lily has needed more oxygen tonight than before. This could mean just a bad night, or it might be the start of her decline. I do well with everything until it feels like she is declining. I try so hard to keep it together, but when it starts to look dark, I almost forget to breathe.

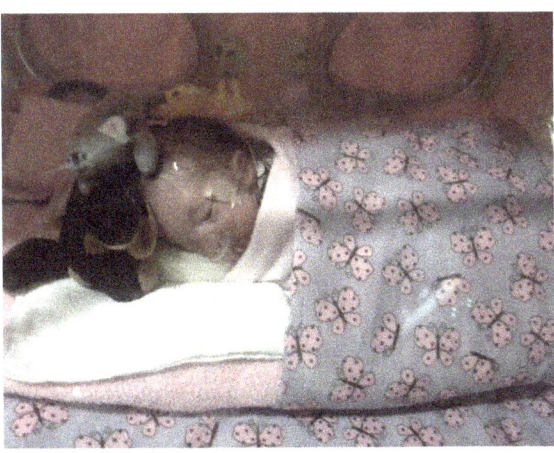

Resting in His strength tonight to keep fighting another day!

I know God's plan is in full swing for Lily. I have to remember that I really only have right now, and I want to cherish every minute. I don't want to go through the motions. I want to live it up and live it right.

I wish everyone could get an extra special Lily moment, but sadly, she can't handle it. We have to manage visits in small increments. She's already a celebrity at the hospital. Everywhere I go around here, people connect her with me. It's rather refreshing to know our story has spread across the hospital.

I'd like to challenge you all not to go through the motions in life. There are too many precious memories to be made...too many stories to be shared...too many moments to love someone. No matter how much this sucks or how long this crazy ride takes, I'm gonna partner with God. I may want to quit sometimes, but I'm reminded of something my basketball coach, Coach Elder, told me numerous times: "Chrissy, you don't always get what you want."

He's so right. I don't always get what I want because it's not about me. It's not even about you. It's about the purpose, the will, and the plan for Lily, Michael, me, and the rest of you. If I had it my way, I'd hold Lily all day long and never let go, but she can only handle twenty minutes to an hour with me and Michael per day. I have to remember it's more than I got with my two miscarriages before her. I never got to meet them, hold them, change their diapers, kiss their cheeks, tell them I love them, or see how God made them to be.

When I reflect on these things, I'm reminded how much God blesses me by drying up my tears and making my heart smile. I love what He's giving us right now. I think when God does decide to call her home, it will just be the beginning for us all. He will inspire us through her story to do bigger and better things, especially when it comes to furthering His kingdom.

♡ LILY'S VITALS
Lily's umbilical cord stump fell off today! Here's her stats for today. Weight: 2 lbs., 15 oz.; length: 15 7/8 in.; head: 27 ¼ cm; and waist: 23 cm.

She's growing, and her spirit is strong. That's just one more reason to praise God. I stand in awe as I watch her. My Warrior Princess is a gift from God for all of us to witness. Please share her story with as many as possible. I'll leave you with a fitting verse given to me by someone I recently met.

Memory Verse 3

⚔ *"The secret things belong to the LORD our God, but the things revealed belong to us and to our children forever, that we may follow all the words of this law" (Deuteronomy 29:29).*

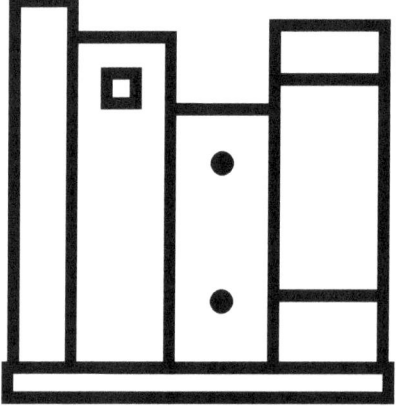

MAY 17, 2010

16 › Generational Love

Today was a special day. Okay, what day isn't these days? My love deepened for this man as he actually changed Lily's dirty diaper. Lily was happy to experience it as her daddy did a fab job! I hope you all get special moments like this.

We must adjust to the sliding-scale outcomes and enjoy the ride regardless. After pouring out my soul through tears this morning, my land legs are back thanks to a friend who allowed me to own my feelings through the vital tool of processing out loud.

> ♡ **LILY'S VITALS**
> Staying at a steady 2 lbs., 15 oz., Lily's heart and breathing stats improved as the day progressed. Dr. Gomez seems to be amazed at our Warrior Princess, and so he should be. We are excited she is eating 25 mL of mommy's milk every three hours.

We know your prayers are helping her fulfill God's purpose. We appreciate the prayers lifted for us! Please remember the other prayer requests needing to be lifted up to Him as God's will continues to play out.

I got a kick out of watching both sets of great-grandparents reading daily devotionals to Lily these past two days. Happiness fills our hearts as we see the precious moments shared between generations, especially Lily's love of listening to us read. Since I am unable to refrain from shopping in the hospital gift shop, I bought Lily more books. I will share our book list for you to gather and read to whomever you wish. Reading is essential no matter what age and stimulates the bonding time we love!

A dear friend emailed a sports-themed piece of soul food called "The Lord's Baseball Game" that matches our current journey perfectly. The lesson taught me that love, faith, and godly wisdom can get us on base, but God's grace will always get us home. We can't get to heaven on our own—we need God's grace and love through our relationship with Jesus Christ to get us there.

I want it stated that if the devil was scared of us before, he must really be shaking now. If not, he should be as masses form with determination not to be moved! Praying for your walk with God! We are blessed with people from all over the world who are sharing their journey as they pray, hope, and walk along with us.

MAY 18, 2010

17 › Roller Coaster Riding

Where do I start while my heart breaks? We can't satisfy anyone's happiness these days. As I've said before, I lack the ability to meet everyone's needs regarding Lily and what they want. By making tough decisions, we have crossed the twenty-three-day mark. Hopefully, everyone will understand that our daughter has guided us through each decision so that we can give her a fighting chance.

> *LILY'S VITALS*
> *She's experienced thirty-five bradys in one day so far. A low heart rate could be a sign of either downhill descent or healing progress. I'm hoping for healing as much as all of you because each episode means there can be brain alterations due to reduced levels of oxygen to her brain and in her blood. Dr. Gomez and I discussed doing another echo and CT scan of her brain for clarification. Keep praying for God to be Big!*
>
> *Huge drumroll, please! Lily's a tiny piglet, hitting a whopping 3 lbs. Hooray and praise God! Let's keep growing, Warrior Princess. The doctor added one-and-a-half mL microlipids every six hours, which has increased her caloric intake. They'd like to maximize her calories by testing my milk and adjusting my dietary needs to meet their goals.*

The ups and downs have us feeling like we are riding five roller coasters simultaneously. Exhaustion has set in, and you could glimpse our carried-away craziness through our recent Facebook post. We released some of our emotion by laughing hysterically with our daughter, and her enjoyment of the moment brought better stats and the fading of bradys. Praise God! I will leave you with the promised list of books Lily loves. These are wonderful books to share with your children, family, and friends. I know all the children of the world will feel the same. I hope you enjoy! Good night!

- *The Secret of the Red Shoes* by Joan Donaldson (Lily's absolute fav book)
- *Precious Moments Gift Treasury*
- *Hello, Pistol Pete!* by Aimee Aryal
- *Where the Wild Things Are* by Maurice Sendak
- *My Daddy and Me* by Tina Macnaughton
- *I Love You Through and Through* by Bernadette Rossetti-Shustak
- *How Do I Love You?* by Marion Dane Bauer
- *What Will Heaven Be Like?* by Kathleen Ruckman
- *Hermie: A Common Caterpillar* by Max Lucado
- *Are You Ready for Bed?* by Jan Johnson
- *Twinkle, Twinkle, Little Star* by Sanja Rescek
- *My First Read and Learn Book of Prayers* by Dr. Mary Manz Simon
- *50 Bedtime Stories* by Tig Thomson
- *One-Minute Devotionals for Girls* by Carolyn Larsen
- *Charlotte's Web* by E. B. White
- *Scripture Prayer Cards* by Beth Moore - *Faith, Hope and Victory*

MAY 19, 2010

18 › Embrace the Storms

Rain...the sweet smell...the renewing quality...the cool, wet drops. God washes away everything. Knowing how detailed He is makes my heart happy, and my soul rests with an unexplainable peace in the storm.

Storms vary in length. I recall my favorite rainstorm with my best friend, Cristin Handlin, in Chandler, Oklahoma. The rain crashed down onto the streets as we danced. We had a blast. Pretending the rushing rapids on the street edge were a water park ride, we submerged ourselves until a couple of officers pulled over to check on us. Our laughter filled the air as we teenagers lived out a little kid's dream.

Oh, how I still love to dance in the rain! God helps me figure out how to love what's happening during life's storms, no matter how intense they are. This revelation may occur after the fact, but more times than not, I figure it out during the storm and dance.

Today, Moosh Moo, my camp best friend from my Camp Champions days in Marble Falls, Texas, shared a site about a little girl with Edwards Syndrome who has made it past her first birthday. Michael and I sifted through the site as we listened to her music. Tears of hope and joy consumed us. Inspired by the beautiful little girl, Michael and I took turns dancing with our princess to the song "I'm Yours" by Jason Mraz playing on the site. The time was short, but wow, was it A-W-E-S-O-M-E! And she loved it! I wish we could have danced outside in the rain. Someday that may be a reality, and what a day that will be!

I can't talk about rain without bringing up one of my favorite country songs, "Bring on the Rain" by Jo Dee Messina. It's been a staple on my playlist through many storms, giving me power and perseverance. There will always be another day, another trial, another mountain, or another battle until I take my last breath. I will have days I feel like a warrior and others where I'm a complete failure. I'm not going to let them stop me. I will not hide. I will face them all, one at a time, no matter what it takes. My God is gigantic and can do all things, so bring on the rain!

♡ LILY'S VITALS
More good news! Keep those praises and prayers lifted up. Lily did much better and had fewer bradys. The doctor added more mommy's milk every three hours. She is up to 27 mL with one-and-a-half microlipids. She gained another ounce to hit 3 lbs., 1 oz.

My heart sings as we conquer day twenty-four of life in one of the numerous miracles through this storm. The facts: her conception wasn't supposed to be possible, her life expectancy was her first breath, and living longer than fifteen days was slim. We praise God as we enjoy our time with her.

With a water pitcher, shampoo bottle, and cloth, we gave Lily her first bath. Thank You, Lord, for these precious moments that are not guaranteed to everyone who faces losing their baby too soon. The doctor's goal is to get her weight up so she can experience life at home with us, and learning to bathe her is one step toward that goal. Let's drop to our knees and pray we can take her home soon.

Last week, we were unsure about moving her home because we were concerned about her passing away at home. Today, we're excited to shift gears and focus on bringing her home and letting her experience her fabulous, colorful room with bright orange sherbet walls. Dreams can come true. Please, God! May everyone stay safe in life's storms. Hoping for many blessings and miracles throughout. Love you all!

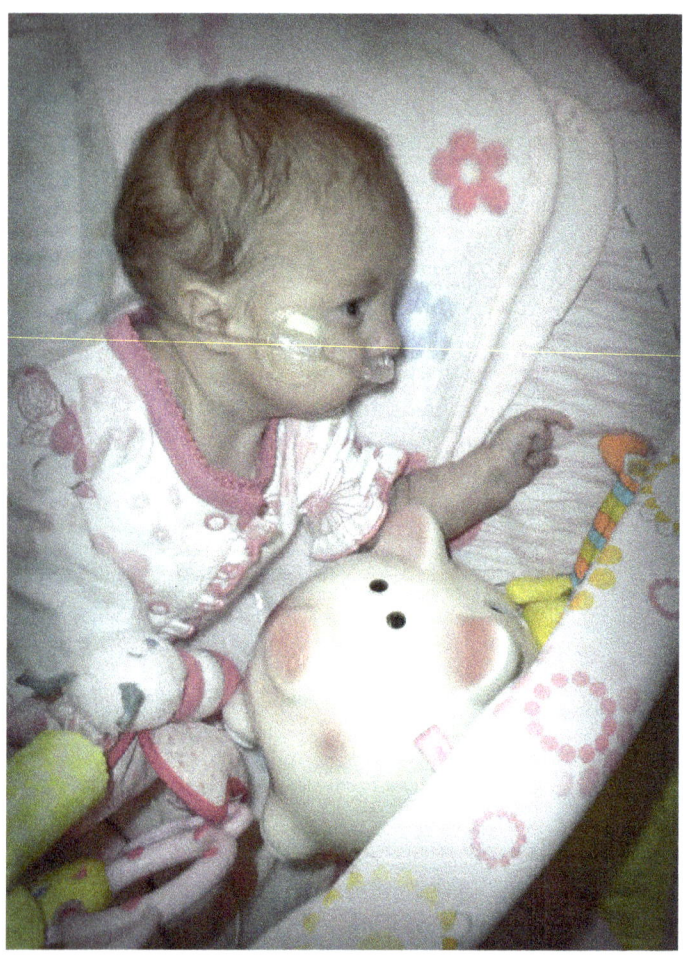

Our tiny piglet growing and saving

MAY 20, 2010

19 › Basics to Grow

Memories of Sunday school and church camp come flooding back when I hear the song "Read Your Bible, Pray Every Day." It's such a simple song with power and wisdom. If you do read your Bible and pray every day, you will grow in knowing God more and finding out how to live life while strengthening your trust and relationship with Him.

Today, we are thankful our tiny piglet has grown. Praise God! She made a big jump to 3 lbs., 5 oz. Hello! Bible readings and prayers continue on the daily just as the song suggests. Soul food is good for everyone to find another level of growth.

If you had projected Lily jumping that much in weight, I might not have believed it. I need to hold onto the fact that my God can do anything He says He can. We are tickled that she put on weight. Lily is like a successful wrestler making weight for the class above. I envision her reaching her weight goal to wrestle that devil. She's saying, "What's up, devil? I got God on my side. What about you?" May she keep winning the battles, and more importantly, the war.

The amount of oxygen in Lily's red blood cells decreased today, wearing her out. This is known as desaturation, or desat, and is common in preemies. We've discovered her bradys and desats increase when she's placed on her left side. She seems to hate sleeping on her left side as much as her daddy does. I was convinced he made up the left-side excuse to avoid cuddling, yet he really does hate it. He's avoided sleeping on his left side while on the couch. When pregnant, I persevered through my flexibility needs and left side dislikes. Perhaps we all share a common dislike for doing what's best for us. God has a sense of humor. Know why? Because we can repeatedly say no all we want until we eventually let Him lead us to the yes!

Dr. Gomez officially ordered the echo of the heart and the brain ultrasound. Let's all pray God blows the medical world out of the water...healing, healing, healing...and revealing the power of His will!

Always remember to read your Bible and pray every day to engage growth! Love to you all. No matter what time you're reading this, may you have a good night or good morning!

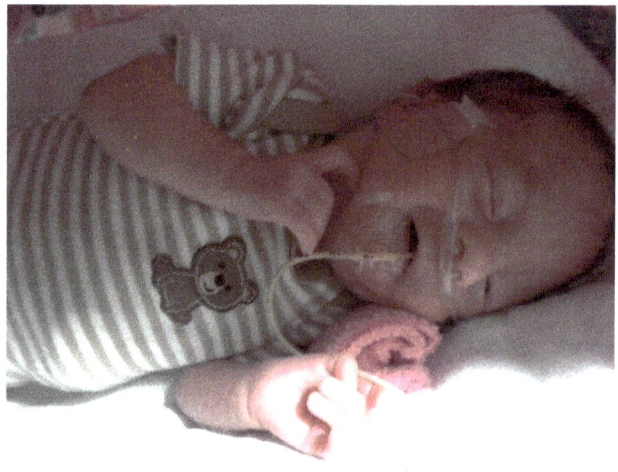

Joy can come in the morning no matter the storm!

MAY 21, 2010

20 › Imprints

We see God's all-knowing and loving ways through the people we meet on this journey. We are blessed God has created moments where we never meet a stranger. Today, Lily and I met an incredible mix of ladies—some for the first time and another we've known for a short stint.

Some argue we know too many people, but I believe life becomes more precious as we increase our radius by sharing God's love and will. Praise God, we get something right once in a blue moon by saying yes to God when He has people for us to meet—a divine appointment.

Lily participated in an artsy creation of her footprint and handprint mold brought to us by one of God's divine appointments to meet people—our RunnersWorld crew, who love us so! They paid Patty Cake's to come help make precious keepsakes that we will cherish forever. God reminds me how He enhances her footprint on the world and spreads His light. I'm in awe of God making her extra special with tiny feet and amazing impact to kick our butts and inspire us to change our footprint on the world.

This reminded me of the "Footprints in the Sand" poem, which has gotten me through all the difficult times in my life. Joyce Brumley, God rest her soul, reintroduced this poem to me when I avoided processing my hardships during my mom's illness. Joyce knew I needed permission to let go and let God and not take on the world's problems. Thinking about one versus two sets of footprints in the sand takes my breath away. No matter what I'm going through in life, God is either walking alongside me or carrying me in His loving arms into victory. He never leaves me! It doesn't matter how many footprints are marked in the sand in any given time on the journey. I have an endless amount of comfort knowing He's with me every step of the way. He knows when I can walk on my own two legs and when I need to be scooped up, resting in His strength.

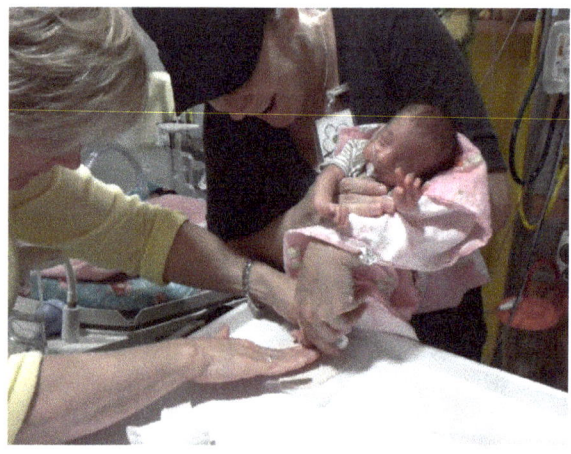

Leaving her mark for keeps!

I've learned this lesson multiple times over the years and am learning it once again. It's like I'm a twenty-year-old still hanging out in the first grade. Wouldn't it be nice if we could retain the information learned or use it for future reference? Praying we all step aside for God to work through lessons He's taught us.

She's been chillin' all day. I love her drive and strength, and I appreciate the lessons she's teaching me as she climbs. I wish she could have been here years ago, but I'll take now!

♡ LILY'S VITALS
Only a handful of bradys means she had a good day. I'm posting early, so her weight will be reported tomorrow. More labs, an ultrasound, and an echo are scheduled for Monday. Dr. Gomez informed me she's doing really well. Hallelujah, Almighty God, for You are here and in this place! They've increased her feedings to 29 mL of mommy's milk. I look at her and can't believe how she is filling out. I love it!

Every woman should own a special pair of red shoes. I bought me some Jessica Simpson red stilettos that make my legs look good (at least in my opinion). Michael and I are going on a movie date tomorrow. I can't wait to take my red shoes for a spin. My little Warrior Princess will be there in spirit. Lily's favorite book, *The Secret of the Red Shoes* by Joan Donaldson, tells the value of owning a red pair. Love you all!

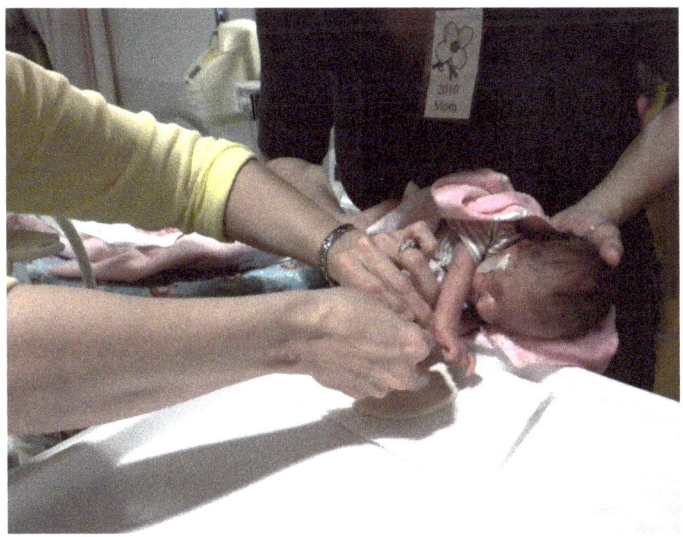

Imprinted for keeps

He comforts and brings peace!

MAY 22, 2010

21 › Step Aside

Want to survive everything life throws at you? Pray that God pushes you aside every minute so that He can battle for you. Stepping aside and letting God is Michael's, Lily's, and my survival tactic. It means we get it right more than we get it wrong. How many times do you step aside and get out of God's way? I'm praying that God helps you move.

Getting in God's way and worrying is easy, but I've found peace in the ordinary moments. Today, Michael and I spent time together cleaning the house, organizing pictures and Lily's new wardrobe, and watching our favorite TV shows. I didn't worry about my baby girl at all. No worries automatically brings the lovely song "Don't Worry, Be Happy" to mind. I've always wanted to be able to let go of my worries, but worrying is my infamous human trait. God teaches us to leave things in His hands so that we can experience true bliss.

I don't want this feeling to ever end. I hope we stay in His will and leave it all with Him. He gives us a feeling of peace, contentment, and invincibility. I hope you reach this state. You'd never want it to disappear. Thank You, God, for continued teachings about getting out of Your way and allowing You to work. May we continue to abide in You and give You the glory. Nothing compares to the hurt of losing a child. Giving 100 percent to Him increases our chances of surviving this situation.

> ♡ ***LILY'S VITALS***
> *Hello, day twenty-seven! How excellent is our Great Physician? He knows more than our earthly ones. We are blessed to spend many days with His fabulous Warrior Princess. Her stats prove how wonderful her break has been from all of us, reducing the possibilities of overstimulation. She hasn't had a brady since eleven this morning. Praise God! The nurse will watch her swollen little eyes. Please lift it up in prayer. She lost a couple of ounces yesterday, but she's weighing consistently at 3 lbs., 3 oz. Her body needs to adapt to the changes, and gaining too much weight too quickly wouldn't be good.*

It's funny to think that most women would love for their clothes to fit too big. Because Lily gained weight too fast for a bit, she started to fit into her clothes too well. It's good she slowed down. I might have to watch my dessert addiction to keep from increasing the calories in my milk.

I hope you all enjoy a worry-free weekend. Make a list of worries and lay them all at the feet of Jesus, who is equipped to handle them. He's the artist, painting a beautiful picture of our lives with the luxury of knowing everything about us.

MAY 23, 2010

22 › Heart Stops

As an alarm goes off, we look at Lily's vitals screen. We see zero for her heart rate and suddenly no numbers at all...my own heart stops as I hold my breath, taking it all in. This happened twice tonight, sending us into panic mode each time with nurses rushing in and my body reacting the same each time. I held my hand near my heart and quietly told myself to breathe in and out while pounding my chest to keep my heart beating. Come to find out (and we're still hoping this was the reason), Lily needed her wires and stickers replaced. Now, that was scary!

Just as we caught our breath, we had another curve ball thrown at us. We thought we had our schedule figured out but not so much. It's not in the cards for us to have a schedule. All parents are nodding their heads right now. We had established a viable visiting schedule to meet Lily's needs, but it's not working. We are putting it in God's hands. Additionally, we need His help in the sleep department since we are experiencing sleep deprivation in the NICU. Hooray! We will take another normal parenting trial.

This is God's way of showing us He takes care of all the devil's curve balls as long as we step aside. There's nothing set in stone on earth except for His love for us. This is day two of bringing up how we should step aside. What's the lesson from today? Step aside! Lily's and my devotional tonight comes from Isaiah 58:11 and gives me hope that He will step in to give us what we need.

Memory Verse 4

⚔ *"The Lord will guide you always; he will satisfy your needs in a sun-scorched land and will strengthen your frame. You will be like a well-watered garden, like a spring whose waters never fail" (Isaiah 58:11).*

> ♡ **LILY'S VITALS**
> *Today marks twenty-eight days of bliss with our sweetheart. Lily's weight had declined to 3 lbs., 3 oz., but she's climbed the scale back to 3 lbs., 7 oz. Praise God! The numbers can be a little off sometimes, but the nurse got the same weight three times. All right! The rest of her numbers are as follows: Lily has grown in length to 16 ½ in.; head: 28 ½ cm; and girth: 26 ½ cm. Lily had an ultrasound on her head today. Hopefully, we'll find out those results sooner rather than later.*

God keeps answering prayer after prayer. Therefore, we ask for prayers for the echo and lab work scheduled for tomorrow. May God blow all of us out of the water by showing us how good He is. Another praise—today at 2:17 a.m., Lilian's future guy BFF, Landon Winters Klenovich, entered the world. He weighs 6 lbs., 1 oz. and is 18 3/4 inches long. Please pray that everything continues to get better, especially with his momma's milk. Praise God for this wonderful addition to Nick and Sheryl's family. We hope our babies will have several playdates in the future. Nick and Sheryl, congratulations to your precious family!

Special note: Lily's one-month birthday is at 8:44 a.m., Tuesday, May 25, 2010. We'd like everyone to celebrate with us by wearing red shoes or clothing all day on Tuesday to represent God's love, Lily's heart, and her favorite book, *The Secret of the Red Shoes*. Make sure to have fun dressing up. We'd love for everyone to say a prayer at 8:44 a.m. in honor of Lily's arrival into the world. How awesome would it be to hear all of us praying at one time? I know God will be smiling as He hears the roar from us. BTW—top the day off with your favorite dessert. The Whittens will celebrate this beautiful day with our new favorite coconut key lime cake from Camille's!

Take pictures and post them to Lily's Facebook fan page, "Lily Warrior Princess." If you don't have a Facebook account, send me a pic via email. We're creating a birthday book where we'll display them.

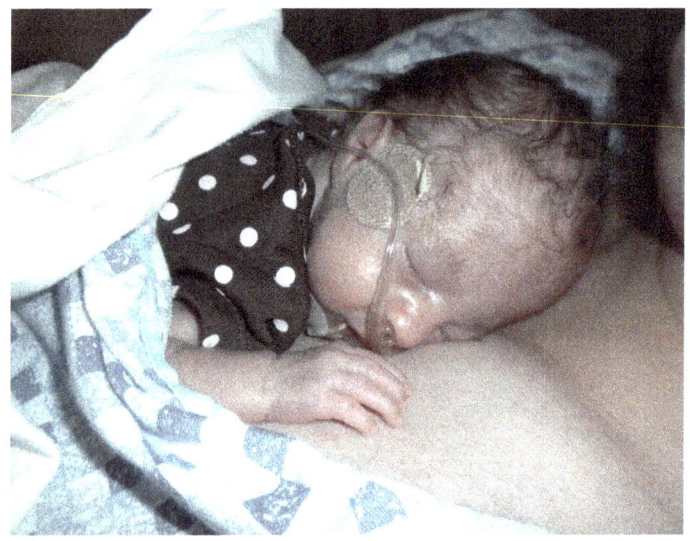

Leaning on and getting rest

MAY 24, 2010

23 › Leaning On Friends

Moments from the last few weeks swirl in my head, and my thoughts finally settle on how I was able to lean on a friend today. We have rockin' friends and family in our life. Today, I was in the twilight zone and feeling overwhelmed from writing on CaringBridge, motherhood, wifehood, friendships, family ties, and more. My girlfriends came to my rescue and told me just to be real. I'm going to continue to be just that—real and raw.

Tomorrow officially marks one month for our adventure. Sheesh, that's a long time. No wonder Michael and I are feeling the strain of sleepless nights and holding our breath. I've been bulldozing through my days like an old car with a hole in the gas tank. We put gas in while it escapes through the hole, never reaching full.

Leaning on others is vital, and boy, have many stepped up to let us lean on them. We appreciate all of you! In honor of leaning on a friend, listen to "Lean on Me" by Bill Withers. Friendship is vital in helping each other through this life. We all take turns needing help in this life and aren't meant to do it alone. Don't be afraid to reach out a hand for another or call someone when you are in need. Remember to make it a two-way street where give and take are equal.

Thankfully, God's helped us get to church each week. Several Sundays, I wasn't feeling it; however, we went to refuel our bulldozers with efficient "gas" for much-needed energy. Fellowship and worship are essential. Listening to Christian music and reading daily one-minute devotionals with Lily helps. What goes in, must come out holds true for what we consume each day. Be aware of what you allow in your life.

One of the best things I've been told is to lean, lean, lean on someone. Two of my Angel Warriors took me shopping for Lilian's special dress for her birthday celebration tomorrow. Lo and behold, we found one at the Build-A-Bear store. How fun is that? It was wonderful to laugh and enjoy time away from the hospital. We let loose and laughed when we saw the most random hairdo. I hate to laugh at someone else's expense, but it was good to release some of my pent-up energy. Sadly, no one got a picture.

♡ LILY'S VITALS
Our tiny piglet weighs 3 lbs., 9 oz., making her one-month celebration tomorrow a wonderful acknowledgement of her growth. God is fabustastic! Dr. Gomez increased her feeding to 31 mL of mommy's milk every three hours and added iron, discontinued her sodium chloride, and increased her caffeine.

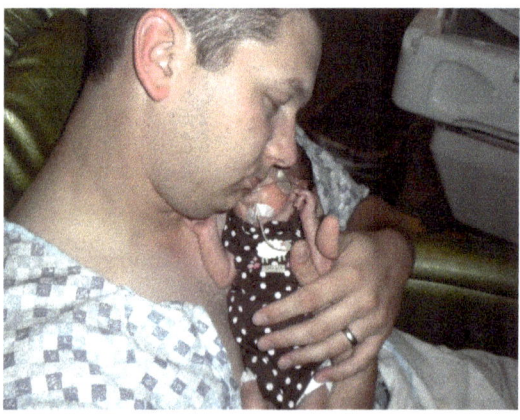

I'll hold you close until I can't.

Through this whole thing, my wish has been for normalcy like other new parents. Fittingly, I got my wish. I cried happily upon hearing that Lily gets her hepatitis B vaccine tomorrow. I don't want my baby girl to hurt, but the vaccine means we get to do something normal. Hooray! It's not your typical birthday present, so please pray for her. I'll post updates when we receive results from the rest of her tests tomorrow.

I love that she's been more vocal today. She's giving us the 411 on how she's doing. It's hilarious, and I love it. She just grabbed her daddy's hand to take a huge poop. She is more like her daddy in this department.

Remember to wear red shoes or clothing, snap a picture, and post to social media (or email me). Enjoy your favorite dessert tomorrow. Love you all!

MAY 25, 2010

24 › One-Month Birthday

I'm singing "Happy Birthday" at the top of my lungs to my miracle. Now, it's your turn. I enjoy the birthday song. It's a simple song, yet it reminds me that our birthday should be a happy time. I love birthdays because we get to celebrate the anniversary of the day we each actually brought great joy and happiness on earth by our becoming. Do you take birthdays for granted? If so, try imagining what it looked like the day you took your first breath. Someone, somewhere felt very blessed to witness the miracle that day and time they first laid eyes on you.

Oh, what a one-month birthday celebration it has been! We still can't grasp how quickly the month has passed since we began this adventure. We are worn out. Lily slept a good part of the day. She had a magnificent time with her parents and grandparents at her small-scale birthday celebration.

We bought her three balloons: a dragonfly (change), butterfly (new beginnings), and red one (one month). We purchased a mini Piglet with red-and-white bows. Lily looked fabulous in her new red-and-white polka dot mini dress from Build-A-Bear. Right now, her rabbit friend is dressed up in her birthday attire. We will never wash it. Her little red socks had a Dorothy-there's-no-place-like-home vibe.

She loved listening to everyone read a variety of books to her. I took lots of pictures and hope to do a Facebook post. She did a wonderful job celebrating. We even sang a nice round of "Happy Birthday." We loved all the pictures shared by those of you who wore red. It means a lot that you would take time to celebrate with us from afar. Thanks for participating and giving us something to smile about while going through the storm.

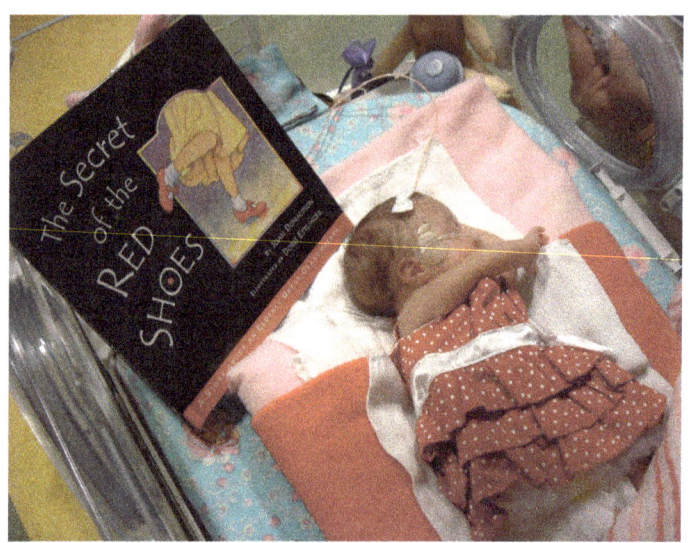

Lilian, one month old, with her favorite book

♡ *LILY'S VITALS*
Bradys episodes increased since Lily was tired. She got her hep B shot, which made her moody and sleepy. We finally got to talk to the doctor tonight. The results of the ultrasound and echo showed no changes.

Let's pray God's will be done. We continue to lift up prayers for more miracles. God has listened and is answering. All her complications are balancing out each other. He knows exactly what she needs.

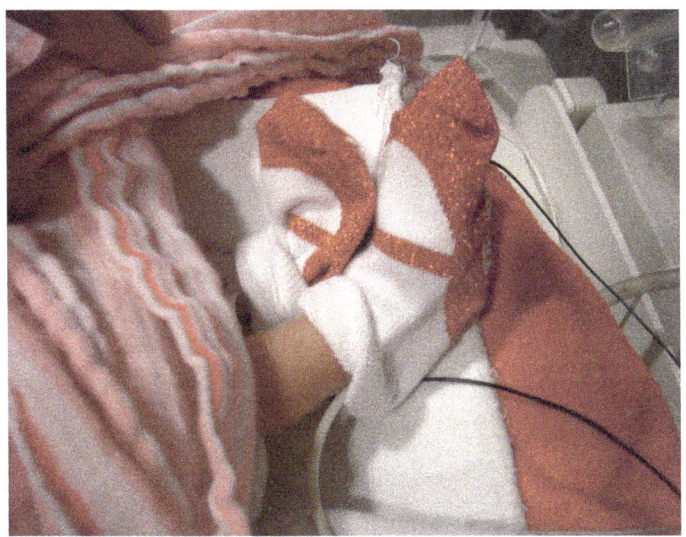

She feels like home!

Lilian's rabbit friend taking her turn in the red dress

Michael and I continue to be tired as time unravels. The daily journey has taken more of a toll on us than we realized. I want more than anything for our daughter to be happy and normal, but no matter what happens, I get the coolest angel I've met to date. Who needs normal, anyway? I'll take my miracle girl.

Another dear friend sent an email with several meanings for Lily's name, and I love the words associated with her: innocence, purity, return of happiness, sweetness, humility, love's good fortune, and Christ's second coming. The email was a small act with a lasting impact. Thank you all for being a small part of our journey. Knowing you care and share whatever God lays on your heart is a huge motivator. We welcome all the soul food, love, care, and comfort for the battle.

MAY 26, 2010

25 › Checks and Balances

We spent time at home tonight after a tough day. I'm now back at the hospital. On top of all that, Lily fought bradys today as well. I completely understand the worn out part. How many times do we all just go, go, go without ever blinking an eye? It seems just when we wake up, it's time to go back to sleep. Time seems to be a spinning clock while staying in the hospital. It's funny how much time you think you should have when you're cooped up within four walls and not having to do regular chores like dishes, laundry, cleaning, or working. There are always things needing attention here.

Keeping everyone updated through phone calls, emails, texts, Facebook posts, and messages can get overwhelming when you feel like you are a broken record with your replies. I have to trek to the cafeteria to make sure I'm getting my nutrition with three meals a day plus snacks to keep my breast milk flowing. No food is allowed in the NICU rooms. I try to pump on an intense schedule of two to three hours between pump sessions of thirty to sixty minutes in length, because it's the one thing I can do for my baby girl. There are doctor visits, medical staff rounds, respiratory checks, meds, tests, blood work, and general care throughout a twenty-four-hour period. I never knew how much energy all this could take from me.

I can't forget the fun things that occupy my time. I get to feed, read, sing, pray, dance, laugh, change, and kangaroo care when Lilian is able. There's a balance to prevent overstimulation, but it's worth getting to do anything with her at all.

We are thankful to do some real-world things lately. It's been nice just to have a normal conversation that doesn't involve answering questions or explaining the situation. Don't get us wrong—we appreciate people caring—but we yearn for normalcy.

God is teaching us to prioritize and slow down. I'm definitely not good about these things, but I'm getting there. Is God trying to get your attention and slow you down? Make sure you listen. You never know what tools you'll receive that you can use for another climb.

I praise God for thirty-one days with our daughter. As I type this, we are into day thirty-two. Keep blowing us away, God! Who would have guessed we'd add our daughter's baby dedication and one-month birthday celebration to our adventure book? It's pretty cool remembering her first breath was predicted to be her last.

♡ LILY'S VITALS
She weighed 3 lbs., 12 oz. but lost an ounce at tonight's weigh-in. She is eating 33 mL of mommy's milk every three hours. Hopefully, she will continue to put on weight to help regulate the temperature in her tiny body.

Hold on to your seat belts because this is gonna take you to greater heights of praise! Dr. Gomez hopes we can take Lily home as early as the end of next week, depending on her stats. Our responsibilities will increase, and we don't know the length of our quarantine from the world. We will have hospice with us. Please continue to pray for God's will to be done. We are conflicted. On the one hand, we get to be home and eliminate some stress. On the other hand, we have to leave the 24/7 care of hospital staff and specialists.

Welcome to our roller coaster ride. I hope your ride is grand and making waves in the world. I will leave you with this question: How are you reaching your full potential for God's purpose for your life? If I have learned one thing (and I'll just guess I've learned about a hundred things or more through this all), it's the fact we can get too comfortable in our life, even during the chaos. Drop to your knees and spend some quality "be still" time to do a reality check of your life. That means all areas: God, church, family, home, work, and self. Include a mental, physical, and emotional check. May God reveal where you are and where He wants you to be. Good night/Good morning!

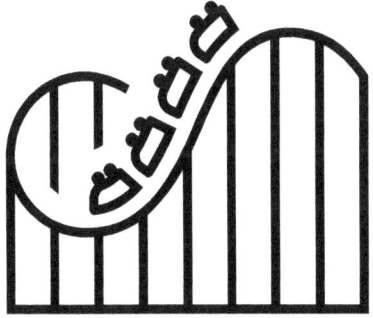

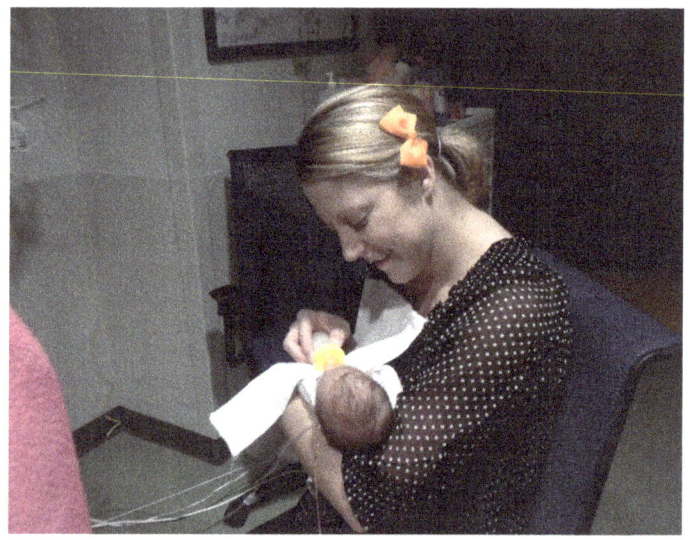

Experiencing a miraculous milestone

MAY 27, 2010

26 › Grace and Humility

Memory Verse 5

⚔ *"But he gives us more grace. That is why Scripture says: 'God opposes the proud but gives grace to the humble'" (James 4:6).*

Today, God blew me out of the water by providing a glimpse into someone else's story. Lily had another rough day, but she pulled through. Praise God! Dr. Groves, the best eye doctor and a Christian man, gave Lily her first successful eye exam, and he prayed with us.

We have a multitude of His angels working with us. Dr. Groves connected us with a godly woman, Lydia Thomas, who is experiencing God's grace and love every day through her daughter's trisomy 18. Lydia and I swapped stories, and I shared an important milestone from today: I got to feed Lily with a bottle of my milk. Praise the Lord! She gulped down 13 mL of the 33 mL. She had previously drunk 10 mL for the speech therapist a couple of days ago. This triumph was grand, but even so, I was humbled to find out that it was a miracle of great accord. See, the lovely Lydia's little girl, who will be five in June, has never taken a bottle and is still on a feeding system.

As I heard Lydia's words, tears welled up and overflowed. I felt for Lydia's little girl, yet her story helped me grasp how grand my baby girl's steps were today in tackling that feeding. God keeps showing me all His wonders step by step. Here I was excited that Lily and I got to share a moment, and come to find out, it was bigger and better than I even knew. James 4:6 reminds me that God gives us grace to be humble. We can easily think we know more than we do or take things for granted.

I hope I can remember that a small step for some is a giant step for others. God, thank You for letting me see that Lily's baby steps in my eyes are really gigantic and explosive by Your intentions. Check to see what's going on around you and praise God for the little things that are meant for huge impact.

♡ LILY'S VITALS
Moving forward from losing an ounce, she is back up to 3 lbs., 12 oz. Wahoo! There was a small issue regarding the lack of poopy diapers, but Lily rocked it out with a nice load a few minutes ago. Praise His name on high! I was concerned when she hadn't but now no worries. Today was rough with the number of bradys and desats because she stayed low on her numbers for an extended amount of time. Simply put, it's not good. I was staying fairly calm; however, I got down when each one lasted longer.

We are giving Lily a three-day-weekend break from visitors. No visitors allowed Friday, Saturday, and Sunday will benefit us as well. I keep reiterating our exhaustion level, but the severity of our tiredness is growing. We all need sleep and rest. It doesn't get more normal as a new parent than this. That's why I'm happy to type it. Normal is what we long for more than anything. I'm reminded not only to sleep but to rest in the Lord. Without rest, we can slip into a pity party. May God keep us in His arms.

I hope you have a restful Memorial Day weekend. Take time to remember those who have left us. I hope they are having a big party with God. If you don't have our Lord and

Savior, Jesus, in your heart, please consider inviting Him in. It's a rockin' time with Him in your life. He's blessed us beyond measure and made it possible to survive this journey.

Grace gives fuel for love to live, which reminds me of a Chris Tomlin song I love, "Your Grace Is Enough." The world can pull us in chaotic directions and create a discontented heart where nothing is ever enough. When we silence the noise and focus on His great faithfulness and how His love leads us daily, we can experience the fullness of His ways and know His grace is enough. Where we are weak, He strengthens us. Love to you all!

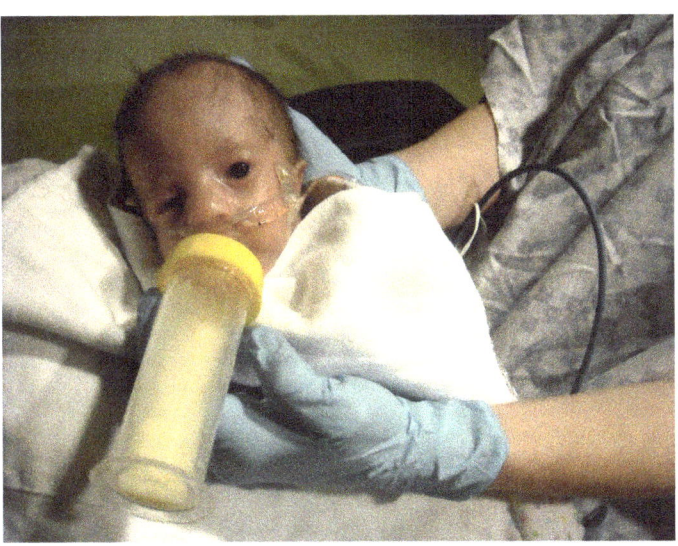

Lilian taking gigantic steps by eating from a bottle

MAY 28, 2010

27 › Surviving and Thriving

Memory Verse 6

🗡 *"Therefore, since we have been justified through faith, we have peace with God through our Lord Jesus Christ, through whom we have gained access by faith into this grace in which we now stand. And we rejoice in the hope of the glory of God. Not only so, but we also glory in our sufferings, because we know that suffering produces perseverance; perseverance, character; and character, hope" (Romans 5:1–4).*

Each day, I enjoy a daily Scripture that's delivered to my inbox to lift my spirits. The above rings true for all of us. I wish we could learn things without having to suffer, but it seems the greatest lessons learned are during the most difficult times. Thousands of stories exist about people around us who suffer through journeys involving cancer, disease, heartache, frustration, and change. What's wonderful to witness is the hope shining through their journeys. I am amazed at the mountains people face and how they conquer them.

I watch people face horrible trials and survive them. Why? Only one common denominator is found...God! God shocks me each day as I watch Lily do incredible things, exceeding the expectations of her diagnosis. She lifts her head and turns it because she wants to. When she looks at the pages of a book I'm reading, I move the book to see if she will follow, and she does. I'm in awe of her and our heavenly Father.

Do yourself a favor by always turning to Him. He knows the number of hairs on your head. He can handle it all. He is omnipotent! I hope you have a stupendous Friday night and Saturday! Love you all!

♡ LILY'S VITALS
We've had a much calmer day regarding her bradys and desats. Thank You, Jesus! Because of the hotter weather, Lily has the top up on her expensive headquarters. It's how she rolls. She's starting to regulate her temperature more, which is fab news. Holler! I'm ecstatic that we are not dealing with a normal child. A nurse observed that Lily doesn't even know she's small. How fun is that? She is consistent in weight again tonight at 3 lbs., 12 oz. Dr. Gomez increased her microlipids to 2 mL.

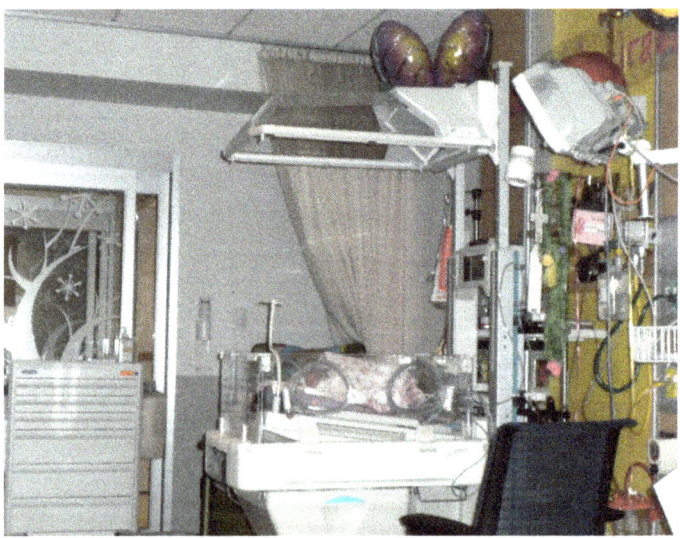

Top up, living in her expensive headquarters, a.k.a. the giraffe

MAY 29, 2010

28 › Perspective

I'm posting early tonight since Michael and I have plans to see *Robin Hood*. I'm uneasy about Russell Crowe in the title role. Kevin Costner should be the last Robin with his outstanding role in *Robin Hood: Prince of Thieves*. Hopefully, Russell Crowe will surprise me.

Lily and I had our first official slumber party. Of course, I've spent almost every night with her but not in the same "room." Since the top was up on the giraffe, it finally felt as if we were in the same room. We stayed up fairly late thanks to Lily's night/day confusion and constipation/squirts from adding iron to her milk. I'm a night owl anyway. Like mother, like daughter, we stayed up and had a superb time dancing around like a sweet elderly dance duo reminiscing about the good old days and worshipping God through praying and singing random praise songs.

Two moments made the day extra special. The first was when I gave Lily sweet smooches on her chubby cheek before leaving for a project. She smiled! It wasn't one of those smiles from gas. It was an actual smile for her mommy. She opened her eyes, looked up, and smiled. I gave her sweet smooches again, told her I had to leave, and promised to return. She smiled once again before closing her eyes. My momma's heart is happier than anything in the world.

As I walked to my car, the "Oh, What a Beautiful Mornin'" chorus from the musical *Oklahoma* popped into my head to sing, so I did! It truly is a beautiful day. It may seem as if things aren't going our way, but with a little perseverance and the right perspective, we see that God is making our situation beautiful. Things are going according to His plan, and I long to be in His will always. When everything is going His way and not my own, true bliss, contentment, and success exist.

A professor once taught me how to look at a situation from all angles. He told me to put a situation in a metaphorical chair and walk all the way around it in my mind. This way, I am not looking at it just one way. I'd like to encourage you all to do the same. Put your situation, problem, or controversy in a chair. Put it in the middle of the room (your mind) and walk around it. You can see the whole picture this way, and then you can discover how you need to handle your situation or understand it better. Good luck, and always pray first!

The second special moment came when Michael gave Lily her bottle and she took 6 ml. Though it was a smaller amount, she kept falling asleep, looking so peaceful in his arms. I watched him change another diaper. I love this man! He is amazing with his sweet daddy's girl!

♡ LILY'S VITALS
Giving her a break always pays off. Her bradys and desats were minimal today. We are so proud of our fighting Warrior Princess. Her perseverance is mind blowing. They have increased her feedings to 34 mL of mommy's milk every three hours. She is thirty-four days old. Hallelujah!

Okay, buckle up. Dr. Gomez told us today they are moving forward with her heart surgeries. He's proposing her PDA surgery for the end of next week. Happy tears! I've prayed for God to give Dr. Gomez and the other doctors the wisdom to take care of Lily. I am completely trusting them because I'm completely trusting God. When she gets to ten pounds, the big surgery to fix the worst hole will be on the table. Please join me in shouting, "Praise the Lord for miracles." She is proving over and over that she's worth more than just letting her slip away into a forever slumber. More happy tears! Continue to pray God provides what Lily needs.

"Sweep Me Away" by Kari Jobe perfectly represents how I'm feeling as her mesmerizing voice belts chords that make you feel as if you are being swept away by our Father. The nights are the hardest, and playing this song brings a ray of light to brighten the dark spaces. Grasping the depths of Him taking my place when He died on the cross for me triggers a stream of tears down my cheeks, praise with raised arms, and overflowing peace in my heart. I long for Him to sweep me away from this endless ringing of bells and unknown timing of Lilian's possible last breath.

He can embrace us with His love, goodness, and sovereign grace. These seem like a continuous theme to our story and perhaps yours. His mercy covers our shortcomings as He embraces us with His unconditional love. I pray He sweeps each of us away from where we've wandered and into the places we are destined to go. He is the answer we are looking for. Let Him sweep you away into His arms where nothing else matters. You can be renewed and reminded of His love for us.

Lily must be channeling her tiger today.

MAY 30, 2010

29 › Freedom

I've sung "God Bless the USA" by Lee Greenwood a hundred times in my life. I am proud to be an American. To be free in this country is not free. The price is paid in full by many men and women along with their families and friends across our nation. Thank you to those who have served, are currently serving, and will serve for our rights and freedom to continue. We remember your sacrifice and service. Michael, Lily, and I hold a deeper appreciation this year because our freedom allows us to receive the best care possible. Praise God!

> ♡ *LILY'S VITALS*
> *Lily climbed to 3 lbs., 15 oz. but lost to be back down to 3 lbs., 13 oz. We shall see what tomorrow brings. She did drink 14 mL of mommy's milk earlier when I bottle fed her. I'm loving it, Father! She has been doing so well.*

We are giving ourselves a break now and then. Michael and I have gotten more time together at home. I completely forgot how relaxing and peaceful our house can be. God blessed our home, and we can't wait until Lily can experience it with us. I get goosebumps thinking about it.

Another reason to be appreciative of others' sacrifices is the opportunity to live freely. I'm happy we have the freedom to worship our heavenly Father without the fear of persecution.

Lily has intensified her vocals the past few days as she communicates with us more and more. Normally, parents wouldn't be this excited, but we are ecstatic for another sign of normalcy.

As I type this, Lily is letting me have it. I'm pumping and typing (hello, multitasker). I can't do anything about her needs at the moment. It's frustrating that I can be taking care of multiple needs at once by pumping, writing, and trying to soothe her with my voice but still find myself failing. She is really being a tigress at the moment. Michael just got here, so he's trying to see what she needs. Man, oh, man, she is really talking it out. He checked her temp (normal) and diaper (wet). Must be that since she is calming down. I don't blame her. I wouldn't want to sit in wetness either!

I see how a mother's desire to take care of every need comes into play. I love it! I hope I can remember I can't be everything to her. I have to leave it in God's hands and let Him provide wisdom for when and how to do things. I'm trusting God completely to help both me and Michael to be what Lily needs. May God help you be everything you need for those in your life.

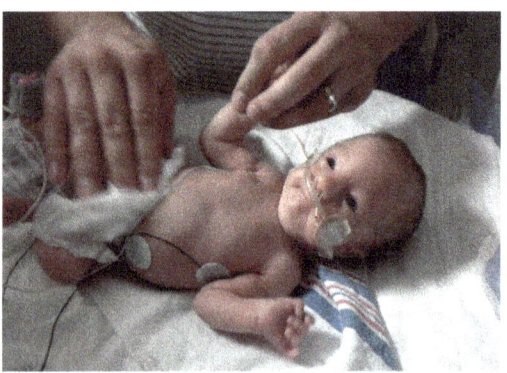

The calm after the tigress fit

MAY 31, 2010

30 › Breathe

Breathe—this has been the theme for today. Lily decided to practice her patriotism by turning red, white, and blue throughout the day. I told her this style of celebrating is unnecessary. I sang as many patriotic songs as I could remember to calm her. She actually turned blue only twice, but once was enough to take my breath away.

A kind family member sent us a jewelry piece inscribed with the word "breathe." My gaze was drawn to it each moment Lily decided she didn't want to multitask. See, multitasking for Lily is breathing, her heart pumping, and her digestion functioning all at the same time. Of late, lack of bathroom functions has gotten in the way of other basic tasks.

Please pray God will give Lily what she needs regarding a position change or fewer meds or whatever. To hear all the alarms clanging after we had such a wonderful break from them has been a nerve-racking ordeal. What might suck the worst? Getting used to things working out, and then boom! A bad day. The good days make the bad ones ten times worse. I'll still take those good days, though, dear Lord.

♡ LILY'S VITALS
She still weighs 3 lbs., 13 oz. She is thirty-six days old and counting. They've increased her to 35 mL of mommy's milk every three hours. Michael fed her a bottle, and she drank 10 mL. Not bad at all. We praise God! When we find out the date of her PDA surgery, I'll post an update.

What can we learn from today? Life can get so chaotic that we neglect many things. I don't know your circumstances, but we all end up in the neglect section of life at some point. At times, I've worked on accomplishing some major projects only to end up neglecting other things. Balance is important to help us be more successful. Look at a scale, and see where you are putting emphasis in your life. Are you balanced? Are you breathing? If not, write out your concerns and decide what is more important. Then breathe and live!

Even though I think I'm breathing, I catch myself when I'm not. I'm praying we all keep breathing along with Lily. Hoping for a better night for Lily and all of us.

P.S. On a lighter note, she did look smokin' in her cute outfit for the day. She even wore her shades. A couple of her pics reminded me of Lady Gaga since her shades were way too big. I love it!

Please, paparazzi, you've had your chance. Now go!

JUNE 1, 2010

31 › Held

Sister Ann Mary visited, and she exudes an air of love and peace wherever she goes. Today, she blessed me with a card displaying a beautiful picture of Jesus holding a lamb. In my mind, I substitute my family for the little lamb being held by the Shepherd. Oh, the joy of being in His presence! I'd love for you all to lift up a prayer for us and all the people who are sick right now along with the medical staff to have wisdom and knowledge in their care plan. May healing occur either on earth or in heaven.

> ♡ *LILY'S VITALS*
> *Shout out loud with us: Hallelujah, Jehovah-Jireh! Lily is an even four pounds tonight. She's been getting a workout with her stomach issues, but today was a much better day than yesterday. She concentrates so hard to get her system moving that her face turns red. She slept more than any other day because the workout exhausted her. She lulled me to sleep just watching her. Pray she will relax and have an easier time with her bowel movements.*

We didn't hear from the heart surgeons today. As soon as I hear anything, I'll post. It will be a quick procedure, and many have told us it's simple. We hope they are right. Good night for now!

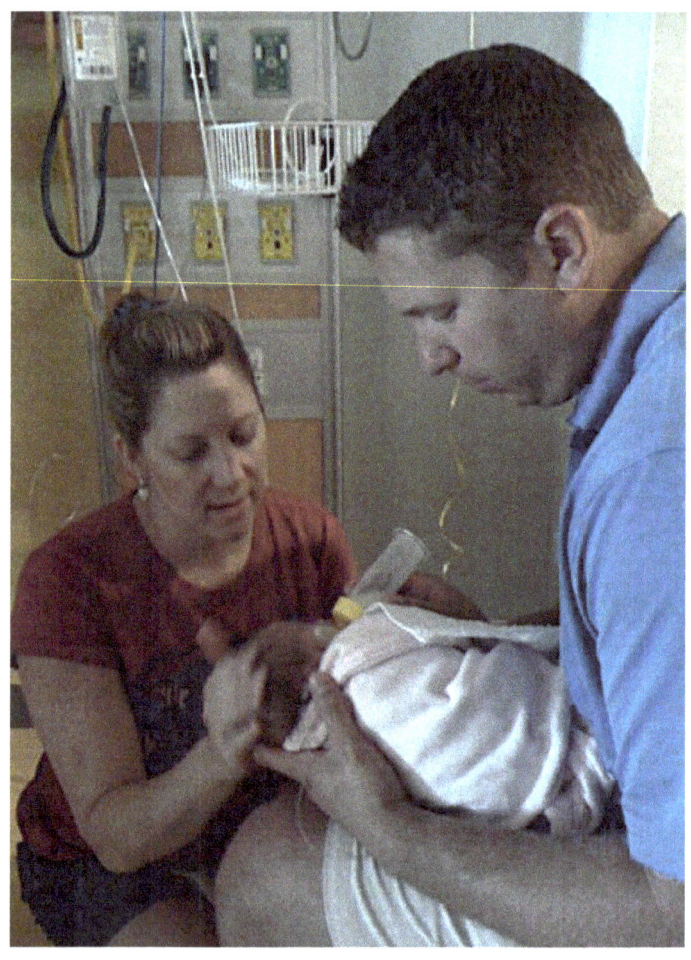

Our miracle, our ripple

JUNE 2, 2010

32 › Ripples

♡ *LILY'S VITALS*
Lily gained another two ounces. Woot woot! She's now 4 lbs., 2 oz. As gas and other things pass through her system, her volume of bradys and desats increases. Her poor lil body, with baby rolls just now forming, works so hard. She is thirty-eight days old!

Her PDA surgery is scheduled for tomorrow, possibly around ten-thirty in the morning or noon. Please, no visitors or phone calls. We would appreciate all prayers. After she is out of surgery, I'll give progress updates when I can. We met with the doctors performing the surgery and feel great peace. I love that God has brought us to this point, and I trust him completely.

My feet drag, and I'm more exhausted than I've ever been. There will be no visitation during Lily's recovery in order to promote healing and growth. We will let you know when visitation opens back up. We hope to go home at the end of next week.

Lily's and my devotional for today reminded me that we are either a positive or negative ripple for people all around us. We are finding out just how far a ripple can go in our situation. Lily has stunned so many, and I pray she keeps sending those ripples out for Him. What kind of ripple are you making? In looking at our life, we've clearly created different forms of ripples. Sometimes, we barely made a ripple, and other times, we've created large waves. I look forward to watching all of us make ripples and spread God's love to as many as possible. We each have gifts to share. Discover your gifts, and let it ripple! Good luck and good night (or good morning)!

JUNE 3, 2010

33 › Heart Surgery

I just pinched myself to make sure I'm not dreaming. Did Michael, Lily, and I really survive this day? A day with Lily's heart surgery? How is it that Michael and I are at peace? Have you ever felt a state of peace so wonderful that you questioned if you were in denial because it felt so dang good? Well, God gave us a great peace throughout the day. I think some nurses and other staff worried more than we did.

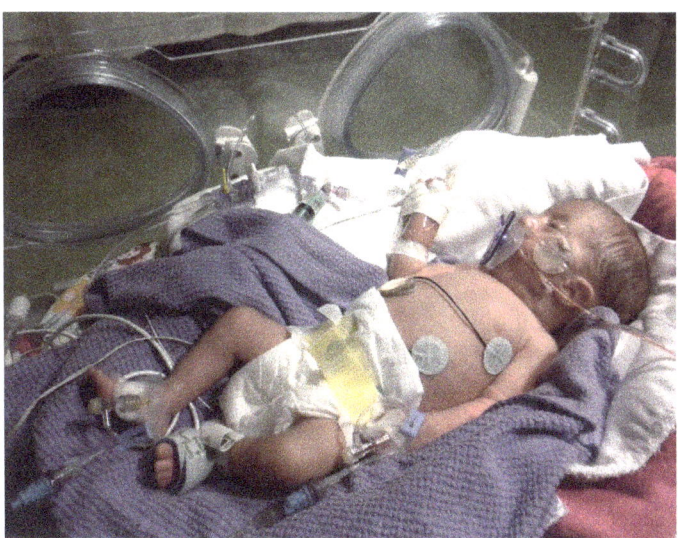

All wired up and ready for her first heart surgery

It felt amazing to fully trust God with Lily's first heart surgery. Wow! I know it's nothing we did. All these prayers sent up in massive numbers by you all have been heard. I believe when two or more are gathered, He hears us loud and clear.

A nurse asked me how I was feeling before the surgery. I smiled big and told her I had a level of peace that almost scared me. See, I don't recall a time when I have found myself as content and peaceful as I was on this day. Let me tell you all this—once you feel this type of peace, you won't ever want to let it go.

I'm not going to lie to you. We're exhausted, but we know we can rest in Him. Can I just say how lucky I am to have a husband who believes in God and relies on Him? Yes, I can and am saying this. I find I'm pinching myself once again to make sure this isn't a dream. My daughter is one of the coolest angels to be born here on earth, and I have a husband no one I know can beat. How did I get so lucky? God's perfect plan for my life! Praise His holy name!

♡ LILY'S VITALS
She hasn't fully woken up today, which is normal after surgery. I know once she really wakes up, we will see the tigress once again. She hasn't had any milk since last night and won't have any till tomorrow. Pray she will remain content and easygoing. With her perfect coloring of a warm olive tone and a touch of rosy pink, she looks more gorgeous than ever due to better circulation and more healing of her body.

Lilian Grace unquestionably has God's love and protection over her. You can see and feel something different about her. I just love it! I'm one proud momma! Thank you all for praying so hard. So many groups from all over were sending up prayers this morning.

Consider Ecclesiastes 3:14—it's food for the soul. We may take the long way to get somewhere and finally realize things we thought mattered end up not having as much value. With God as our foundation, we can seek and find His purposes for our life and discover another level of fulfillment. Everything He creates has purpose and will endure forever, producing limitless joy.

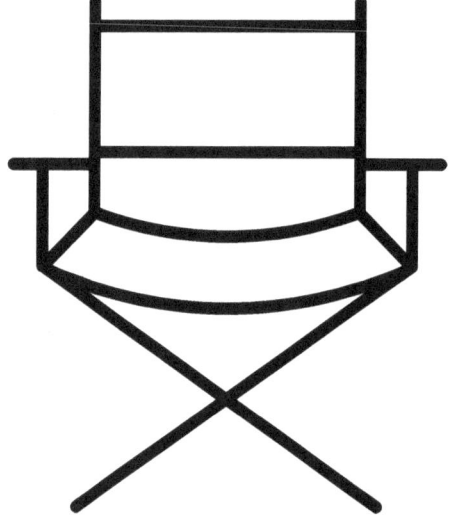

JUNE 4, 2010

34 › Walking Around the Chair

Honesty is the best policy in life! I have to admit, the last day or so (much longer, really) has not been easy by any means. Lists help me organize my thoughts, so I've written down some of the things we've been dealing with over the last several weeks.

First: Lily's PDA heart surgery and her recovery time. She shows us she is the best Warrior Princess ever (in my opinion). The doctors are slowly removing the equipment and lines from her. It's not easy to see your child connected to so many wires and motionless at times.

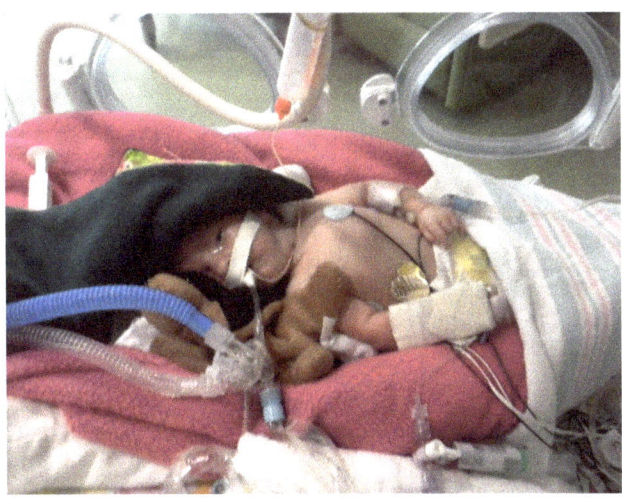

Recovery takes time.

She is becoming aware of her surroundings. When she first opened her eyes, the look on her face was like, "What in the world just happened to me, Momma? This is messed up." I can relate from all the times I've woken up after surgery. You feel as if you've been run over by a train. Her color continues to improve, and she is as pretty as can be. The doctors say she's doing well.

Second: Schedule? What schedule? I know all parents can relate to having a chaotic schedule that changes drastically from moment to moment just for the fun of it. This is one reason I did not post on here yesterday.

Third: With a heavy heart, I resigned from my amazing job with Oklahoma State University (OSU) Extension, 4-H Youth Development. I've worked there for five fun-filled years and met some fabulous people. Though it's tough leaving, I'm upgrading my job description to being my Warrior Princess's mother full time. I've trained my whole life to be ready for this special gift from God. I want to thank all my "substitute" kids in the 4-H program for helping shape and mold me into the parent I am today. I'm gonna miss going to camps, conferences, and events. To my volunteers and parents—thanks for handing your kids over to grow and learn.

Fourth: The roller coaster ride! We are finally connecting with other trisomy 18 families. While it's wonderful to find this source of support and inspiration, it also breaks my heart. These families, especially the kids, are incredible. They battle every day with emotions no one can understand unless you are in our shoes. Seeing these kids makes me cry both happy and sad tears. Happy tears because the kids are alive. Sad tears because we don't know how long we will have them on this side of heaven and the fact that they don't get to be like other kids.

When this sadness overtakes me, I ask, what is normal, really? Our kids, who have trisomy 18, are a blessing from above like any other child. They carry out God's will just like anyone else. Yes, their road is tougher (and for the ones in their lives), but they have such a ginormous impact on God's kingdom.

I know I will continue to struggle. When Lily has problems, I hold my breath and wonder just how long or how hard this life will be. By any measure, this does suck. I praise God for giving me small things like Lily taking a bottle, smiling, crying, trying to poop, her eyes opening so she can see me when I talk, and many more.

Fifth: Knowing our daughter may not be here for long. This one towers over all the others. I just want her here with me forever. She is the most amazing thing I've ever known in my life. All I want to do is pick her up and hold her to my chest—to protect her. I want her to be a "regular" kid who talks, walks, and does all sorts of things. Instead, I have to realize she's in a different category, with a bigger and better spirit than anyone I've known and the opportunity to make a bigger and better impact. I will struggle, but I will remain in the now, live it up, and cry when I need to release the pressure on my heart.

Sixth: Making sure we do the right thing for Lily. This is tough because we really don't know. Only God does. We continue to pray for God to guide us through whatever she needs. I'm trying to run next to her, not ahead or behind.

I know I'm rambling, but I guess I needed an outlet. We deal with many more things, but these made this list. We love you all. Whenever you find yourself struggling, pick up that load and set it in our Father's hands. He knows exactly what to do with it. He knows our every need. Giving it to Him may seem hard, yet it gets easier.

Lately, I've felt robbed—robbed of a normal pregnancy, birth, and baby; robbed of my job; robbed of what I used to think family was; robbed of sanity (perhaps I never had it); robbed of time. Typing this entry has given me a sense from God that I have not been robbed. He has given me a pregnancy, birth, and child that has blessed His kingdom and our family and friends; moments from my job with 4-H that prepared me for motherhood; and opportunities to witness my family members growing and changing as their hearts are ripped and torn to be healed and made stronger. My family grows stronger and individuals mature. Time with my daughter, which I was told we wouldn't have, tops the chart. God has given me fruits of the spirit and moments to be still and know He is God.

I took my own advice and placed things into a metaphorical chair, walked around it in my mind, and altered my perspective. This doesn't mean I won't fall into complaining. It means I'm trying to feel the uncomfortable times because they allow me to be in the now. Praise God!

Be like our Warrior Princess! Fight for your life and enjoy it. Stop trying to fill your life with unnecessary stuff. Start living because God has blessed you with breath and health in your body, mind, and soul. I'm trying to stop taking things for granted and appreciate my blessings. Thanks for hanging in there on this long entry. I love you all. I love the Lord for teaching me (though at times I wish I could have a spring or summer break). I'm holding tightly to the promises in Proverbs 3:5–6 and Jeremiah 29:11. I'm trusting His plans for me and praying I always find joy in the process of living those plans out regardless of the outcomes. I know He will guide me as long as I seek Him.

JUNE 5, 2010

35 › Reality Check

For most of today, Lily looked swollen and seemed off. I wanted to pick her up but knew I shouldn't. Her IVs were still attached, and she needed as much rest as possible. As I was cleaning my pumping equipment this morning, Lily had a brady and desat. I am not proud of what happened next, but I think it shows my exhaustion level.

I froze with the equipment in my hands. I stared at the monitor as tears rolled down my cheeks. I could only stand motionless. I did nothing. Nothing at all. My precious baby girl could have slipped away. Perhaps that would be easier for us both, and we wouldn't have to face an unknown future.

More tears as I type this. I'm scared that I may not be capable of doing this, but then God rescues me and reminds me that it's not about me, Chrissy, trying to make it on my own. It's about Him carrying me in His arms and trusting Him completely.

I went to my cousin's baby shower, and I was scared of how I might feel during it. Would I be a mess, crying at the littlest things said and gifts seen or build up anger or bitterness from the happiness around me while I'm dying on the inside knowing my daughter is going to die? Family and friends were kind with their warm, comforting hugs, sweet thoughts, and prayers. Being there actually lifted my spirits. I was just having a bad day leading up to the baby shower. I wondered if Lily would ever get to play with her cousin, Waylyn, or any kids at all. Dang it! More tears. Man, this life is tough, but it would be worse without her.

On another note, I will say that Michael and I had fun tonight. What did I just say? Fun! I didn't know we could still do that, but we can. We scored free tickets to the Talons game. We had a blast with our friends, the Downings, and arena football is my new favorite sport. Hughley (number three) is my favorite player. I just love his name. Say Hughley five times fast and try not to smile. Getting out was a nice change. I didn't have to answer questions or help soothe someone or be strong and brave. We yelled and danced, acted silly, and took fun pictures. Thank You, heavenly Father, for the break!

And as I type this, my hubby opens the curtain (I'm pumping), holding our precious daughter to his chest. Tears consume me. The moment takes my breath and makes all the bad moments melt away. Seeing him be the best daddy a man could be makes my heart laugh and dance. All the other stuff is manageable and makes it worth living through when I see this. She's a daddy's girl. She looks so much better after resting. I'm speechless seeing her strength. She is the biggest rock star ever and could run a hundred miler!

To conclude, do I want my daughter to slip away so it will all go away? No! Do I want to change some of our circumstances to make it easier? Yes! Will we survive the horrible moments? As long as we keep trusting God and leaving it in His hands. This is our life now. As long as I give myself a chance to process things on the not-so-good days, then I won't dwell.

Good night with lots of love!

JUNE 6, 2010

36 › Refinement Through Fire

> ♡ *LILY'S VITALS*
> *Weight: 3 lbs., 14 oz. (She has lost weight, but that's understandable with surgery.); length: 18 in. (She has grown, Praise God!); girth: 26 cm; and head: 29 ½ cm.*

Lily lived through her worst day so far. She battles hard, and she looks tired and worn. Though her eyes are swollen and her body limp, a smirk can be seen from the corner of her little lips. Her spirit is strong—she's not defeated. Michael and I spent family time together after surviving more of her episodes. This helps us endure the hard times. We love her so much. We understand God knows the hour, minute, and second when she will earn her wings. We just have to enjoy the time we have, even through the bad parts.

Lily is not able to have visitors right now. We appreciate your loving us from afar. We will keep you updated when we can. Pray for us for strength, energy, peace, understanding, and God's will. Remember, we are strongest on our knees. Always look up with your eyes focused on Him. If you ever want to be mad at someone for the bad things happening, be mad at the devil! Think about Psalm 66:10–12, one of the favorite verses of a dear friend, another Warrior Princess.

Memory Verse 7

🗡 *"For you, God, tested us; you refined us like silver. You brought us into prison and laid burdens on our backs. You let people ride over our heads; we went through fire and water, but you brought us to a place of abundance" (Psalm 66:10–12).*

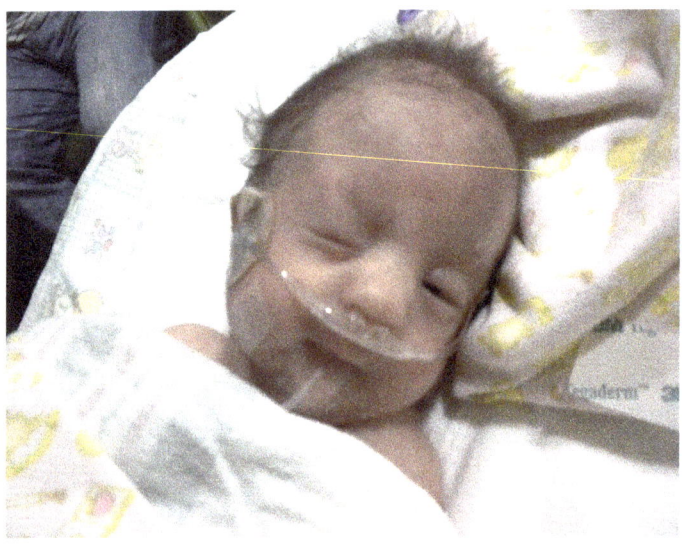

Baby girl not losing her spirit

JUNE 7, 2010

37 › Enduring

We've cried more in the last three days than all our days combined. No parent should have to go through this journey and see these horrible things. No one can fully relate unless they've been through it. I wish words could make it all better, but I don't even have words to type this entry tonight.

Pray for us like before and know we appreciate everyone doing so from afar. Our lil' Warrior Princess is finally getting some much-needed rest. Her oxygen intake has been increased to a hundred. We hope to get some sleep tonight. We have no words to speak right now. Please keep this in mind when we don't answer.

We are trying to endure the rough loops and find the good in them until they are over. We have no clue where this journey is taking us. We continue to trust God. We know He is working in so many lives right now. Please pay attention to what He is doing in your own life. Don't waste this miracle.

Tomorrow at 8:44 a.m., Lily turns forty-four days old. We have been immensely blessed by our Father to have time with her. This pain, suffering, and craziness will pass, but we are scared out of our minds. Pray God will give us the wisdom to help keep Lily in a good place. We love you.

JUNE 8, 2010

38 › Release and Relief

I may have hit my "this is too much" level after Lily's episodes Sunday night and Monday morning. I originally told myself I wasn't going to share our middle-of-the-night terror, but I feel more peaceful now and am moved to share pieces. On Sunday at 1:35 p.m., I got a call from Lily's NICU nurse telling me to hurry to the hospital—it was time. They were struggling to bring her back up from a brady and desat. My heart was ripping apart, especially since I knew she might leave this earth without Michael or me with her.

Not too long after that call, the nurse called back to say Lily had come out of it. Tears streamed down my cheeks. This would only be the first of many episodes. The next one happened after I ate supper in the cafeteria. I saw my daughter turn gray, a color that no one should ever see, especially on her child. I thought I was really going to lose my mind this time, but God was with me. Now buckle up, because this next one will not be easy to read. When I held Lily during kangaroo care, she went down fast. I couldn't stand to see her that color again, so what did I do?

I cried as I held her as tightly as I could. Then I started singing hymns. I whispered that she had more than earned her angel wings and could go. We turned the monitors off and pulled the cannula out of her nose. Let me be clear—this sucked. I bawled as my heart shattered. I will not share the rest, but I felt my daughter go through the process of dying. I wish this on no one, not even the devil.

I thought that was it. We gave her a way to go and not

suffer. And what does my daughter do? She's stubborn like me and decides she isn't done. She cries, and it's the most glorious sound. I instructed the nurses to turn the monitors back on and put her oxygen back in. We tried to say goodbye, but it wasn't her time. By the time Michael reached the hospital, she had leveled out and was sucking on a pacifier. I watched them in amazement. I didn't know how she could still be here, not after everything I had seen. I am more of a believer than ever. It really is all in His hands, no matter what we do.

After that, I couldn't sleep or eat. People tried to help me, but I couldn't get the images of Lily dying out of my head. Michael also experienced some of the episodes. One of the nurses raised her oxygen intake to one hundred, and we have not had an episode since. Please God, have mercy and grace on us for that not to happen again. I pray that when our daughter does earn her wings, it happens while she sleeps.

We have been told that Lily is starting the dying process. Please remember we have had forty-four days with her. We choose to appreciate each moment we have with her. She is the most amazing gift anyone could ever receive. She made us a mommy and daddy, for which we are so thankful.

LILY'S VITALS
She gained a little, weighing in at 4 lbs., 1 oz. We need prayers for her to poop. I know it's not an ideal prayer topic, but we really need her to since her last one was about thirty-six hours ago.

She still looks gorgeous, especially with her color tone returning to a soft glow versus the gray. Michael and I have been doing kangaroo care with her as much as possible. We want her to be comfortable and to know how much she is loved.

I hope this wasn't too much to read. I was moved to type it tonight. We love you all. We still believe we are living out God's will. We pray God does a miracle...that He is huge! We don't know when this journey will end, but pray that we have peace, love, and joy during and after it. This truly is the hardest thing (we believe) anyone has to face. I pray for healing for your hearts as they break right along with ours. We love you all!

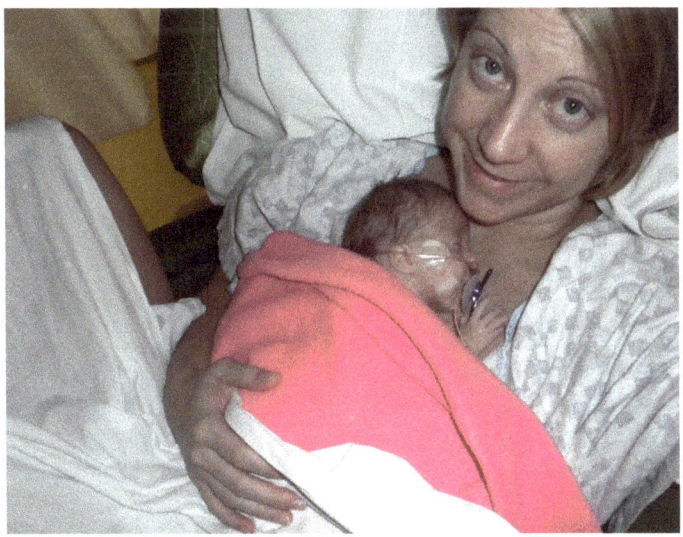

Relieved after a night of horror

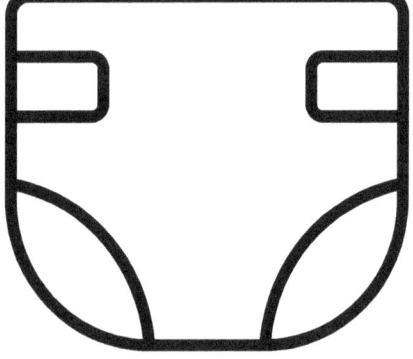

JUNE 9, 2010

39 › Prayer Request Granted

I know I just did an entry last night, but I am shouting, "Holy, holy, holy!" My God is Big, and He answered my continuous prayer that Lilian could poop finally. After forty-five hours of no poop, she filled a diaper. Praise the Lord! She got some much-needed relief. Please keep praying her bowels move and God's will be done. No suffering! Love you all!

PS: God is so good at hearing us, especially when we align ourselves with His will. Unanswered prayers can be just as good though, because God knows our future and doesn't want us to suffer. He wants to help us fulfill His purpose. Though I'm thankful for the answered prayers, I'm starting to understand and appreciate the unanswered ones. Remember to align yourself with His will and trust that He knows what's best for each of us.

"This is the confidence we have in approaching God: that if we ask anything according to his will, he hears us. And if we know that he hears us—whatever we ask—we know that we have what we asked of him" (1 John 5:14–15).

JUNE 9, 2010

40 › Unwavering Praise

Thanks for all the prayers and well wishes. Today, we have cried and cried as the realness of her life expectancy shortens; as our storm's strength builds; as our shattered dreams of normalcy slip away; and as our worn spirits lack control. Because I want to make more special memories with our sweet Warrior Princess, her grandparents spent time with her tonight. Oh, how my heart aches for them.

I wish I could make this journey be full of freedom, total health, and unlimited time for all. Her grandparents haven't experienced the restrictions and heaviness with their other grandkids or the idea of what having them would be like. I long for a normalcy far from our current hospital and T18 journey where they can hold her, watch her accomplish milestones, and be in the moment.

My girlfriend, Nikki, encouraged me to listen to the song "Praise You in This Storm" by Casting Crowns. The song lifted my spirits and spoke to me as I mentally pictured the storms raging around us. We are going to praise God no matter how strong the storms escalate or the number of occurrences we face. The length and strength are unpredictable. Still, I will fall to my knees and raise my hands high anywhere that I am. He is worthy to be praised come sunshine or rain. I cannot do this journey without Him leading me through the known and the unknown. He will never leave me while calming the stormy waters.

We have no clue how much time we have left with Lily. We pray that if and when it is her time to fly that she will do so peacefully and without pain. I praise God for giving us this time we've had with her. I still hope for a miracle and that she will be with us here forever, but I have to be real and know her purpose may be fulfilled soon.

I am mad at Satan and no one else for making this the worst experience ever. I praise God for providing for us always and using this situation for good. He has shown His strength, His face, and His guiding hands throughout this journey, and we could not survive without Him. Pray Michael and I have wisdom to make decisions that are in Lily's best interests. I hope we do not have to go through what happened earlier this week.

Throughout this process, we have been blessed with new relationships, love, and strength. But Lily has been the greatest gift of all. Praise His name on high for all eternity no matter the storm or sunshiny day!

JUNE 10, 2010

41 › Leap of Faith

The roller coaster ride took an upside-down loop today. Michael and I needed to make some major decisions this week, and we've talked things out and tossed options around trying to decide the best way to go. I've tried to get the memories of Sunday night out of my head so that I could help make the right decisions. Remembering that we are on borrowed time, I chose to simply push through my brokenness, insecurities, and indecisiveness by stepping aside for God's plan to continue while she is still breathing. Prayer time and communication with my hubby brought great relief.

Michael and I wanted Lily to be held by her grandparents, great-grandparents, aunts, and uncles before we took the plunge on a drastic measure. Lily has been on major oxygen this week, and we have to limit her time on it to avoid damaging her body. Starting to wean her off means she might progress quickly to death. With this knowledge, my fear kicked up a notch and made it difficult for me to know what the best thing for her would be.

This has been the first time through this process where I have had no clue what the right decision is. So far, I've trusted God completely. I could sense Him and feel His peace flowing over me, making it easy to trust. While I know He has never left me, I feel that I have been left to fend for myself. The following thoughts play over and over in my mind: If we keep her on the high level of oxygen, then she will fade away. If we wean her off, she might plummet into death.

So I prayed. Last night, I prayed. This morning, I prayed. Michael and I continued to discuss ideas. He wanted to bring her home, but I wasn't sure of my abilities. Keeping her on the current oxygen level seems very selfish and chicken. Taking her off means I have to let go and let God show His power and plans. Wow! Talk about a hard road.

Do you know what God has done for us in this situation? He gave me peace by bringing individuals to speak wisdom and tell me to face the music. I've listened to those people and accepted what needs to be done. We are weaning her off the high oxygen levels to give her a chance to fight the way she has shown us she can.

No matter how hard it is, I know I must leave Lily in God's hands. She will have a better chance in His hands than in ours. Please keep us in your prayers. I am scared out of my mind and can hardly sleep. My chest is tight as my mind races. I'm continuously reminded to trust my heavenly Father, who knows what's best for her. I'm watching the monitor as I type this to encourage myself to let go and let God, for He either needs her to remain on earth or fly to heaven. His peace is all consuming and washes over me like a flood.

Since early evening, we've been dropping her oxygen levels. I praise God because she's staying at a hundred. It's amazing how she can improve in one moment and then turn worse the next. Let's continue to trust God and His will for Lily. No matter what the future holds, let's enjoy the present. Whether Lily comes home depends on my strength and her doctors' release. I need prayers to conquer my fear of a repeat from Sunday night and the ability to stand strong as her caretaker.

One more thing—at Fellowship Church of Tulsa (where we attend), we are part of a building campaign. Michael and I decided to tithe using 10 percent based on my past salary from the OSU Extension Service that I no longer make. Practicing sacrificial tithing will be harder with Lily's medical expenses and my voluntary unemployment, but we have already seen God's faithfulness in our finances. Within the last twenty-four hours, we were given the exact amount of our monthly pledge. We have earmarked this money for food during our hospital stint. Praise God for taking care of us in everything.

For me, trusting God is an easy decision despite the hard road. I will continue to trust through the ups and downs. What happens when you trust God? You expose yourself to miracles and peace beyond comprehension. Thank You, God, for never allowing me to get too comfortable and for not leaving even when You are quiet. Be still and know!

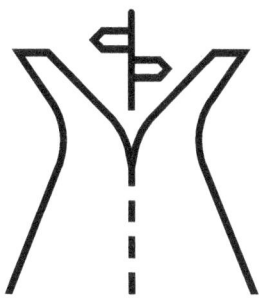

JUNE 11, 2010

42 › Noise and Light

We are far from perfect, and I let the situation get the best of me today. When the threat of losing Lily seems close, I hover near the edge. It's no one's fault but my own. I get protective, mad, and short-fused over things I should just let go. When an individual wasn't hearing my words nor pleas over the phone, I snapped and lost my mind. This escalated to high-volume screaming and uncontrollable crying in the NICU solarium, a secluded, quiet cube where families can escape on the NICU floor. I wish I could be perfect in my reactions, but the last time I checked, my name was not spelled J-E-S-U-S. I will work on it, but I need people to understand I'm barely hanging on.

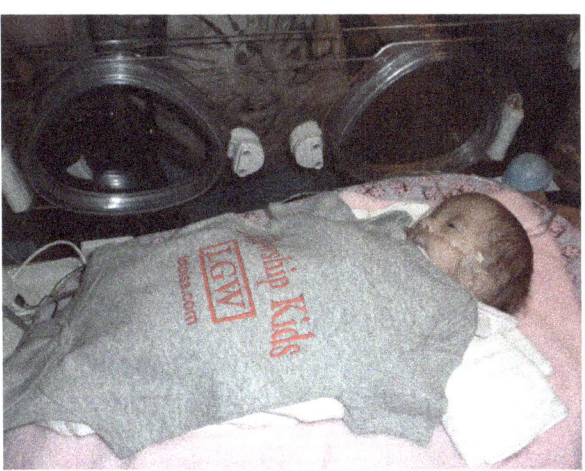

Shining bright and touching lives

After a long twenty-four hours, Lily is exhausted from the bradys and desats related to her digestion issues. I just want to scream and cry out my frustrations. Every time those alarms sound, I hold my breath and move into action trying to get her to breathe and pump...breathe and pump...breathe and pump. Having others to help us would be fabulous, but we barely have energy for ourselves and Lily. We watch everyone's heart breaking, and it hurts just as much.

Lily's and my devotional brought tears of joy owning Lily's purpose but still wishing hardship didn't have to be part of the package deal. Based on Matthew 5:14, we can be a light in a dark world by living out obedience to Him. Lily is that light. She's taking one breath at a time to fulfill His purpose. It's a human desire to want to check out. This journey is hard with an endless supply of darkness. We must remember He has purpose in our light for the darkness. Be the light!

JUNE 13, 2010

43 › Imperfect Empathy

Not having internet access last night stopped me from typing a journal entry. I wasn't expecting to need a break from writing, but it turned out that I did. There's much to say about renewing the mind, body, and soul. Michael is very sweet and encouraged me to go to the movies last night. I finally listened and went with my friend, Pam. God knows just when I need things, and He provides. Oh, how He provides!

> *♡ LILY'S VITALS*
> *Lily has made a 180-degree turn today. I get to report praise to God because she looks and seems to feel wonderful with eye swelling at a minimum, warmer coloring of her skin, and little squeaks from within. She's showing us just how tough she can be. Bradys? What bradys? We could live like this forever. Please, God, continue to bring miracles of healing and peace for Lily and all of us. Lily weighs 4 lbs., 4 oz.—only an ounce below her pre-surgery weight. Woohoo! My body shakes from crying out with praise that our daughter is forty-nine days old today. Wow, God, You take my breath away and sweep me off my feet. Thank You! Thank You! Thank You! This part of the roller coaster ride makes the bad days bearable.*

One of my favorite cherished sisters sent me the song "Come to Jesus" by Chris Rice. It energizes and moves me while I think about getting to go to Jesus. My heart melts and I want to come to, sing to, fall on, cry to, dance for, fly to Jesus for all my life. I may not always get my relationship right with some of you. I may not say the right things or communicate my feelings the right way. Know that I do love you. I am far from perfect but know that I don't go a day without thinking about others and putting myself in their shoes. I have to remember that this type of compassion and empathy is a gift from God. I see others' pain, and I hurt for them.

Always remember to come to, sing to, fall on, cry to, dance for, and fly to Jesus. We all have a past and things we struggle with every day. What matters is our relationship with God. I don't ever want someone to think I hold their past against them. We all are perfect in God's eyes.

May each of you know how special you are. I love you! Most importantly, our Father has the most love, unconditionally, without a price tag, for each of us when we say yes to Him. Where else can we get something so huge for eternity? Nowhere! The ultimate gift is to be reunited with Him and others who have gone before us. Giddiness consumes my spirit imagining such a reunion! Have a beautiful Sunday.

JUNE 14, 2010

44 › He Is for Me

Okay, prayer warriors, we have some lil' babies at the hospital in need of prayer. Two of the babies are in major trouble. Two weeks ago tonight, we were in the same place, and my heart breaks for their families. Eli, who moved across the hall, is fighting for his life. Please keep him and his amazing family in your prayers on this tough road and rough week ahead.

> *LILY'S VITALS*
> *Lily gained another ounce to reach 4 lbs., 5 oz. Yes, Lord! She has returned to her pre-surgery weight. More bradys and apnea episodes are caused by her lack of poopy diapers. Let's lift it up in prayer. Nothing is too small for our God!*

Now, I must tell you about the song "You Are for Me" by Kari Jobe. I've listened to it on repeat through tears and surging emotions of comfort, peace, tranquility, clarity, and hope. The notes can sooth your spirit while reminding you of who God is and what He can do. Tonight, the lyrics of this song ring truer than ever. Watching these families face their fears and the horrors on the roller coaster ride they never signed up for is hard. God reminds me that He is always for me and for them. His truth and promises are pure and woven in my heartstrings forever so I don't forget.

I said this before, and I need to say it again. Why do we question God when we should question the devil? Unfortunately, the devil prowls around this earth. When we are confused, it is from lies the devil shouts at us, plain and simple. Our God is not a God of confusion. In confusing situations, in difficult situations—be mad at the devil. That's what I'm doing.

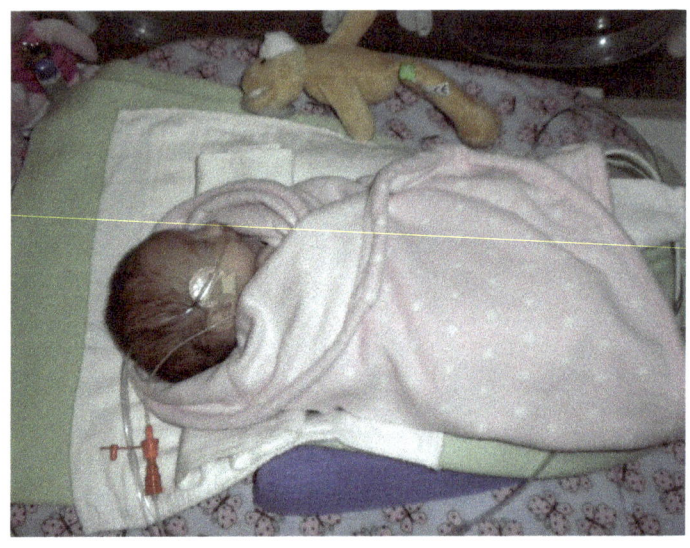

Getting rest knowing He is for her

JUNE 15, 2010

45 › Still Standing

Where do I stand? I stand upon my Rock, my Savior! Today is day fifty-one of Lilian Grace's life. Tears roll down my cheeks. God has indeed taken my breath away.

Am I ready to bring Lily home? I'm conflicted—50 percent of me is overflowing with joy because our daughter gets to experience the atmosphere of our home, which is something we thought would not be possible. The other 50 percent of me is scared completely out of my mind. Lily has a new line of machines letting us know her heartbeat, apnea episodes, and oxygen levels. She will be on continuous oxygen and a feeding pump. With so many things to remember, I pray we do remember them all!

Today, Miss Lily finally got to take her nursery pictures. Tears of joy flow as I help change her and position her for a picture. She was a natural in her bright floral jumper as her eyes lit up and lips curved upwards with a sweet smile knowing she was getting to come home. Her left hand appeared to sign I love you. You mean we get something normal? Yes! Praise God for the big and little things in life. Praise His name on high for giving us a team of doctors, nurses, respiratory therapy specialists, and other specialists to provide the best care for our Warrior Princess.

For fifty-one days, it's felt like summer camp or a 24/7 slumber party with all my peeps in the NICU. I'm going to miss all the incredible people here. I have a new appreciation for their sacrifices, passions, and path. Thank God they have chosen this field! My daughter is still here because of their desire to help others and follow God's lead.

I've realized more now than ever that grasping your path and taking in the good, the bad, and the ugly prepares you for your purpose. I've heard story after story and can tell you that God plucked each one of us to be exactly where we are. He doesn't create bad things. If we pay attention, we see He goes before us to help us grow and so others can see Him. It brings a longing for heaven, where there's no place like home. I hope when God calls us home, we get to enjoy being with our heavenly Father for eternity. Until then, we will have joy in the now.

> ### ♡ LILY'S VITALS
> *She's the biggest she's been so far—4 lbs., 7 oz. Hallelujah! She's spitting up like a normal baby. She has shown us the spirit of a true Warrior Princess by never giving up. I have no idea how long we will be blessed to enjoy our daughter here on earth. I do know that I'm going to give it everything I've got to make it the most joyous adventure ever. May God continue to be with us through the ups, downs, twists, and turns.*

We're buckling up with our eyes wide open as we trust God to guide and direct us through this new chapter. We love you all! We know we've been strong on our knees. Keep in mind God wants to be in our life every day through a one-on-one relationship with us. Ecclesiastes 5 reminds us to follow through with our vows and make sure to guard our steps. When we don't get what we want, God is giving us what we need.

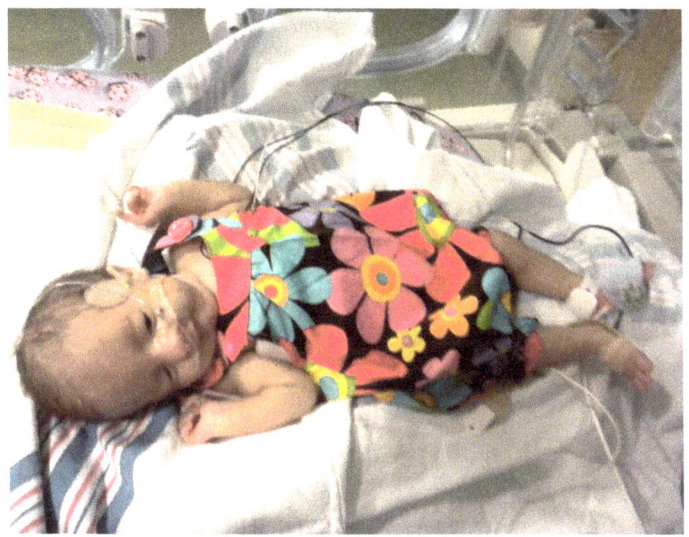

Blooming and ready for her close-up

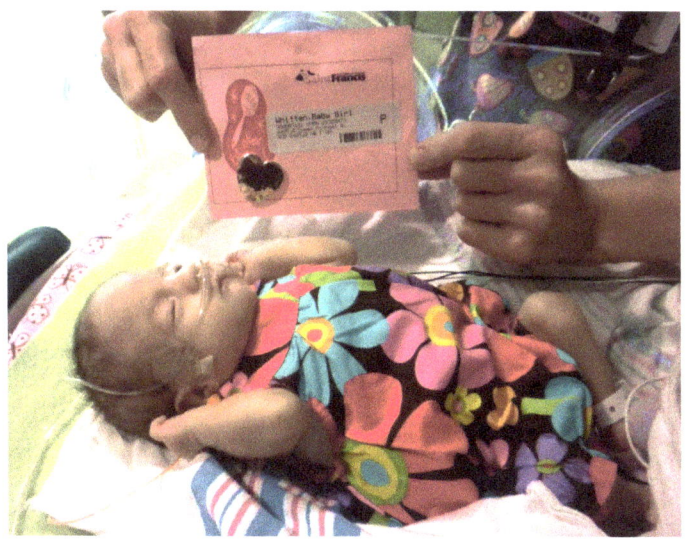

Praising God to be going home

"Fulfill Your Vow to God"

Guard your steps when you go to the house of God. Go near to listen rather than to offer the sacrifice of fools, who do not know that they do wrong.

> *Do not be quick with your mouth,*
> *do not be hasty in your heart*
> *to utter anything before God.*
> *God is in heaven*
> *and you are on earth,*
> *so let your words be few.*

> *As a dream comes when there are many cares,*
> *so the speech of a fool when there are many words.*

When you make a vow to God, do not delay in fulfilling it. He has no pleasure in fools; fulfill your vow.

It is better not to vow than to make a vow and not fulfill it.

Do not let your mouth lead you into sin. And do not protest to the temple messenger, "My vow was a mistake." Why should God be angry at what you say and destroy the work of your hands?

Much dreaming and many words are meaningless. Therefore stand in awe of God.

(Ecclesiastes 5:1–7)

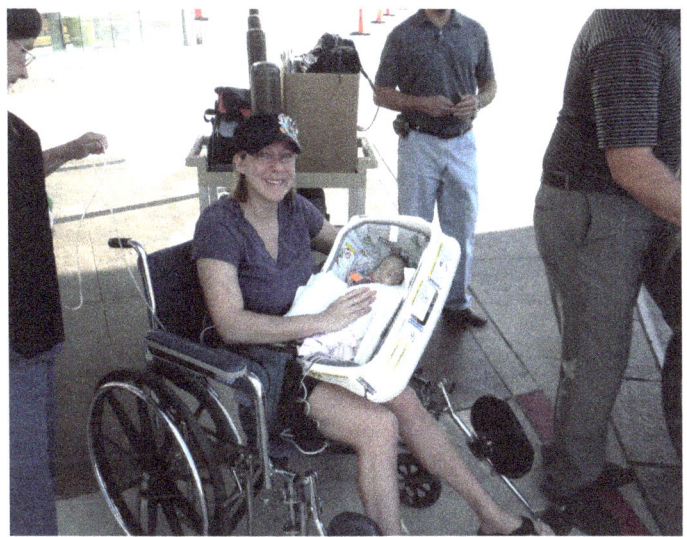

Joy unspeakable and full of grace

Standing in His grace and joy

Home Sweet Home

JUNE 16, 2010

46 › Home

I forgot to grab the extra-supportive buckles when I said we were buckling up for this ride. Today was a repeat from yesterday's crazy, stressful ride. I'm as exhausted and out of breath as if I'd run three marathons in a row. What's the lesson learned? Preparation! Thank God I love to plan because this adventure needs a well-thought out system.

We will load our living room with necessities. Lily has an awesome nurse named Michelle, who will stay overnight five days a week. Both the home health care and equipment companies are wonderful. I already had my first meltdown this morning when I couldn't figure out what was causing Lily's machines to go off continuously. Between my lack of knowledge in the medical field and the ability to adapt to the non-stop noises, I was drowning. Thankfully, Joel, the home health care worker, came to my rescue and walked me through the basics of the machines. Praise God!

Getting used to the new bells and whistles is tough but manageable. Lily's breathing and pumping has been unstable today. I got her to rest without problems this afternoon by playing continuous classical music and relaxing next to her. I'm hoping for more moments like that. We have many who are willing to help, but we are quarantined right now. Please be patient. Lily has her first doctor's appointment next week, and we will discuss the length of our quarantine. May we continue to figure things out and enjoy this time together. I love how God has given us one of the desires of our heart—to be parents. Praise His name on high!

JUNE 17, 2010

47 › Sweet Moments While Resting

It's Lily's fifty-third day in the world and second day home. I'm trying to do special things for her between her sleepy nap times. Our schedule today has involved the following:

- Playtime for twenty minutes with her cute toys and jungle gym;
- Morning nap with mommy and Lily chest-to-chest for an hour and a half;
- Watching a kids' TV program in her sweet lamb sitter for ten minutes followed by an hour nap;
- Mammoth pillow time for a two-hour nap;
- More naps;
- Watching the NBA Finals, World Cup, and US Open.

We had a fairly busy day with an emphasis on napping, which is good for her healing and growth. I'm trying to post more pictures on Facebook, but it's not happening right now. I will get them up as soon as possible.

We have had the normal spitting-up business. Yay for normal stuff! The not-so-normal stuff, like hearing the alarms on her equipment, is wearing on me. I've taken three naps and just woke up to pump again. My naps have been the best kind—chest-to-chest with Lily. Thank the Lord for these sweet moments among the stressful stuff.

Since today's focus was rest, I was reminded of Matthew

11:28–30 and singing "Come unto Me" on Sundays. I always enjoyed singing it in choir. I didn't know how essential it would be to have this song embedded in my memory to help me embrace the importance of rest. He will lighten our burdens when we come to Him for rest. He gives us a rest like nothing else can provide for us. His yoke is indeed easy! Thankfully, God carries our burdens. I want to pass them on to Him because this path is far from easy, and I am tired. Lots of love to you all.

Memory Verse 8

 "Come to me, all you who are weary and burdened, and I will give you rest. Take my yoke upon you and learn of me, for I am gentle and humble in heart, and you will find rest for your souls. For my yoke is easy and my burden is light"
(Matthew 11:28–30).

JUNE 18, 2010

48 › Survival Mode

Ever feel like you can't remember how life used to be before? Today, I tried to remember what it used to be like before Lily, before pregnancy, before marriage, before college, and so on. It's hard to remember what it used to be like.

I've heard people say they wish they could go back to this or that. I have to admit I'm glad I don't have to go back. As each chapter has been written, I've learned lesson after lesson. I wouldn't want to go back and do it all again. Thinking about this makes me realize I've been in survival mode for a lot of my life.

Why do I say this? Well, I've always tried to push through whatever I'm going through, a.k.a. survival mode. If Lily has taught me one thing—and let's be clear, she's taught me several things in her short life—she's taught me to stop trying just to survive and to live in the now because we don't always get tomorrow.

Today was a pretty good day. We are praying for more poop, which is common in our life right now. I can't even imagine where it's all being stored in her tiny body. Lily hasn't gone poop in two days, causing reflux.

I finally posted the rest of the pictures after upload failures. If I missed one, I'm not even going to apologize because there are so many already. I hope you enjoy a glance into our adventures. We've had some good ones so far. Here's something to melt any bad day or feeling away:

Love translated in just a look!

Daddy's girl at bath time

I haven't seen much daylight lately, but tomorrow I'm destined for a much-needed walk while Michael is home during the day. May we all learn to live in the now and live it up! God is fabutastic in painting a marvelous picture for us and showing us how to take advantage of each moment.

P.S. Someone asked me if it is wonderful kissing a miracle every day. Kissing my miracle angel from above is the most exhilarating pleasure I will ever have. She is a treasure like no other. I hope you get the same feeling from your little ones. My hubby even sends chills down my spine when he gives me a peck on the lips. Life is soooo grand!

Slowing down and trusting God

JUNE 19, 2010

49 › Slowing Down

Weariness made for a semi-lazy day until tonight. We've cleaned and organized. Well, not all of us. Lily has mostly slept. She is now wide awake and ready for the night with her big, wide-open eyes and giggly spirit. When I lay chest-to-chest with her, she will fall fast asleep. I just love watching her eyes droop and feeling her body relax against mine as she surrenders to a peaceful sleep.

We've been catching up with paperwork and filing. Man, it's crazy how much paper we waste. I just hope the amount of paperwork we have to fill out slows down. Being buried in paperwork reminds me of how the devil throws so much at us and wraps us up where we can't see ahead.

I remember reading a story about a climber falling and hanging from the side of the mountain in the pitch black, trying to figure out how he was going to get out of his predicament. Come to find out, if he would have just stopped and reached down, he could have touched the ground. How true is this for our life? If we could just slow down, we could see how to get through things by trusting God.

Anyway, tonight is our first official night solo. The nurse is here five nights a week, so it'll be an interesting night without her. I will say, last night I was up and down a lot anyway, so tonight shouldn't be any different. Michael has become quite a helper. He lined up all Lily's meds in her special syringes. Praise God for a wonderful husband and father. I couldn't ask for a better man to take care of our daughter and me. He is such a fabulous provider and gives us lots of love! The biggest thing—and ladies, this is most important—he is a godly man. He has become the spiritual leader of our household, and I couldn't be more honored and blessed. Praise the Lord! I love watching Lily and her daddy together. She loves him and stares at him with her big, gorgeous eyes. Their bond takes my breath away. I hope you all have such wonderful memories. Happy Father's Day to all you fathers out there.

"What Makes a Dad"

God took the strength of a mountain,
The majesty of a tree,
The warmth of a summer sun,
The calm of a quiet sea,
The generous soul of nature,
The comforting arm of night,
The wisdom of the ages,
The power of the eagle's flight,
The joy of a morning in spring,
The faith of a mustard seed,
The patience of eternity,
The depth of a family need,
Then God combined these qualities,
When there was nothing more to add,
He knew His masterpiece was complete,
And so, He called it...Dad.

(Author Unknown)

JUNE 20, 2010

50 › Gratitude on Father's Day

I thought I might completely lose my mind during our long night marathon. Did I ever have it to lose? Anyway, Lily's monitors went off throughout the entire night. Michael came in as relief pitcher in the early morning so I could sleep. Just love that guy a whole lot.

Michael went to church, and I stayed with Lily-bug. While we were alone, her heart rate soared to 210 and her temp increased to 99.5. We haven't seen a heart rate that high since the beginning, and I freaked out a little pacing and biting my nails while my heart raced and my mind swirled thinking about what it could all mean this time. Could she have a heart attack or stroke with her heart rate being so high? I needed relief, and God calmed me down as I listened to our pastor on podcast. When Michael got home, I called the NICU. They directed me to the monitoring company and pediatrician.

What was the problem? Still the same thing: poop problems. Lily hadn't had a real poop in four days. It's been crazy that poop has taken over my conversations lately. We prayed, emphasizing poop again. What did our heavenly Father do? He's given us three poopy diapers since three this afternoon. Praise God for poop once again! I didn't realize how much poop can control the heart rate and temp for lil ones.

Michael had a wonderful Father's Day with his daughter. They watched tons of sports today. I got a timeout to spend quality time with my dad, mom, brother, sister, sister-in-law, niece, and nephew watching *Toy Story 3*. Loved, loved, loved it. I even cried at the end.

Spoiler alert: Watching Andy play with his old toys one more time did me in. How many of us wish someone paid attention to us or appreciated us? I want you all to know how much we appreciate you. Without your love, support, and prayers, we wouldn't be soaring through this.

God continues to teach us many valuable lessons through His attention to detail every day of our lives. He has provided more than perseverance, love, and comfort. He's provided money when we needed it, food for our nourishment, and strength to survive this incredibly difficult ride. I thank Him a million times to infinity for always thinking of us.

Today, being with my family brought tears to my eyes. I love them so much and have missed spending time with them. It's crazy how quickly things can change. I am so glad they invited me. I needed them more than I would have thought or let myself admit.

Try to take moments with those you love. You never know how much it means to them. When I got home, I grabbed Lily and held on tight. God has given me almost fifty-seven glorious days with my daughter. Adjusting to our situation hasn't gotten easier, but it has gotten easier to enjoy the good moments. I've given her a million kisses just because I can. Thank you, God, for no one could have given me this but You!

JUNE 22, 2010

51 › Teamwork

Oh, boy, has it been a day in the twilight zone. I have to admit, sometimes I'm tired of learning. I keep going, but sometimes I yearn for a break. We are moving forward and switching from a night nurse to a day nurse. Please pray the new shift will work for us since the night shift was unsuccessful.

I can't believe yesterday, Monday, June 21, 2010, was my original due date. Wow! Talk about surprises and blessings all twisted together. Lily is almost fifty-eight days old, with seven days at home and now one day into her development. I couldn't be prouder than I am right now. She is way more advanced than her diagnosis predicted.

Lily is going to have bad moments mixed with good ones. Life as we know it will never be the same. I have to admit that the new T18 moms in my life are a godsend. I talked to two of them today to help me get through some things. Thank you, ladies! This road wasn't what we signed up for, but I praise God for preparing us and providing others who have walked the road before us.

Today, a kids program we watched focused on teamwork. Oh, I love the concept where more is accomplished as a team than as an individual. This reigns true in all aspects of my life. Who are you teaming up with? Is it working?

Michael and I are learning what's working and what's not for our team members. I know it may seem crazy, but sometimes I wish I didn't have to speak up. It gets hard. I know we would not be standing on our own two feet without God and our support system.

"Family of God" is an old hymn from my church choir days that keeps playing in my head. The family of God, all over the world, has stepped up and out making sure we are not alone or without our needs being met. I'm learning that we are all human and deal with trials differently. What I love is when God brings the right people from His family to be His hands and feet. Not everyone is meant to be part of every season. I'm beyond blessed to be part of His family. Hundreds have played a part in helping me get where I am today. Again, this journey is not meant to be done alone.

Lily has been rolling through the diapers, and shoo wee, do they stink. Hallelujah for more answered prayers! Puts a huge smile on my face. She's been more vocal today and is cracking me up as always. I couldn't love someone more if I tried.

We go to the doctor on Wednesday. Lift up those prayers for God's will to guide and direct her doctors and nurses in giving her the best life possible, full of potential and health.

JUNE 22, 2010

52 › Cartoons

It's not meant for me to post tonight. This is my third attempt. Somehow, I keep deleting my words. But here's one more try.

Lily is fifty-eight days old, with seven days at home, and living it up enjoying cartoons. Her hands wave, and she chatters at me as she tugs at her nasal cannula and feeding tube. Just now, she told her daddy to get out of the way with her squeaks and hand motions. Hilarious!

We've turned her oxygen down to .03 liters per minute of oxygen flow. Pray it keeps going well like it has today. It would be such a relief not to have oxygen tanks that could blow up the house. We aren't allowed to burn candles, so I'm a believer in the Scentsy products more now.

We're planning a huge celebration on Friday when Lily will celebrate two months of life. Praise God and hallelujah! Here is what we posted on her Facebook events page:

Lily's two-month birthday is Friday, June 25, 2010. We are celebrating by wearing green all day. She is going to wear a beautiful Tinker Bell outfit from Build-A-Bear. The green represents life, growth, moving forward, and celebrating the 4-H program (since I had to depart from it). So grab your green and help celebrate our Warrior Princess making it to two months! Make sure to post or send me pictures of yourself in green. Also, make sure you eat something extra healthy that day. You are worth filling up with good stuff. Remember, a car can't go without gas. Make sure to take care of yourselves. I think we all take ourselves for granted sometimes.

Feeling chosen and lucky to be her parents

JUNE 23, 2010

53 › Proud Parents

Lily is growing! Lily is growing! God is Big! She weighs 4 lbs., 12 1/2 oz. Praise God, we rocked the doctor's appointment. I am shouting out loud because I don't know how many moments we'll get. Yay! Thank You, God, for a back entrance to go through at the doctor's office to protect her.

The chaotic morning had me scared something might go horribly wrong. Why would I feel like this when God truly has provided this whole time? When we got to the doctor's office, we had a blast getting compliments about how adorable Lily is. Yay for celebrations and wonderful compliments! My heart jumped up and down, dancing and singing. We are proud parents of our Warrior Princess, who rocks everyone's world. God, how did we get so lucky to have her here? Thank You for choosing us to be her parents.

After hearing about other T18 kids and their parents, I have more praise for God supplying us with doctors who care about moving forward with Lily's care. Other parents and kids are not so lucky. Let's lift them up in prayer and ask God to send doctors who care and want to help these beautiful babies have a healthier life while on earth.

This road sucks at times, but there are good moments, too. Since life is unpredictable, I'm grabbing my family and soaring high in the sky, creating moments like a dance in the living room, a fashion show photo shoot, a movie marathon outside, or crafting projects with her hand- and footprints until we don't get to anymore. Grab your family and soar. Soar above all the crap this life can bring sometimes.

"Soar Like an Eagle"

Did you know that an eagle knows when a storm is approaching long before it breaks? The eagle will fly to some high spot and wait for the winds to come.

When the storm hits, it sets its wings so that the wind will pick it up and lift it above the storm. While the storm rages below, the eagle is soaring above it.

The eagle does not escape the storm. It simply uses the storm to lift it higher. It rises on the winds that bring the storm.

When the storms of life come upon us—and all of us will experience them—we can rise above them by setting our minds and our belief toward God. The storms do not have to overcome us. We can allow God's power to lift us above them.

God enables us to ride the winds of the storm that bring sickness, tragedy, failure and disappointment in our lives. We can soar above the storm.

Remember, if we are really honest with ourselves, it is not the burdens of life that weigh us down, it is how we handle them.

(Author Unknown)

JUNE 25, 2010

54 › Two-Month Birthday

Lily had a rough time late Wednesday night and all day Thursday, turning blue a few times. I spoke too soon about things looking up, but I'm not gonna let it get me down. We will soar above this storm and remain excited about celebrating Lilian Grace's two-month birthday later today!

Her outfits are ready. The *Tinker Bell* movies are queued up to watch. Michael is bringing home a birthday surprise—an actual birthday cake with a Tinker Bell theme. We are excited to celebrate with her just as our little family—Michael, Lily, and me!

We love sharing our life with others, but it's important to do family things together. I'm so big on large family gatherings, but I am starting to appreciate the smaller and more intimate moments. I think our heavenly Father loves His one-on-one time with us even more.

I'm leaning on God more than I ever thought possible. He has been so good to us, and we have not gone without. Even in the middle of Lily's bad day, my hubby took over so that I could use a massage gift card one of my dear friends gave me. Holy moly! I had some knots in my shoulders and lower back, and the massage therapist kneaded until she got them out. I appreciate that my body can carry the load no matter what kind of stress, good or bad. Though the massage worked out some of the tension I was carrying, I know I still have to feel the pain that comes before healing. I fell asleep as the calming music and mesmerizing scents swept me away. I thought about Lily and cried. Not being able to shake the feeling of "is it already time" playing continuously really sucks.

No matter how many normal things we get, there's a huge, dark cloud hanging above us. I do pretty well living in the present, but the bad days make that cloud darker and more real. Here's to sunshine and no darkness as we pray Lily has better days. As I sing "You Are My Sunshine" continuously, I love how much happiness she brings by making all the bad fade away with her light. I wish I wouldn't ever have to live without her sunshine, but I am realistic and know we are on borrowed time. I hope she knows just how much I love her to the moon and back and for all eternity.

We love you all! Remember to wear your green and take pictures!

Happy two-month birthday to our real-life Tinker Bell!

JUNE 25, 2010

55 › Faith and a Fundraiser

Lilian transformed into Tinker Bell wearing a precious Build-A-Bear metallic green dress with touches of purple ribbons, glittery silver wings, and Mary Jane socks while holding a pixie dust wand. The vibrant green, lavender, pink, and white cake her daddy brought was a dream come true with her very own Tinker Bell accessory flying over a flower nested on top of the cake. Pictures are on Facebook. We'd love to see the pictures of you wearing green to add to her birthday book.

Thank You, God, for giving us two full months with our Warrior Princess. Words cannot describe what I feel today. I can only say I am truly speechless, which does not happen often. To be at this point is a miracle. God has shown us many stages of the storm. We have many more to go through, and He keeps providing.

Last night, I was down, letting Lily's bad days play continuously in my mind while trying to process and be positive for whatever the day would bring. It felt wrong, somehow, to enjoy the good moments of celebrating another monthly birthday while the bad lurked, waiting to attack at any moment. I must continue to trust God and leave it all in His big, strong hands. He is experienced beyond a million men combined. He loves me, and He loves you. Oh, how I love to be in His presence.

Cheers to God for giving us Lilian and showing Himself to us every day. I keep thinking I'll wake up and all our magical moments will have been a dream, like story time has ended. Though our journey has been hard, I am blessed beyond measure. Continue lifting Lilian in prayer, and other kiddos who are sick or have a syndrome. I'm asking God to be Big!

> **LILY'S VITALS**
> She wore out easily, dealing with lots of poop and reflux at the same time. We tried to wean her off oxygen and then realized it's not time. Her oxygen is now at 12 liters per minute. It feels like a crazy dance where we move forward, backward, sideways, turn, and jump in no particular order.

We've finally gotten shirts for Lilian's fundraiser. The funds help with her care and future therapies when insurance does not cover it. Thank you to everyone participating. We may do another order later but no promises. On the front side of the shirt is a heart, swirls, and a dragonfly with the words "God Be Big," "Lilian Grace," and "Ephesians 3:17–19." On the back side, the word "Lily" and words of the verse are emblazoned along with a cross with Jesus.

Memory Verse 9

"So that CHRIST may dwell in your hearts through FAITH. And I pray that you, being rooted and established in LOVE, may have power, together with all the Lord's holy people, to grasp how wide and long and high and deep is the love of Christ, and to know this love that surpasses knowledge—that you may be filled to the measure of all the FULLNESS OF GOD" (Ephesians 3:17–19, all caps added by author).

JUNE 26, 2010

56 › Learn and Grow

When you read 1 Corinthians 13:4–7, substitute your name for the word "love." *Chrissy is patient, Chrissy is kind. She does not envy, she does not boast, she is not proud. She does not dishonor others, she is not self-seeking, she is not easily angered, she keeps no record of wrongs. Chrissy does not delight in evil but rejoices with the truth. Chrissy always protects, always trusts, always hopes, always perseveres.*

Gulp! Ouch! When I did this exercise, I realized it's not all true. My prayer is for it to become true. I hope that if Michael and I can help Lily see anything that it will be to always look in the mirror for a reality check with God. We will never be perfect, but we can always keep learning and growing.

We've had several bad days in a row, but Lily looked so cute in her pictures anyway. Sadly, they do not show the whole truth. They do show a family doing their best to keep it together while loving each other to the fullest. What they don't show is the behind-the-scenes reel of a family struggling as the alarms clang when Lily's oxygen levels crash and her heart rate drops below fifty. I'm glad you all can't see it because living it and reading about it are different. It's a lighter load when you don't have to be in the trenches.

I've heard through the grapevine about a couple of T18 kids going to the hospital. My heart aches for them. Leave it to the devil to bring forth our fears to paralyze us. He brings ridiculous struggles, such as people and our behaviors, to steer us in the wrong direction. I'm done with people pleasing and letting the devil win small battles. I want to live out 1 Corinthians 13 as I am patient, kind, protecting, trustful, hopeful, and persevering. I do not want to be envious, boastful, prideful, rude, self-seeking, easily angered, or a keeper of wrongs.

Lily crashed many times during the night, but my tears had dried up. I looked at our pictures from yesterday and couldn't help but want more of those moments. I may sound like a broken record, but I want a lot of things I know I can't have. The tears flow now as I look at Lily and ask God to keep being Big and even to heal her completely. This may or may not happen, but the most important thing I need to remember is that He has the best plan.

Everyone who has followed our journey and supported us through the T-shirt fundraiser has been such a blessing to us. Everyone blesses us even more as we share our climb up this mountain. I hope this journey strengthens you for your own climb. Love you all!

JUNE 27, 2010

57 › Triumphant at Church & Home

Our little family attended church together. We didn't give anyone a heads up. We were excited to do this with God and to worship together and celebrate our triumph over the not-so-good days that can break us down. The alarm brayed a handful of times, but Michael did a good job of silencing it. Though today was special, the activity wore out Miss Lilian, creating lots of nap time.

The service stirred my emotions of victory, joy, peace, and triumph as we shared this special day with other believers. I didn't think we'd ever get to be at a service with our very own child God gave us, holding her in my arms. Pastor Matt even had us come to the front. The last time I stood there, we asked people to pray over us for a surgery back in January. I'm not sure what I said when I was up there, but I do know this: say yes to God, and He will take you on an unforgettable adventure. God is unbelievable!

Michael and I keep our feet rooted in Christ like a tree rooted deep in the ground. He is our source of essentials for survival, and we grow stronger as our relationship with Him matures. Our family trees bear fighters throughout time with lineage in the Cherokee and Chickasaw tribes. This tree symbolizes our roots and our intent to keep moving forward with God's strength. We are His warriors, battling whatever confronts us. Our church and family have been the hands and feet of Jesus, reaching out like branches. They rejuvenate us (at the hospital, at home, and at church) and encourage us to press on each day toward triumph.

"Rooted and established in love"

Now for something even more special that is very personal. We've been working on breastfeeding since the pediatrician told us to try for five minutes at a time. The special part is that Lily cried, then decided to try and get after it. Praise God! I know it will be a long time before she can breastfeed without receiving supplemental formula, but this is a special and gigantic step. Thank You, God!

JUNE 29, 2010

58 › Settling into a Schedule

Sorry I have not posted in the last couple days. I promise to start back by Thursday. We are settling into our busy new schedule. Praise God that Lilian Grace is feeding from a bottle. Full details, hopefully, tomorrow, and if not, then by Thursday. Love you all.

In the meantime, I'd like to encourage each of you to meditate on Psalm 46 daily. The verses are rich in providing essential soul food for your spirit and helping you remember to be still and know He is God! Love you all!

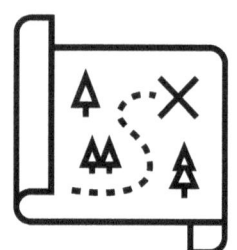

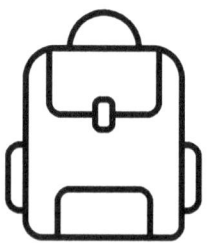

JUNE 30, 2010

59 › Obstacle/Opportunity

Memory Verse 10

🗡 *"Then Jesus declared, 'I am the bread of life. Whoever comes to me will never go hungry, and whoever believes in me will never be thirsty'" (John 6:35).*

After days of changing our schedule, we are adjusting and feeling a little more human. Late Sunday night, we moved all Lily's contraptions to our bedroom so that we can sleep in the same room. Lily was acting up with her unsettling squeaks growing louder and the continuous restlessness of tapping her arms and feet on her bed, but I hadn't encountered any major problems. When it was time for her eleven o'clock meds, I couldn't find the feeding tube we use to administer them. Not seeing the tube coming out of her nose created a moment of panic. Where was the tube? I dropped to my hands and knees to search and pray. I crawled around the bedroom, finally finding it leaking milk onto the carpet. I immediately called home health care to ask for a nurse to come by and put in another tube so Lily could eat. Well, guess what? They couldn't get someone out. They suggested we go to the ER.

They had showed me how to insert the feeding tube before we left the hospital, but I did not feel comfortable shoving it down my daughter's nose and neither did her daddy. I do a lot of stuff, but I found my line and couldn't force myself to cross it. We were not taking her to the ER where the chances of finishing her off were high with so much exposure to those who are sick.

What did we decide? We got her mini-medicine bottle that holds 20 mL and started feeding her Sunday night. We had two beautiful days feeding her without any reflux until last night when Michael and nurse Celeste fed her.

Am I gonna let those few times stop us? Not a chance! I know God is providing for us! I think it was meant for the tube to be removed unexpectedly and for the nurse to be unavailable so that we'd dare to try something new. Lily had a couple apnea and desat episodes, but these happened when she was still connected to the tube. Pray she will get stronger. I'd love to overcome this completely.

We are feeding her 20 mL every two hours. Though this schedule is a little crazy, it's worth it to have one less tube coming out of her. May this beautiful dream continue. I'm just so proud of her. Her daddy and I are a little worn out from the new schedule, but I'll figure out how to do it even on little-to-no sleep. It's worth it all! We go back to the doctor next weekend and will see if the bottle feeding versus the feeding tube changes anything.

She looks gorgeous with her rosy cheeks like Aurora in *Sleeping Beauty* and is changing so much in her expressions and filling out as we find ourselves on day sixty-six! Hallelujah! If you look at her adjusted age, she's just nine days old. I have to admit, she's doing pretty normal things. Our verse tonight, John 6:35, is totally what God is doing for us as He provides for our every need. He doesn't let us go without help. We lack for nothing.

Another praise God: Lily's heart specialist is filing paperwork to be in our network. Since she is not covered by our insurance, it's almost $1,200 every time she's seen Lily. Praise God for taking care of us and for all who ordered shirts. We have received over three hundred shirt orders so far and love all the support! We thank you!

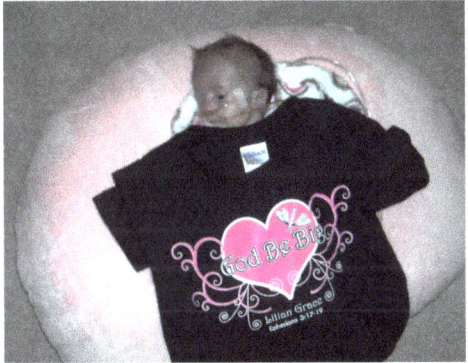

God's proof that He is being Big!

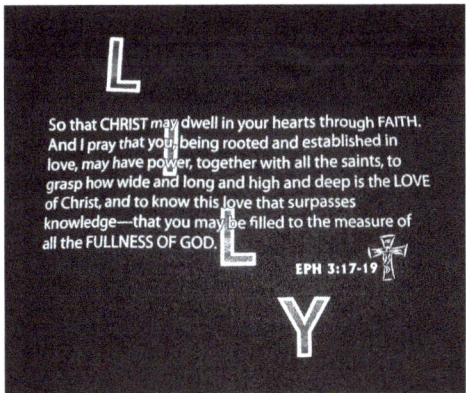

Back of Lily's T-shirt

JULY 2, 2010

60 › Shine Bright

"Go Light Your World" by Kathy Troccoli is a beautiful song I used to sing back in the day. I now sing parts to Lilian Grace all the time and love that I can share a song that continues to encourage me to always let His light shine no matter what is happening on my journey. People need His light in this dark world to give hope, comfort, and strength. We each can let His light shine bright by fulfilling His will in our life. We have to be willing to use our gifts and go into the world.

God is showing us so much through our journey with Lilian Grace. She takes my breath away by the distances she's conquering in her life. I praise God she is still feeding from a bottle when she shouldn't be. We are actually getting more of a normal parenting experience with her because she cries so hard when she's hungry.

Hold on to your seats! Lily moved up from her little baby medicine bottle to a 35 mL bottle, and within an hour, she had consumed an ounce of milk. With tears rolling down my cheeks, I praise God, for You are magnificent and miraculous in all Your ways. Little Lily is showing the world just how fabutastic You are in the small things—those things that are small to us on a normal basis anyway. To top it off, she is starting to roll over and move her head fairly well.

Even with this triumph, we are not without struggles. Lily battles breathing and heart-pumping issues at times. Pray she'll continue to grow, bottle feed, and gain weight.

Lily's Grandpa Whitten let us borrow a postal scale to

weigh her. We placed a book on top of the scale, and then we set Lily on top of the book, which was hilarious to watch. She weighed 4 lbs., 11 1/2 oz. without clothes. At her last doctor visit, she weighed 4 lbs., 12 1/2 oz. with clothes. We are so proud of her weight gain. Bottle feeding sessions can burn too many calories. How many women would love that easy workout to burn calories? I would!

I learned today about an experiment done on plants. One group of plants was spoken to while the second was not. Both groups were given the same care otherwise. The group that heard the grower's voice flourished and thrived. All I can say for Lilian's sake is praise God, He gave me the ability not to shut up! Hoping it has played some part in her successes.

We are taking visitors now and ask that you call before coming over to help limit her daily exposure. She is really challenging herself with new strides, and we want her to flourish. Please make sure you are not sick and have not been around anyone with a sickness. A cold to Lilian could mean death. If you have been sick, you need to wait at least a week from the last known symptom before coming by. Hopefully, that doesn't scare you.

Praise God for giving us the ability and the opportunity to let His light shine through us. Let your heart blaze for Him. We are trying to do just that in our own walk. We love you!

JULY 3, 2010

61 › Another Round

I will continue to rejoice when we experience good times, even though I know a bad day will probably follow. Yes, Lily had a very bad day sprinkled with good moments. The bad means she had two apnea episodes, feedings were crazy, and breathing was fair. Ahhh! Okay, got that out. Now, for the good—Lily dressed in her watermelon outfit for an awesome photo session with actual fireworks personally delivered to her by some church friends as the backdrop. Even in the midst of the darkness of our day, she looked super cute.

Tears flowed off and on today as I tried to adapt to having the air knocked out of me over and over. We will not be defeated by the waves rolling over us. We cheer as Lily reaches sixty-nine days at 8:44 a.m., Saturday, July 3, 2010. God has given our sweet miracle Warrior Princess life beyond the predictions made about her. Thank You, Lord, for breaking through and giving us a life with her, no matter the length.

Michael and I long to show Lily our love and give her the best moments we can. Her great-aunts and great-uncles are holding her now. Another unexpected issue that arose today was my camera. Somehow, I messed up and deleted pictures with great moments of my aunt, grandma, cousin, and me feeding Lily with the medicine baby bottle. Oh, well, I gotta pick myself up and dust off. Such is life.

BarlowGirl's fabulous song "One More Round" embodies what we do every day as we try not to get beaten down by life. I feel like each knock down builds my strength because I lean on God more and more. I cannot battle alone. With Him, I will be able to keep fighting round after round to victory. I may not want to keep going at times, but I'll keep fighting one round at a time as long as He keeps bringing me to and through them.

So I will celebrate the positives to the extreme and cry as a release about the negative. May we all look to the positive and try our hardest to survive when we get knocked down. God is in our corner coaching, encouraging, and celebrating! When we are weak, He gets to be strong!

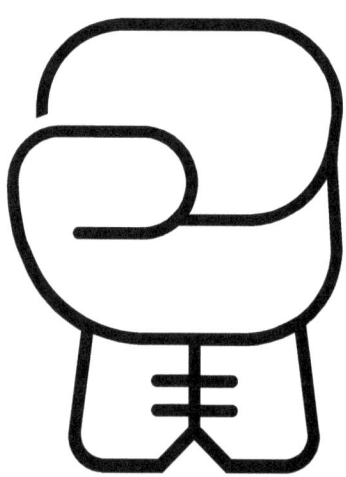

JULY 4, 2010

62 › Our Little Firecracker

> ♡ *LILY'S VITALS*
> *Lily is doing better than she did yesterday, but she's still having not-so-great moments where breathing struggles and semi-low heart rates are tiptoeing on the edge of becoming a problem. I'm thankful it's less traumatizing today because the drastic changes give me a wrecked digestive system, and it brings my spirit down being continuously reminded the end is lurking nearby. I pray we can work with her doctor and figure out a better game plan for our Warrior Princess's current issues. A fabulous mommy gave me great information regarding our T18 babies having UTIs when congested or respiratory issues arise. I need to discuss with her doctor about getting a urine test. Pray God will give us wisdom about what to do.*

On a bright note, my cousin, Jenea, made Lilian Grace the cutest skirt ever. I went to Walmart and bought stars to put on her onesie to complete her holiday outfit. She's going to be decked out tomorrow, and I can't wait. I love dressing her up. Lily makes everything look fabulous. We will upload pictures to Facebook ASAP since the files seem too big for CaringBridge.

We hope you all have a blast celebrating one of my favorite holidays. There's nothing more exhilarating than fireworks. Camp Champions made it so special for me during the three summers I worked there. Working there was completely amazing! I just have one thing to say to my CC peeps: "Purple."

Since it's Independence Day, I want to encourage you to take a closer look at the Pledge of Allegiance and soak in what it really means to speak it out loud. It should be more than words taught to us, memorized, and recited at school, club meetings, games, or events. Walking our talk is a much-needed approach in this life. I love you all and hope you have a Happy Fourth of July!

Firecracker Lily

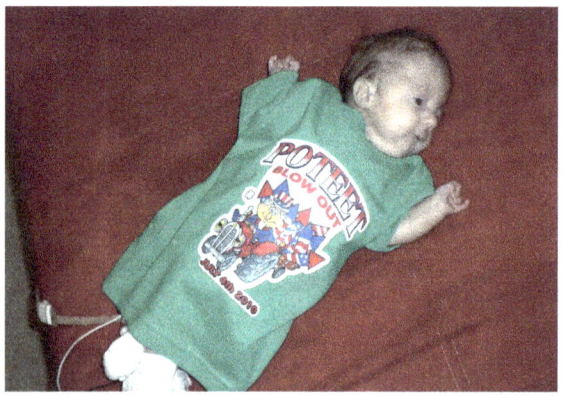

Lilian wearing her family shirt with pride!

JULY 4, 2010

63 › A Mother's Intuition

As Lily's mother, I officially mark July 4, 2010, as Lily-bird's tantrum day, when she dissolved into multiple ear-splitting fits. I remember hearing other kids at church and other functions, but it's a surprise to hear our child misbehaving that way at church. Her tiny vocal cords let loose during the service. On one hand, it meant something was wrong, but on the other, we celebrated because it was something a normal kid does.

We had a traumatic midday experience when the cannula broke and we didn't have a backup like we assumed. We got through it with help. It's frustrating not to be able to fix something at all. God is so good to make moments like the one today turn into valuable lessons about preparation and seeing yourself (to deal with yourself).

We finally called our pediatrician. Thank God, he gave us his cell phone number. Any person who takes a call on the Fourth of July ranks high in my book. I updated him about Lily's episodes over the past four to five days. He thinks she is recovering from a bug. Oh, my poor, lil' Warrior Princess, watching you fight yet another big issue crushes me.

I feel vindicated—I knew something wasn't right. I thought she had a bug, but who am I to know for sure? This is a first rodeo for me. We pray she has a full recovery so that she is strong enough to continue her T18 fight.

One thing is for sure, dressing up Lily is entertaining. Thanks to my cousin for giving her an adorable firecracker tutu. I jumped into supermom mode and ironed stars onto one of her plain, preemie onesies so that it would match. I was pretty happy with my crafty work, and she looked amazing.

Michael and I worked on a hallway project to display Lily's photos and some of our things, and I'm very happy with the result. I'll have to take pictures and upload to Facebook. Completing the project and cleaning calmed my nerves. It's always nice to see things in place and clean. Ahhh! I love it! Cleaning is my drug.

Anyway, Lily watched her first fireworks show during her TV time. I hope everyone had a safe and fun time. With my love of fireworks, the Fourth of July has always been my favorite holiday. I absolutely love the sparkle.

P.S. Thanks again for the support from our T-shirt fundraiser! If you have sent extra with your shirt order or a separate donation, we appreciate you so much. You are a true blessing for Lilian Grace and us.

JULY 6, 2010

64 › Back to the Hospital

A mother's intuition is strong and a godsend. I knew Lilian Grace was not herself for the past five days. We've struggled and cried and wanted to pull out our hair. Lily just wasn't being Lily.

I couldn't shake my gut feeling any longer, so I called to get an appointment. Dr. Gordon was available at 9:20 a.m. yesterday, Tuesday, July 6, 2010. I reported all her symptoms and kept probing about getting her tested for a UTI or anything for that matter. By the way, thanks to my T18 mommies who encouraged me to get her checked. We will find out tomorrow if she has an infection.

Oh, yes, I jumped ahead. We are back in St. Francis Children's Hospital. Can I just say something totally morbid? Okay, I'll go ahead. I cried tears of joy when I walked through those doors again. I've been going like a crazy woman the past three weeks at home.

There is no place like our second home, appropriately renamed Hotel de Lily, where we have everything we need to take care of our precious baby. Walking through those doors lifted the weight of the ginormous elephant sitting on my heart and lungs. I get to take a break. I get to breathe. I prayed for a break, and God is giving me one. Now, I'm not at all happy that my daughter is sick, but I'm happy we are in a place that will help her be my baby, the one we know and love and not the miserable one I can't help. Oh, praise the Lord!

She actually didn't go back to the NICU. We were very

sad, but every rainstorm does have a rainbow. We have graduated to the second floor—the regular one for kids. Since I am pumping, I get three meals a day, and we have a shower and toilet in our room. The simplest things make such a difference. I told them they can let us stay as long as possible. I see this as a little vacation for Lily and me, with different people to share our story this time.

It turns out I was right about her not being right. Her hemoglobin level was way down, which explains why her color and energy levels haven't been right. She has a possible UTI, and we will provide an update after we get the results tomorrow afternoon. Lily received a blood transfusion, and she's already looking so much better. Praise God! We may be here for seven to ten days if she has a UTI. Pray she will have complete healing and kick the other issues coming her way in the butt!

We are at seventy-two days. Actually, seventy-three in eight hours. Hooray for Lily, the glorious miracle from God! May you all find the positive in the midst of the negative. May you see God's hand moving in your life. He is so fabutastic for caring so much for us all. I just love Him whole bunches. He's kind of a big deal to us!

♡ LILY'S VITALS
Weight: 4 lbs., 10.78 oz.; length: 52 cm/20.5 in.; head: 30 cm/11.8 in.; chest: 28 cm/11 in.; girth: 29.5 cm/11.6 in.

JULY 7, 2010

65 › Deeper Waters

I forgot our devotional book at home, so Lilian Grace and I found a new one called *VeggieTales: 30 Very Veggie Devos About Kindness.* The entry I turned to used Philippians 4:6 as the focus verse, and the instruction to pray about everything fits our situation perfectly. We are encouraged to give our worries to God regarding knowledge, attitude change, or whatever. If we lack it, ask Him.

The devotion gave us affirmation about doing the right thing. The doctor threw out options for us to consider regarding Lilian Grace. Once again, we found ourselves facing tough choices that can affect her. I decided I wasn't going to worry about it. I expect God to give me an answer on what we should or shouldn't do.

When Michael got here in the early evening, we discussed her options, and I told him not to worry...that it would work out...we'd get a clear answer. I prayed about it and gave it to God. Not even thirty minutes later, our pediatrician called to check in after hours. After updating him, he gave us advice and direction. There you go—we got our answer.

I'll tell you, it isn't easy making a decision to go into deeper waters with our Lord, but it's totally worth the risk. He takes care of us better than we could ourselves. Undeniably, He loves us. I'm starting to really get the hang of being still and letting go. I hope you try it and see how spectacular it feels.

♡ *LILY'S VITALS*
She has a bacterial infection in her urine and blood. Her platelets are too low, but her blood count is up to ten now, and her gorgeous color is returning. Thank God! She's been gulping down milk without spitting up and sleeping more. Hooray!

If anyone would like to see us, we are in room 203 at St. Francis Children's Hospital. We ask that you stop by only if you aren't sick and haven't been exposed to anyone who has been. I'd greatly appreciate it if you would contact me via email for a heads up if you can visit.

Lots of love! Remember to be still and let God take control. He does a better job than we ever will!

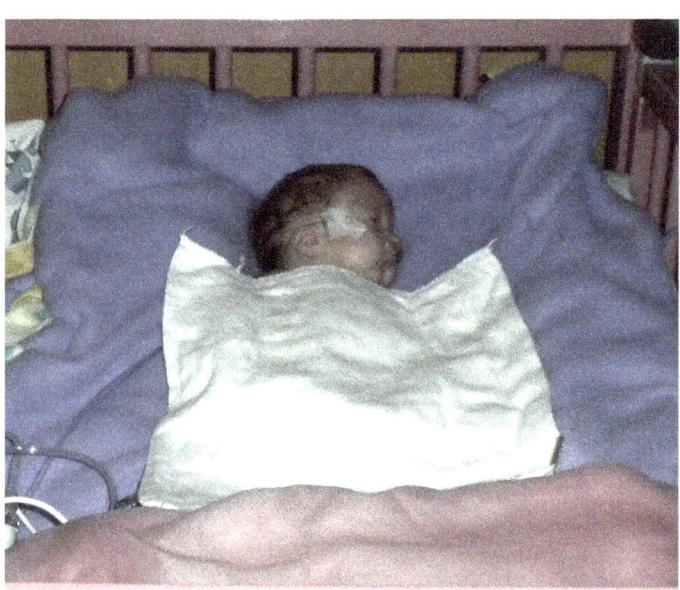

Catching up on rest at her second home

JULY 8, 2010

66 › God's Strength

During college, my girlfriends and I saw Michael English perform in a riveting live concert. His song "In Christ Alone" painted a magnificent picture of how my relationship with Christ truly means everything for surviving and thriving on this journey. I learned that consuming soul food was a way I could build my relationship with Him and make it through anything, and more importantly, that without Christ, I am nothing. When I trust Him, there is glory and victory in whatever life brings. Bad, good, no matter what, Christ alone is my strength and hope.

People keep asking me how I can make it through this. How can I still be standing? Well, I've given this answer before, and I'll give it again. Michael, Lily, and I have nothing to do with our strength. God gets the glory. We are just lucky enough to be living His will out loud.

Holding Lilian earlier today put a huge smile on my face. She is definitely of God. His light shines through her, and watching people see her is magical. They can't help but be lifted up. Is this because of her? No, God made her extra special to show Himself to us through her. Lilian Grace is rocking it out, battling strong today. The antibiotics have been successful and started her plumbing working again. Praise God! We shall see what the doctors say tomorrow. We are looking up and trusting God with whatever happens.

May God keep blessing us with His strength, love, mercy, and grace. May He continue to bless you through all of this as well. We know you may have hard decisions to make, but He never leaves us. He is always here. Make Him your main source. He will always be your strength in times of weakness. Let His glory shine bright in the darkness!

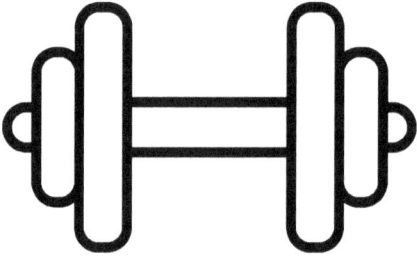

JULY 9, 2010

67 › Tears and Comfort

Lilian Grace is 4 lbs., 14 oz.! Almost five pounds! Oh, Lord, You are amazing! We love You! Though she's extremely tired, somehow she releases a good, loud cry when hungry or going to the bathroom, just like a typical woman when she needs to do something. What can I say? We are blessed with dramatics.

The loud crying reminds me of the familiar chorus from "It's My Party" by Leslie Gore about crying if you want to. I would cry, too, if I were in her state. I actually have cried too many tears to count. I'm reminded that this is not a party for the most part. Thankfully, there are many blessings to celebrate that trump the chaos and setbacks.

I love how crying naturally comes to her when she's in need. Have you ever gotten to a point where you just want to cry because your need runs so deep? God gives us tears for our hearts to unload and recharge. A good cry cleanses the soul. If you keep it all bottled in, you will explode. At least in our case, that's what has happened.

God is the ultimate listener. I love getting in a closet and turning on the water works. I don't even know what I'm crying about at times, but the Holy Spirit does. I feel lighter, less stressed, and whole again after my release session. Take time to let go and give yourself a gift. Be still and let your heart unfold before God and release all the weight. You deserve to be whole and feel lighter in your soul. Take time to cry it out. God is ready to comfort and recharge you.

Lilian's bacterial infection has remained. The doctor

changed her antibiotics, and we hope the new medicine will kick the infection in the butt. Man, does she know how to fight! I just love how God prepared her already. All that kicking and moving inside my tummy must have trained her for this. I guess I need to be thankful she was so active during gestation. Remember, God eventually brings us to thanksgiving for the very things that once brought us pain. It's all meant to take us to the next level!

JULY 10, 2010

68 › Five-Pounder Club

Goodbye, four-pound world...hello, five pounds! Oh, yes, Lilian Grace weighed in at 5 lbs., 1 oz. today. We made it to another milestone, and I'm so proud of our Warrior Princess. God, keep shocking all of us. I hope she keeps gaining, growing, and adapting to whatever comes her way. Lord, guide and direct her mind, body, and soul.

Now for the not-so-fun part: the bacteria has spread to her heart. She has vegetation at the pulmonary valve, a.k.a. bacterial infection located in the heart. The usual course of treatment is four to six weeks of intense rounds of antibiotics. I wasn't planning on such a long break from home, but I want Lilian to have the best care here at St. Francis. They are doing a fabulous job. Praise God for their expertise and continued sacrifice.

God gives Lily the ability to fight as she goes up and down. One hour she looks horrible, like a ghost fading away, almost lifeless, and the next, she's the most precious angel and supermodel who came to the earth with her rosy cheeks and bright eyes ready to conquer anything. May this battle be won by Lilian Grace with God in her corner. I wish she could catch a break, but for now, she will keep her boxing gloves on.

I told Michael we must be doing something right because the devil just won't leave us alone. I'm not giving in. I may look like crap with messy, oily hair and darkened eyes sunk in and feel as if I'm on my last leg with little-to-no sleep and mentally exhausted from the high levels of stress, but my mind and heart will continue to love Jesus and give Him all the praise. Yes, I'm tired. Yes, Michael is tired. Yes, Lilian is tired. But we will rest in Him as He gives us strength.

Even though we face another bump in our path, perhaps we can back up and fly right over it. Life happens, and we are only in charge of our reaction to it. So we may not be "on" at all times, but even so, we will adjust when necessary. Life happens to all of us. Don't ever think your problems aren't as bad. It matters. You matter. Each of us has had to go through one more thing at different times. Hang on tight! Try to enjoy it no matter what because bad stuff happens. There's no way around it. The following quote helps me get through difficult situations: *"You've gotta dance like there's nobody watching, Love like you'll never be hurt, Sing like there's nobody listening, And live like it's heaven on earth."—William Purkey*

Anyone who knows me knows how much I love to dance. There is just something about it. When music plays, my body just reacts. Depending on the beat to the song, my hips move side to side or everything starts swaying as the notes play. It makes me happy and reduces my stress. Do me and yourself a favor—crank up your favorite music and let go. Let the music move you. I have a feeling it will make you smile.

Here's to all of us finding the music in any situation—good, bad, or ugly—and letting our dance moves get us through it. Do not let the problem defeat you!

JULY 11, 2010

69 › Dreams, Nightmares, and Grace

Pinch! Pinch! Pinch! It's not working. Pinch! Pinch! Pinch! Well, I thought I would try to see if I could wake myself up, with no luck. I love the part that's a dream (our life) when we get to experience normal parenting and family stuff. Lilian Grace is hard to resist and draws everyone in. She exists with an abundance of light and strength flowing through her. One of her nurses bought her the cutest mint chocolate chip Build-A-Bear bear with two outfits: one with a tasty ice cream treat on the top and frilly skirt of chocolate brown and green mint.

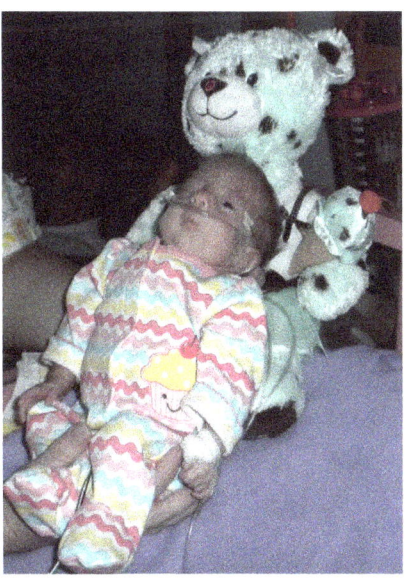

Double scoop of sweetness

The other part, the nightmare, I want to wake up from. It's the part where we have bad moments with Lily's health and tough decisions to make. I wish I could pinch myself hard enough to wake up in my comfy bed at home. I guess this is just part of the plan where I must continue to adjust.

Lilian Grace's IV line blew today. They attempted at least six sites for a new one without success. There's not even a site to do a PICC line, which leads us to yet another traumatizing decision: should we put in a central line or not? I feel sick about it all. If we don't do this, she can't get the hard-core antibiotics she needs to kick the bacteria out of her heart and body.

Now, we are looking at a six-to-eight-week treatment plan. The doctors will insert a central line into a large vein located in her neck. Pray God guides the doctors and nurses when Lilian Grace goes under for the procedure. I trust God completely because He knows her needs more than any of us.

I thought I had no more tears to cry. A little while ago, I started praying over her as I fed her. Tears streamed down my cheeks just as they do now as I type this entry. I want to take away her pain. I want her not to suffer any more trials. I want her to be healthy, to get to be a normal kid. May God continue to hold and guide us.

To top it all off, I may have a hernia from the surgery Lilian and I went through in January. Neither one of us can catch a break. I am calling my OB tomorrow to see what I need to do. Pray Michael makes it through all this. If Lilian and I both are in the hospital, it may be too much. I guess this means we are continuing to scare the devil. Boy, is he trying to finish me off. Unfortunately, he picked the wrong blonde Energizer bunny to mess with. I may feel like I'm drowning in a hundred feet of water, but my Lord and

Savior makes sure I don't stop swimming.

Lilian should have surgery some time tomorrow. Keep her lifted in prayer along with everyone who will care for her before, during, and after surgery. God be Big! God, heal this lil' angel, who has more than proven time and again she is a Warrior Princess and missionary for You.

Tonight, I'm thinking of a song I used to sing, "Who Am I?" by Point of Grace. I wonder why God entrusted this massive responsibility with me? I pray His light can always shine through in my joyous to darkest hours. I feel like I'm nobody, yet He keeps calling me to rise up for another challenge to hopefully show you who He is along the way. Oh, His grace surrounds me and walks me through the fires. I'm here. I'm sharing. I'm hoping you see Him woven in our journey.

Do you see Him in your life? Do you feel Him near you? Do you hear Him? I don't always see, feel, or hear Him, but I know He is here! He's holding me through Lilian's journey, equipping me. He's doing the same for you! Hold on to Him! Let His grace be sufficient for you.

JULY 12, 2010

70 › Central Line Surgery

How are we doing? Each of us would answer the million-dollar question differently.

Lilian Grace...Trusting God...
- She looks as if she ran a couple hundred milers back-to-back in twenty-four hours.
- Praise the Alpha and Omega for getting her through surgery without needing a ventilator. Yay! She appreciates making it through!
- She has found her voice and is letting us have it.
- She is finally sleeping after eating 60 mL within two-and-a-half hours.
- Pray she keeps moving forward from all this junk.

Michael...Trusting God...
- He looks as if he decided to run with Lilian but forgot to hydrate.
- He is frustrated and may mess someone up if they look at him the wrong way.
- He has no tolerance for lazy people.
- He has cashed out to avoid additional stress.
- On the verge of losing it, he went home for a much-deserved break.

Chrissy...Trusting God...

- I look as if I decided to go seventy-eight days without sleep and then thought I'd join the other two just for giggles on the back-to-back hundred milers.
- I'm eating my weight in sweets. My favorite is coconut M & M's.
- When watching the nurses dress Lilian's surgery sites, I felt I might do the following at the same time:
  - Vomit;
  - Sweat to death;
  - Pass out;
  - Have a coronary;
  - Cry enough tears to fill the ocean;
  - Explode;
  - Jump out the window; and/or
  - Yell at the top of my lungs.

What a day this has been. Before Lilian Grace went into surgery, the lack of communication with hospital staff left us stressed. At one point, we had another little girl's paperwork. Her name was similar to Lilian's first name but with a different spelling and different last name. During this scary moment, I told myself God is not a God of confusion. This is not of Him. He will take care of us three. He is not over this mass chaos. He will get her through the surgery. I tracked down a nurse and made her aware of the mix up. Thankfully, another staff member had caught the error and corrected it.

We did not come this far for it to end here. Though there was a lack of communication, they got her in, and the surgery is successful at this point. Praise God, and please let it continue to be good! They've moved us to Floor B, Room

021 (B-021) among the cancer and surgery patients. Getting jostled around from room to room is a pain but good for the soul! It's another opportunity for growth. My new philosophy is not to get used to anything and to take change in stride. It comes our way constantly and keeps my hair growing and my heart pumping. I'd like for you to consider these comforting verses:

Memory Verses 11-16

"Peace I leave with you; my peace I give you. I do not give to you as the world gives. Do not let your hearts be troubled and do not be afraid" (John 14:27).

"In peace I will lie down and sleep, for you alone, Lord, make me dwell in safety" (Psalm 4:8).

"Even though I walk through the darkest valley, I will fear no evil, for you are with me; your rod and your staff, they comfort me" (Psalm 23:4).

"For the Spirit God gave us does not make us timid, but gives us power, love and self-discipline" (2 Timothy 1:7).

"Come to me, all you who are weary and burdened, and I will give you rest. Take my yoke upon you and learn from me, for I am gentle and humble in heart, and you will find rest for your souls. For my yoke is easy and my burden is light" (Matthew 11:28–30).

"Search me, God, and know my heart; test me and know my anxious thoughts. See if there is any offensive way in me, and lead me in the way everlasting" (Psalm 139:23–24).

JULY 13, 2010

71 › A Date with My Mate

Praise God for rest—we received more than we thought we needed. Michael and I got away from the hospital for a while and went to his company dinner to meet three other couples. We actually had a wonderful time. When I first climbed into the truck, I did not want to leave Lily. It's not easy leaving her alone without one of us there with her.

We left her in the amazing hands of Amy Goforth, one of our NICU nurses, newest close friend, and Lilian's godmother. I was able to relax knowing Lily was in better care than any child I know. I took the advice many have given me and took a break. We went to Michael Fusco's Riverside Grill, where we ate incredible food. Wow! I ate a lot. Yummy! Plus, the company was entertaining and enjoyable, and I definitely want to do it again in the future.

Lots of sleep helped Lilian move back into the five-pounder world. She lost a few ounces after I originally reported the milestone. She is growing and eating enough for ten babies. Not really, but our little piglet can't get enough. Hello to seventy-nine days today, Tuesday, July 13, 2010. God has provided the entire way. We are so blessed.

I'd like to encourage all parents to have a special dinner away from the kiddos. You owe it to them to take time for yourselves and get re-energized. They know when we are down. Without a doubt, they feed off our energy.

Please continue to keep Lilian's progress in your prayers. We are only a day out from surgery, and we're told the third day is usually the worst. We are looking forward to watching her grow. I promise I will get the latest pictures up ASAP, though it may be this weekend.

JULY 15, 2010

72 › Strides and Support

Calling all little piglets! Calling all little piglets! You must be able to down 43 mL within thirty minutes, and then less than two hours later, down 22.5 mL more. Oh, yes, our little piglet has quite the appetite! The only struggle is deciding when to stop so that we won't trigger her reflux. She's had no reflux so far today. Praying for continued success. She literally downed 22.5 mL within seconds. Thanks, God, for continuously blowing us away with her abilities.

Lily looks much better. After receiving another blood transfusion Wednesday morning, color has returned to her tiny body with rosy cheeks, and she has a happier spirit filling her big eyes and a smile that lights up the room. I questioned her lifeless, pale looks and irritated attitude the night before. She looked beyond drained and hopeless in her hospital crib. Guess I'm blessed with extra senses. Go, God! Thanks for making the mother gene strong. He's made us like super heroes to take care of His precious children here on earth.

Of course, by eating so much, Lilian has gained weight to reach 5 lbs., 6 oz. Her weight fluctuates, but I'm excited we're remaining in the five-pounder club! Hoping she keeps moving forward, ounce by ounce.

Tonight, I had a late night visitor who is like my sister. We laughed and reminisced about fun times we've had together. It was a wonderful time of fellowship, and our time together reminded me even more of the importance of taking time out from the various hats we wear. For example, I am Chrissy—daughter, sister, wife, mother, granddaughter, cousin, friend, best friend, and jokester. All these roles make me who I am, but I need to be still and know God's in charge of each one.

God intended for us to be here for one another. I have such amazing family, friends, church family, and more. We know without a doubt we wouldn't be trucking along in this journey without the influences and support of everyone. We each play a vital role in one another's life. We all wear a multitude of hats. Are you lifting people up or tearing them down? Do you inspire or deflate people on their journey? Are you taking time out from all the hats you wear?

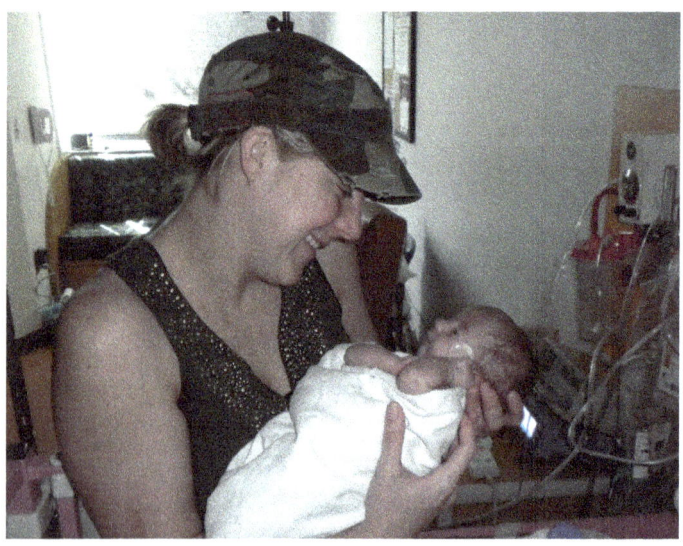

My favorite hat I wear is being her mother.

JULY 16, 2010

73 › Strong Women

To be (blank) or not to be (blank). How would you fill in the blank? I could say I'm angry, happy, sad, fed up, scared, excited, amazed, ridiculed, jealous, a drama queen, or hurting. The list could go on and on and on.

Yesterday, Thursday, July 15, 2010, I was in a weird place. The doctors decided to take Lily off oxygen. Say what? No oxygen. Are you C-R-A-Z-Y? I wasn't very hopeful that it would work. She's had to be on oxygen since birth.

I know. I wasn't living in a positive place. The doctor was seeing if she could be off the oxygen since there has to be a balance to avoid damage to her eyes, lungs, or other organs. Guess what? She's rocking it out. My heart overflows with astonishment and praise. Now, she has an oxygen tube flowing next to her in case she needs it, but this is a huge step for a girl with the tiniest feet and lungs I've ever seen!

I know she loves not having a cannula. She has ripped it out of her nose and tossed it off to the side over a couple dozen times. As I watch her, I see she is truly my daughter because when she doesn't like something, she just doesn't!

She roars when she's hungry, and she's eating almost two ounces of breast milk mixed with Neosure formula almost every feeding. Hello! That's just whacked out and miraculous at the same time. Thanks, God, You keep blowing my mind and expectations out of the water.

Praise God, Lily's numbers are staying at an acceptable range. May this continue to be real and not a dream. She deserves to be a normal baby who gets to experience all this life has to offer. The world is a better place with her in it. Oh, shivers run down my spine. I love being in her world! May God continue to guide and direct all who help her. She has not lightened up on her fighting powers. I understand this may not last forever, but I am so privileged to ride along and fight beside her.

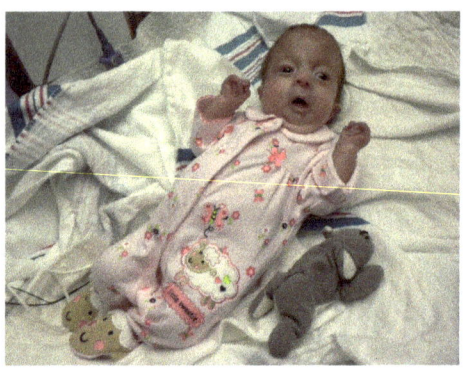

Her fighting powers are going strong.

Forget my doctor appointment next Friday. I am going straight to the surgeon about my hernia issues. I see the doctor on Monday. Please remember us in prayer. All this has sent me over the edge. Sorry if anyone has dealt with me as "not-my-best" Chrissy. Hang in there with us as we've had a heavy load to process.

For all the ladies out there, even if you've read Proverbs 31:10–31 before, read the verses again and let them be a reminder. My great-grandmother, Edith Cooper, was this type of woman, and I aspire to be more like her. She always made everyone feel they were extra special. Oh, how I miss her wisdom, comfort, and example.

"The Wife of Noble Character"

A wife of noble character who can find?
  She is worth far more than rubies.

Her husband has full confidence in her
  and lacks nothing of value.

She brings him good, not harm,
  all the days of her life.

She selects wool and flax
  and works with eager hands.

She is like the merchant ships,
  bringing her food from afar.

She gets up while it is still dark;
  she provides food for her family
  and portions for her servant girls.

She considers a field and buys it;
  out of her earnings she plants a vineyard.

She sets about her work vigorously;
  her arms are strong for her tasks.

She sees that her trading is profitable,
  and her lamp does not go out at night.

In her hands she holds the distaff
  and grasps the spindle with her fingers.

She opens her arms to the poor
  and extends her hands to the needy.

When it snows, she has no fear for her household;
  for all of them are clothed in scarlet.

She makes coverings for her bed;
  she is clothed in fine linen and purple.

Her husband is respected at the city gate,
  where he takes his seat among the elders of the land.

She makes linen garments and sells them,
  and supplies the merchants with sashes.

She is clothed with strength and dignity;
  she can laugh at the days to come.

She speaks with wisdom,
  and faithful instruction is on her tongue.

She watches over the affairs of her household
  and does not eat the bread of idleness.

Her children arise and call her blessed;
  her husband also, and he praises her:

"Many women do noble things,
  but you surpass them all."

Charm is deceptive, and beauty is fleeting;
  but a woman who fears the LORD is to be praised.

Giver her the reward she has earned,
  and let her works bring praise at the city gate.

(Proverbs 31:10–31)

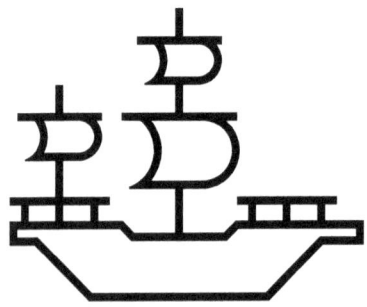

JULY 17, 2010

74 › Worn

I hate to give credit to the stinkin' devil, but he is really fighting back. This past week, we experienced extreme levels of highs and lows in all areas of life. It's time for me to take a break from writing on CaringBridge. When I write again in a week or so, I will post an update on Facebook. Though I love you all, I need to chill out and get my attitude right.

Trying to write from a positive perspective feels fake when all I want to do is scream at the top of my lungs. It takes more strength than I have right now. Lily needs for Michael and me to be at our best because she feeds off us. I ask that people—all people—contact me before visiting. Lily can handle only a small number of people in one day. By regulating her day, her routine doesn't get all jacked up.

She's worn out and hardly eating. None of us can comprehend how the littlest things wear her out, such as the mere presence of people. I can't watch our little girl go up and down like this. She deserves to have her environment as perfect and peaceful as possible. Please set up a time to visit out of respect for her needs. No more unexpected visitors, or we will tell you to come back. This wears on us, more so on me than Michael.

Lily is back on oxygen. She's sleeping more and unmotivated to move. She screams at us now and then. I change her diaper, try to feed her, and pick her up to comfort her, but what it boils down to is she just wants quiet.

I know my not posting will cause some to call, but please,

let us have some much-needed downtime. We are extremely tired from being in the most stressful situation anyone could ever face. We never get a true break from having to make major decisions.

I've seen a side of humanity I do not care to see. I have felt more insignificant than I ever thought possible. I am not—let me repeat—I am not mad at any particular person. I need an attitude adjustment. I don't like the person I see in the mirror right now. Presently, I see someone playing a little violin. Poor me. How dare they do this or that? How dare they feel they are entitled? Blah, blah, blah. The list of songs goes on and on. It's not fair for me to jump down someone's throat for looking at me the wrong way.

When we keep doing the same things and expect different results, it's called insanity. I really should have bought myself a straitjacket for my birthday. It would be very fitting for our journey.

Everyone deserves to take some time for themselves, so I will. I appreciate the continued thoughts and prayers along with the supportive acts of delicious food, gift cards, and generous donations. We have people around us who get it right and others—well, not so much. Remember to think before you speak. I have failed at this too many times. God never meant for us to do things on our own, and I'm making strides by leaning on Him and others.

I hope you all enjoy a break as well. I know you have been reading and experiencing this journey through our thoughts and feelings. I hope you never go through something like this. It's not right. It's messed up. But I do know this—Lilian, Warrior Princess, is our little missionary. The world was meant to know her. I pray she gets to live for a very long time and continues to teach us.

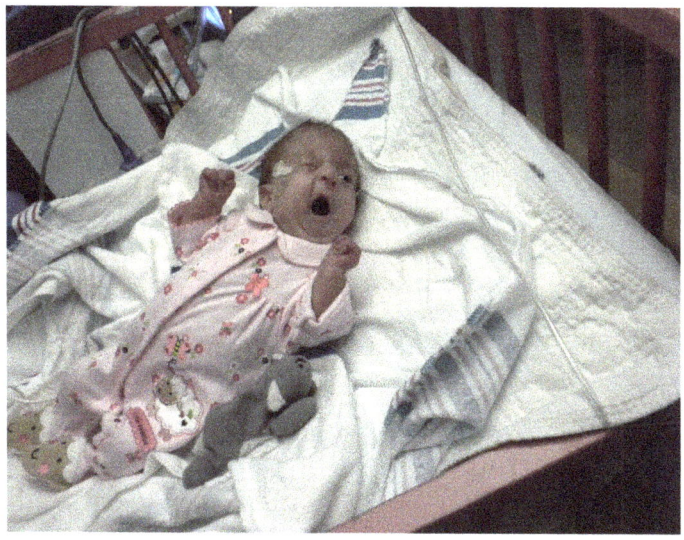

The yawn of a Warrior Princess

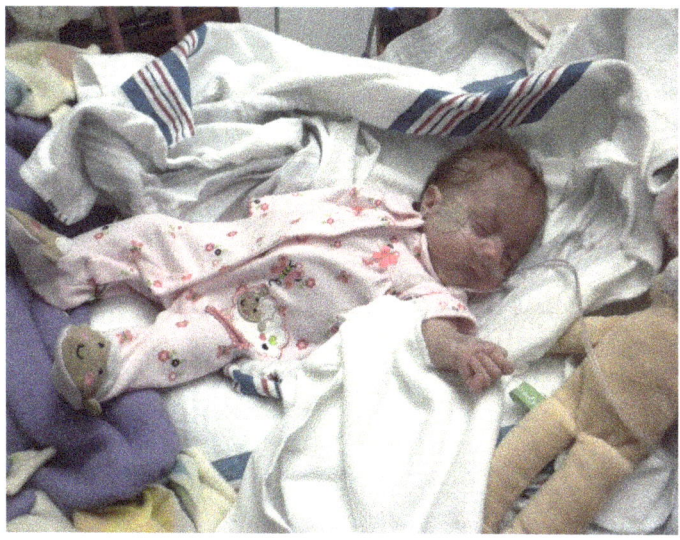

Worn out but not giving up

May you go back and read other entries. I know some people tell me they read, but they ask me the same questions that are answered in the entries. Plus, they argue with me that I haven't said something on here that I have, and I kindly direct them to the date and entry for proof. I've shared everything I possibly could with everyone. Poor Lily-girl has had more pictures on Facebook than a lot of people I know.

So please see this as a nice break. I believe we all need to stop and be filled up because empty is a scary place to be. Try to give more than you take is the philosophy I want to illuminate. May you each be blessed, and live, live, live! I'm working to put on the full armor of God because the times are getting crazier and crazier.

We need to prepare ourselves for anything that comes into our world, and God's armor will give us the protection we need. Love you all! Go to the following website for great material on the armor of God:

http://www.crossroad.to/Victory/Armor.htm

"The Armor of God"

Finally, be strong in the Lord and in his mighty power. Put on the full armor of God, so that you can take your stand against the devil's schemes. For our struggle is not against flesh and blood, but against the rulers, against the authorities, against the powers of this dark world and against the spiritual forces of evil in the heavenly realms. Therefore put on the full armor of God, so that when the day of evil comes, you may be able to stand your ground, and after you have done everything, to stand. Stand firm then, with the belt of truth buckled around your waist, with the breastplate of righteousness in place, and with your feet fitted with the readiness that comes from the gospel of peace. In addition to all this, take up the shield of faith, with which you can extinguish all the flaming arrows of the evil one. Take the helmet of salvation and the sword of the Spirit, which is the word of God. And pray in the Spirit on all occasions with all kinds of prayer and requests. With this in mind, be alert and always keep on praying for all the Lord's people.

(Ephesians 6:10–18)

Three-month picture

JULY 25, 2010

75 › Three-Month Birthday at Home

Lilian Grace celebrated her three-month birthday under the sea dressed in her Little Mermaid Build-A-Bear outfit with a shiny purple seashell top, iridescent green tail, and radiant red wig. I've never seen anyone love a wig as much as our sweet Warrior Princess did wearing her tiny one. She hawk-eyed her cousins when they took turns wearing her wig for pictures.

We wore calming blue to represent the sea of support for our little Warrior Princess. While leaving the second floor at St. Francis Children's Hospital, we joyfully noticed that the floor decorations there matched our three-month theme.

In our journey, the waves can be harsh and treacherous. Our Captain, the Most High God, will provide the instruments we need to navigate through threatening waters. Seeing all those sea creatures and water-themed art pieces, tiles, and pictures in the hospital hallway reminded me of this and inspired me to persevere homeward.

Her daddy ordered adorable sea creature sugar cookies made with extra sweet frosting (black and white whales, sunrise seahorses, gray sharks, and purple passion jellyfish). She was fortunate to celebrate and share the delicious cookies with some of her aunts, her uncle, and her cousins. The kids enjoyed listening to fabulous tales of the Little Mermaid's adventures, while Lilian intently watched my every move and gazed at the vibrantly colored graphics as I read and turned each page.

Our little mermaid stared intently at the vibrant storybook.

Lilian, three months old, proudly wears her wig.

We are grateful God has given us three months with His little missionary, despite our mixed feelings about leaving the hospital again. But Praise Him, Lilian got to enjoy a little monthly birthday fun with the next level of her family. If we would have stayed at the hospital, this time with them would not have happened due to the rules and regulations at the hospital.

I wish we could create memorable celebrations with everyone, but it's not possible right now. We will continue to swim and praise God for the treasures we can discover, unearth, and cherish. A great lesson to learn is not to take for granted the time, ability, and means you have to make special moments happen. It doesn't have to be a big production. What matters is taking the time to get together while you can and making beautiful memories living life together, creating everlasting joy and love.

Memory Verse 17

"The God of peace will soon crush Satan under your feet. The grace of our Lord Jesus be with you" (Romans 16:20).

The Scripture above gives me hope that God is in control and Satan will not win. I needed this reminder after the week I've had. I'm happy I took a break from writing. The temptation to write crept in a few times, but I held firm to my decision.

Lilian Grace has ridden her usual roller coaster regarding her health. One minute she's healthy and happy; the next, she struggles to breathe, and her heart rate skyrockets. This past Thursday, the doctors at St. Francis decided we should head home. Everyone seemed excited except for us.

Being in the hospital has given Lily professional care, enabling weight gain and achieving the best version of herself.

Michael's and my nerves dramatically change at home versus the hospital, and our stress levels soared with the news of heading home.

We are administering antibiotics to deal with the bacteria still located in Lily's heart. I didn't know I'd get a high-intensity, emotional workout administering these meds through a central line. I seem to sweat every time since the risk of complications or death is high. As I type, Lilian's heart rate raced to over 200 bmp, her temp increased to 99.9, and she's breathing hard with attitude. Once in a while, she chirps to let us know she's still here.

We are hard on ourselves because Lilian deserves the best care. I've said to myself on repeat since coming home, *Chrissy, what do you want to be when you grow up? A nurse? No! Chrissy, what do you want to be when you grow up? A nurse? No!* It's funny how God takes you on several paths to bring you full circle, even when you feel incapable.

Administering Lilian's medicines to prevent congestive heart failure was scary at first, but now it's nothing. She sucks on the needleless syringe and swallows like a champ. Wow! He really has taken us through extremes to make sure we can handle all the steps. I know this—I'm ready not to go any higher. I'll continue to climb however long or high He wants me to, but I thought it appropriate to say out loud just in case He was wondering.

I hope I'm getting my attitude right after a week-long break. I know now more than ever that I'm never going to bring happiness or satisfaction to someone by the decisions I make. I will not apologize for creating opportunities with people. Lilian Grace has a mission. I want to enjoy this journey, even the scary parts that make me want to scream, throw up, or quit. Last time I checked, I do not need someone's permission to share my daughter with whomever we choose. Just thought I would throw that out there.

We are home, struggling with scheduling, administering medication, and dealing with feedings. Some of this is the most normal thing in the world, which I absolutely love. The more normal it gets, the happier our hearts are. Michael would like to get some sleep. I get tickled about that. I told him that not getting sleep is exactly what new parents go through. Yay for us!

Lilian Grace will receive major antibiotics through her central line every six hours for at least five more weeks. We do not have nursing staff right now, and I have to admit that I'm not too sad about it. Though the help would be nice, there's something to be said about having our house to ourselves. We have the infusion company on call, and RNs are just a phone call away. In fact, we have already called them about the problems we've had with the oxygen tank the last couple of days. Our supplier helped us get that fixed hopefully for good.

We have many appointments coming up with her pediatrician, heart specialist, and urologist. Lilian has reflux in the urethra, a potential culprit for the major bacterial infection she's battling. Continue to do two things: pray for God's will to be done and live your life out loud. We shouldn't waste the time God gives us. We love you all!

P.S. With my surgery coming up this week, I may not post daily so that I can prepare. I have a huge hernia that looks like swiss cheese in my abdomen. It formed after January's surgery and then my subsequent C-section to have Lilian. Just fantastic, if you ask me. Pray God will guide the doctors, nurses, and staff to make this pain go away. Also, I need to look different. Right now, my poor tummy hurts more than I want to admit, and I look like I'm five months pregnant. This too shall pass!

JULY 27, 2010

76 › Powerful Name

In church on Sunday, we sang about Jesus being the light of the world and king of the earth. We sang His name over and over. The repetitiveness gives me God-chills thinking about the power just singing His name has over us. The simplistic song came to mind just a bit ago when Lilian Grace's heart rate soared above normal. I sang and prayed and sang some more, swaying as I held her to calm her heart while filling my spirit with all that the name of Jesus embodies. Just whispering the name Jesus brings power and an all-consuming peace that covers me from head to toe in this hard moment like a shield to deflect any harm coming our way.

The song "Healer" by Kari Jobe also came to mind. It's been on repeat for most of our days. I do believe He is our healer. I trust Him even when I don't feel like trusting Him. He brings contentment and oxygen through the trials and fires. I won't be burned because He is taking care of me. I may not like how the journey unfolds at times, but I know He has the ultimate plan, meeting all my needs and making all things turn out for the good.

I'm standing here with the full armor of God. Nothing is impossible for Him. He has us all in His hands. I believe He did not bring us this far to strand us. He is doing His magnificent will.

At Lilian Grace's checkup yesterday, she weighed 5 lbs., 12 1/2 oz. She had all her clothes and a diaper on, plus she had a major poo later that could have made her weight higher. We do know she's still over five pounds though. Praise God! The checkup went well, which is why Michael has had no sleep tonight. When we have good, the bad follows, like Lily being up throughout the night. Isn't that about par? It could be the full moon or just how this part of the path is meant to be. I asked Michael if he's prayed tonight. He told me he was praying for Lily to go to sleep. I replied that he's not praying for the right thing. Praying, praying, praying for healing, comfort, and peace.

I have surgery at eleven this morning to repair the large hernia. I know it seems like we can't catch a break. I laugh now because it's just one more thing we have to face—another kind of giant. As I type this, the alarms peal in the other room. In Jesus Christ's name, I ban all evil from Lily, this place, our life. I repeat the prayer as the alarms sound again. Man, we must be doing something right. You better be scared, devil, because my feet are planted in Him!

Jesus is taking care of us; He will take care of you. He's abundantly equipped to provide for our every need. Trust Him! Love you all!

JULY 28, 2010

77 › Momma's Surgery

I had surgery yesterday. It's kind of kicking my butt just a little, and I'm very sore. On another note, I met a very interesting lady who inserted my IV so well I didn't even feel it. With all my surgeries, I can now call myself an expert, so I let her know she's the best I've ever had. She told me her husband prays every morning for her to give amazing IVs! Yes, every day! How special is that? How many of us pray for our spouse or significant other to soar throughout the day while blessing others? Thanks, God, for this golden nugget among the nutty things I'm going through.

Lilian Grace looks amazing with her sweet baby rolls. Those chubby cheeks invite a thousand little smooches! Our dogs, Vega and Trinkie, agree and wanted to give their puppy kisses all away. We were blessed to get some pictures of them all together while Lilian tried to pet both of them. They have loved her since first sniff.

We still have ups and downs, but she continues to take our breath away. She is one tough cookie. Praise God for making her perfect in every way! She's still bringing down the house with her food intake. I just love it. The girl consumes over 300 mL per day from a bottle. Can I get a shout of praise for God? Who knows if we will get to do this for long, but I'm going to enjoy it while it lasts.

Sadly, I have to dump all my milk for twenty-four hours due to the anesthesia. Oh, yes, I get the joys of pumping and now dumping. It seems like such a waste, but I wouldn't want the stuff to pass through Lily and cause her harm. I'll just buckle up and figure out how to keep pumping through my recovery. Thank God for this wrap around my waist. It helps!

Well, that's a quick update. I'll leave you with one funny from my sister about yesterday. Supposedly, when ice came up in recovery, I sang, "Ice, Ice Baby!" It's true that what goes in must come out. Leave it to me to bring a classic rap song back to life for some laughs. Love you all!

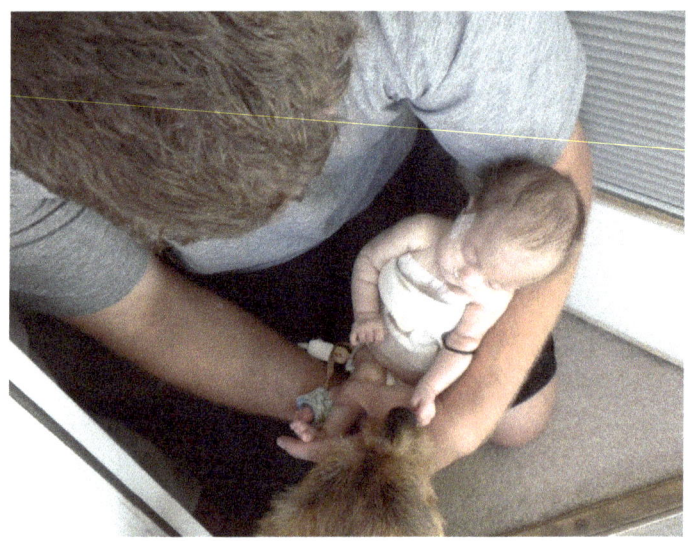

Love at first sniff

JULY 29, 2010

78 › Serenity

My in-laws, Monty and Janese Whitten, gave me an awesome bracelet with the Serenity Prayer on it to remind me to take things one day at a time. There's a large percentage of things I have no control over and need to give to God in prayer. I will work on the things I can change like my attitude and reactions to everything. God has been good at helping me see the joy and goodness in the hardest of times. I'm a continuous work in progress.

Lilian is growing and changing so much. It's wonderful to watch all the other lil' babies born around her growing as well. I can't imagine someone seeing these babies and not believing in God's existence.

♡ LILY'S VITALS
I'm keeping it short today. The nurse came yesterday to draw blood. Here are her vitals for this week: Weight: 5 lbs., 8 ½ oz. on our scale from Babies R Us; head: 32 cm; chest: 30.5 cm; girth: 32 cm; and length: 18 ¾ in.

As for me, my pain has intensified, so I've increased to two pain pills every four hours. Lily won't get my fresh milk for a while longer. Thankfully, God blessed us with a mega supply in the freezer. Thank You for abundance, Lord!

JULY 30, 2010

79 › Blood Transfusion

I guess the entry I attempted to type earlier was not meant to be read. Sometimes, I wonder why things won't post on here. I have to let it roll off, just like everything else going on right now. I do need to stop, count my blessings, and remember to keep trucking forward. I repeat over and over: I trust, God! I trust, God! I trust, God!

No matter the outcome of our life with Lilian Grace, I will continue to trust God. I will trust Him for all eternity. Nothing can separate me from Him—nothing!

Lilian Grace is back in the hospital for a blood transfusion to raise her hemoglobin numbers. Her heart may be the culprit on the blood loss. She may have another infection, which could be from the central line. This is one thing we had feared. I'm just giving it to God. I hate that she faces yet another obstacle.

As I look around, I see how we spend our time on negative thinking. Why? Why waste so much energy? I want to spend the time I have left with my husband and child on positive things. Buckle up, trust God, and figure out how to enjoy the ride. It's not easy, nor will it ever be.

My life feels out of control right now. I hate being out of control, especially with medicine. I'm taking pain meds while trying to keep it together through a crisis. Thank God for the people around me. Lily and I couldn't have made it to the doctor's office yesterday, then to the hospital, without help. I really had to get it together after taking pain meds a short time before it all started. Let's just say that if anyone wants a dark comedy on their hands for the fall lineup, we've got some material. Our life is definitely a series I haven't seen before.

May God be with Lilian's team. May she get full healing if that is God's will. I hope for the best and realize we all have limits. I've got to remember—it's in His hands, and I trust Him. Love you all!

P.S. Michael is with Lilian at the hospital. I'm at home recovering. I'll give updates on here and/or Facebook.

JULY 31, 2010

80 › Separation Anxiety

1, 2, 3, 4, 5, 6, 7...100...223...1,000...Keep counting. Keep moving forward! Today was one of those days when I wanted to grab us all and jump into a wormhole to another life.

Lily is hooked up to more stuff. They really don't know why she's breathing so hard. Her oxygen numbers are up, she's eating occasionally, and she's had two blood transfusions. I'm trying to recover from surgery, Michael's trying to deal with both Lily and me down and out, and Lily is trying to survive. Man, if that isn't a day, I don't know what is.

I can't be at the hospital right now, so I feel out of the loop. We sat down together with the doctor this afternoon, and I sure felt the pain from my surgery. The doctor wanted to know what lengths we are willing to go to for Lily. Here's where we stand: whatever allows her to fight for herself is as far as we will go. There's nothing we can do to keep her here. If she is meant to be here, then she will remain. If she is meant for heaven, then she will fly and earn her wings.

Why does this have to be so heavy? I love being her mother, and Michael loves being her daddy, but it gets hard—really hard. No matter what, we have to watch her experience these crazy things in life. We have no power to take away her pain or suffering. I watch other parents with their kids, and I know all we can do is encourage, teach, and hope for the best. We can't make them be someone different or make different decisions. They have to stretch, learn, grow, and hurt. God intended for us all to learn and grow, and sometimes the lessons are painful. We, as parents, want to jump in, but it's meant for us to step aside and let our kids learn. I hate feeling useless and defenseless. I have to trust my Father and know He has a plan.

I pray God guides each of us in our walk as individuals, partners, and parents. Parenting is the toughest job one will ever have. Sometimes, you just want to jump ship and swim to a deserted island to escape it all, which is normal and natural. Whoever said parenting was easy was never a parent, in my opinion. It's the best and worst of everything. Thank God, the good times outweigh the bad.

Lilian weighed 5 lbs., 13 oz. today. She's straining to catch a breath, and it's exhausting her. During today's visit, she didn't seem like herself. I know she doesn't understand what is happening, especially when she is used to me being with her 24/7. When I read and sang tonight over the phone, Michael said she reached for the video of me as if I were there to scoop her up and hold her. I'm bawling right now. I just want to give her everything, the best of the best, and whatever will make her better.

Not getting to be there is so hard, and what's even harder is thinking about life without her. Those thoughts steal my breath. Please, God, be with her. I know whatever Your will is, is what should be. Help us have peace about it. They are running test after test, hooking her up to all sorts of wires and machines. Thanks for supporting us from a distance. I'll share another update in my next entry.

JULY 31, 2010

81 › Battling Toward True Rest

"True Rest"

My dear child, I know you're weary
With nothing left to give.
You've worked long and hard
Now you feel frayed and worn.
Come with Me to a quiet place
Away from all the noise and busyness.
Let Me wrap My arms around you,
Enfold you in My love.

Let Me whisper peace to your heart's storm,
Soothe your troubled brow.
Listen to the love song
I composed just for you.

In Me is true contentment.
In Me you will find what you long for.
Come with Me to a quiet place
And receive rest, strength, and peace.

(Margie Casteel)

I came across this poem called "True Rest" by googling "dealing with stress." Oh, for us to get rest from the craziness of life and the turmoil around us. May we all wake up and figure out how to make things run smoother.

We didn't find out much more today. The growth on her heart has shrunk, with her valve shrinking as well. We didn't hear back from the heart specialists. We hope to have an update from them by Monday or Tuesday. Her blood count was up around eight. She still has quite a few things hooked up to her. Michael has been great about surviving hospital life. It's definitely not his idea of a good time. We hope Lily won't be in the hospital for long this time.

It's funny how mad they get at such a young age. She really wasn't impressed when I finally showed up this afternoon, and she looked away almost the whole time. I tried to explain that taking care of myself allows me to take care of her, but I don't think that got me anywhere. I'm looking forward to my time at the hospital tomorrow night. May my daughter forgive me and let me back into her little world. I am getting ready to post some pictures since she looks much bigger. I meant to do it earlier but needed to do other things.

I think we finally grasp how to administer medicine ourselves at home. May God give us knowledge and continued strength to do what Lily needs. It looks as if we won't have any more major news until later. One good thing is that Michael was able to get her oxygen level down again. Praise the Lord! May we all have peace tonight. We all have giants to face, and the battle is wearing us out. May you get some much-needed rest. Love you!

AUGUST 3, 2010

82 › Quarantine Season

Sneezing, check. Congestion, check. Viral rash all over her body, check. Eating habits all over the place, check. Cough, check. Running a fever of over 102 throughout the night, check.

Lilian Grace is finally passing the viral infection she caught. Who's to blame? No one! Michael and I could have brought it home. What do we need to do? When we go home, we must quarantine ourselves again, possibly until her next surgery. To think, to us a common cold or viral infection is nothing. To Lilian and her T18 buddies, it means a hospital stay, super antibiotics, and sometimes, sadly, death.

God graciously helped her fight through this battle and gave me a wake-up call. During this whole time of not knowing how long we had with her, I wanted as many people as possible to see her. Oh, how I wouldn't survive if the reason Lilian wasn't here was because of my need for everyone to see her. Here we are again—you will have to bear with us and watch from a distance.

What sucks most about a viral infection? There's nothing any of us can do to make it run its course any faster. Pray it will leave Lily's body immediately. She has been a different baby while going through this. I'm the type of mother who kept asking the nurses to check her temp, but she was only 98 or 99. Of course, last night, I felt she was hotter, but I didn't ask them to check her since I had asked for temp checks several times with no result of a high fever. Lo and behold, she ended up over the 102 mark. Lesson learned. I don't care if I've asked a million times for a temp check, I'm going to keep asking. You can never be too safe!

I've been back at the hospital with Lily since Sunday night. Let's just say my surgery site is not better for sleeping on the hospital room couch. I will be glad to be back home. We now see, even more, the importance of routine for Lilian Grace.

I'm going to take this quarantine season to learn how to cook better and get my act together on practicing yoga and Pilates again. Hello, Chrissy's culinary school from cookbooks and Chrissy's yoga/Pilates study time. Here we come. I look at this time as a renewing period. Instead of focusing on what I don't get to do, I'm looking at our time as a positive adventure for Michael, Lilian, and me to learn new things and revisit something I used to love.

What have you wanted to learn over the years but never did due to time restraints? Join me during this time and do it! Learn something new or renew your passion for something you used to enjoy. Let us know in the CaringBridge guestbook what you will be doing and how it is going. This will be fun for all of us.

LILY'S VITALS

She weighed 5 lbs., 12 oz. a couple of days ago. With bumps of fat on her arms and legs, she is our little roly-poly. I love it! She weighs today, and we'll see if the viral infection has reduced her weight. She's on super antibiotics, and we will add two antibiotics—ampicillin and gentamicin, until August 20 at home. She has several doctor appointments coming up.

THE FIGHT 237

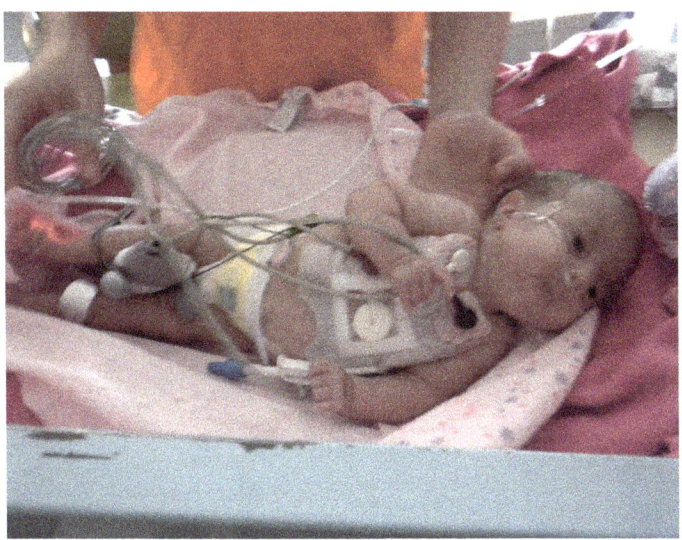

Our little roly-poly chillin'!

Lilian is a movie star with her own team to help her get better. Praise God for people who sacrifice and dedicate their lives in the medical world. It is a tough place to be, and they are amazing for doing it. Lilian is here because you accepted a calling.

I'm hoping this fever doesn't postpone us from going home today. It's amazing how God changes your heart and desires. All I want is to be home. The things that scared me before now seem like nothing. Praise God for helping us adapt and providing the right equipment. He is being Big! Hallelujah!

AUGUST 3, 2010

83 › The Silversmith

I must have misplaced my red glittered shoes because we are not going home right now after all. Talk about a turn for the worse. Lilian had a bad afternoon and evening. After this, we may be here for some time. Her heart rate skyrocketed to over 220 bpm. So many people were going in and out of the room. Praise God for people who care!

She had fever again, bathroom issues (going a lot—go figure), coughing, and all the other symptoms of this viral infection. Even though this viral thing is kicking her butt, she still fights on. I am so proud of her for bringing a whole new meaning to the name "Warrior Princess." I think they should put Lilian Grace Whitten as the definition in the dictionary!

I find hope thinking about us as silver in the following story. I picture God refining us in His own image through the fires we face regularly in this season.

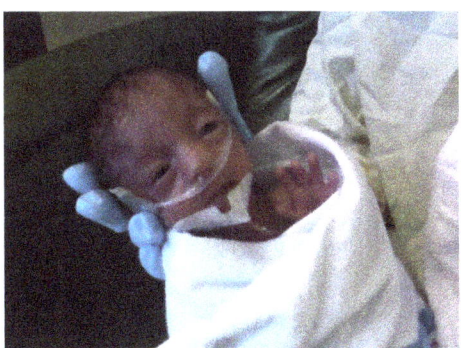

Worth being in the fire

"The Silversmith"

Some time ago, a few ladies met to study the Scriptures. While reading the third chapter of Malachi, they came upon a remarkable expression in the third verse:

"And He shall sit as a refiner and purifier of silver" (Malachi 3:3).

One lady decided to visit a silversmith and report to the others on what he said about the subject. She went accordingly, and without telling him the reason for her visit, begged the silversmith to tell her about the process of refining silver. After he had fully described it to her, she asked, "Sir, do you sit while the work of refining is going on?"

"Oh, yes, ma'am," replied the silversmith. "I must sit and watch the furnace constantly, for, if the time necessary for refining is exceeded in the slightest degree, the silver will be injured."

The lady at once saw the beauty and comfort of the expression, "He shall sit as a refiner and purifier of silver."

God sees it necessary to put His children into the furnace; but His eye is steadily intent on the work of purifying, and His wisdom and love are both engaged in the best manner for us. Our trials do not come at random, and He will not let us be tested beyond what we can endure.

Before she left, the lady asked one final question: "How do you know when the process is complete?"

"That's quite simple," replied the silversmith. "When I can see my own image in the silver, the refining process is finished."

(Author Unknown)

AUGUST 5, 2010

84 › Calm Before the Storm

I've been singing "He's Got the Whole World in His Hands" off and on all night, changing the words to fit our situation. Yesterday, Lilian looked like her healthy self again. She was gorgeous in every way despite the viral infection. I sent several pictures to family. I was so thankful God blessed us with a wonderful morning. This happened to be the calm before the bigger storm.

Lily started going downhill and just couldn't get back up. We tried to figure out what to do. The viral infection had spread to her lungs. She couldn't breathe no matter what we did. She turned all sorts of colors, and then gray. Tears rolled down my cheeks. Was this it? Was this really how it would end? Part of me wanted to encourage her to stay and fight—the other, to fly. She has been through so many fights in her life already. I just hate watching her suffer. The bottom line is, it just sucks.

We ended up moving to the PICU (pediatric intensive care unit for infants and children up to seventeen years old), and our experience has been just as wonderful as our other stays at the St. Francis Children's Hospital. Praise God for these amazing people who enter our world. Thank You, God, for them all. For giving them a heart to help Your people and to be here for Lilian Grace.

We had to make yet another major decision—to intubate or not. Our goal continues to be doing whatever allows Lilian Grace to fight the good fight. I prayed so hard. There's a fine line as always for us. Do we keep her here or let her go? What would help her do what she needs? Without help, she was for sure going to die this time.

We got answers from the PICU doctor, cardiology team, and our pastor. All advised us to intubate and give her a shot at getting through this infection. Let me tell you how God did this with our pastor, who does not believe in assisting a person to keep her here—meaning if she has to be solely dependent on assistance, then no. Therefore, it's definitely from God when even he said to intubate. The heart doctors will talk to us about the chances of beating the bacterial/viral infection and give us a status update for her much-needed heart surgery. Please pray that God will guide all of us in her care. Pray she and the rest of us do His will.

This morning has been rough already with her current complications. I shivered in the cold room, not knowing how to pray. I just kept repeating over and over and over, "I trust You, God! You did not get us this far to leave us. I trust You, God!" Whatever is going to be will be, but it sure doesn't make this road any easier to walk. In the last twenty-four hours, I have proven that I can cry even more than ever before, continue to praise the Lord, and pump milk for my little girl. W-O-W!

Man, it's tough to breathe sometimes. This has been the craziest, most bizarre story anyone will ever hear. I will say that no matter what, God has us in His hands. He perfectly timed the devotional I read to Lily today. It confirms His existence for me once again as I read the reminder—God doesn't make anything without great thought and breathing life into its very existence.

Hang on. This ride is going to rise and then plummet as we walk through it. We will not be moved off course. God doesn't make anything or anyone by accident. All things are for a purpose whether we ever understand or not.

He is with me always, and that's enough for me. Thank You, dear Jesus, for planning the tiniest details to help me through this life and to be Lilian Grace's mommy and Michael's wife. May I not let You down! Love you all.

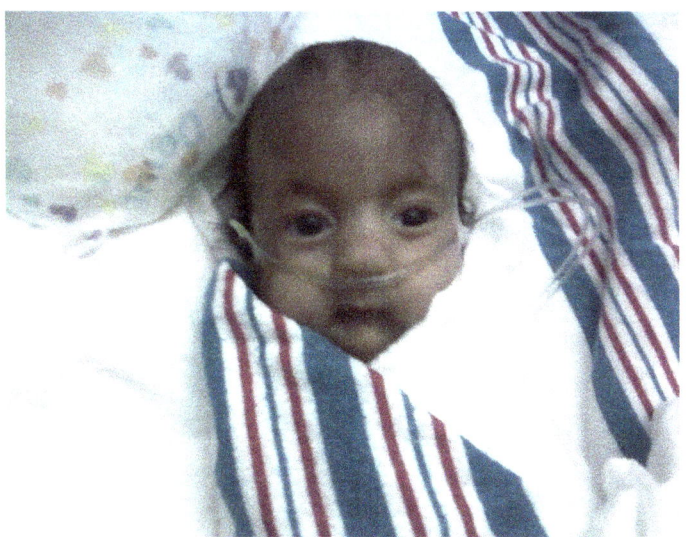

The storm disguised as perfection!

UPDATE: Lilian Grace fought the good fight and earned her wings at 6:19 p.m. on the day this entry was shared. I was heartbroken in my loss on one hand and praising God for her healing on the other. As we weathered the worst part of this storm, I could feel God's peace and strength embracing us. Watching my sweet baby girl transition from earth to eternity was horrifying yet peaceful in a way I never imagined. She got to be in my arms then Michael's. As we took turns holding her, I managed to sing every worship song I had ever memorized until she breathed her final breath. In the upcoming entries, I share more details about her final milestone on earth—death to eternity.

AUGUST 6, 2010

85 › Rest in Peace

Rest in peace, my beautiful sleeping beauty!

> *Now I lay me down to sleep*
> *I pray the Lord my soul to keep*
> *If I die before I wake*
> *I pray the lord my soul to take.*

God gave us the second coolest miracle to ever walk this earth. Jesus was the first. Lilian Grace gave more than someone who had lived on this earth for eighty years. Predicted not to live past one second, she conquered and lived for 103 days. We love her and rejoice for her as she rests in our Father's arms, where we yearn to be.

Lilian's celebration service will be at ten in the morning, tomorrow, Saturday, August 7, 2010, at the Cornerstone Church, 8801 West 41st Street, Sand Springs, OK 74063. We ask that you send money for the First Annual Warrior Princess Trail Run (April 25, 2011) instead of flowers.

The race will celebrate Lilian's life while raising money for T18 families and NICU staff because of the special things they do for all God's lil' miracles! We will do this annually on her birthday (April 25)!

I don't know how long I will continue to write on CaringBridge. I will write soon about our precious last day. I just need to take care of her service first. We love you all and appreciate all the love and support you've given. All your prayers were heard by God. He gave us time. He gave us our Warrior Princess, and she touched us all. Remember what you have learned through this, and keep it in your hearts and minds.

AUGUST 7, 2010

86 › Celebration of Life

I woke up early, feeling untouchable and strong. I worried I might find myself in a straitjacket at some point, yet I felt more aligned with my purpose than ever before. Today, I was turning a dream (one God had given me during my REM sleep at the hospital) into reality. This amazing dream about Lilian's celebration of life felt prophetic and real, even though she was still alive at the time.

I'm thankful I didn't disregard the dream when it came to me one night in that dark hospital room. I immediately made calls to the people God had appointed in my dream who were to speak and sing during the celebration. This gift was another way God prepared me for Lily's departure. It was extraordinary to experience something I had dreamed about, but it gave me great peace and much-needed encouragement for the days of grief that followed.

Only God could get me up on stage at my daughter's celebration of life less than forty-eight hours from her last breath. Only God could provide me with the strength to carry on. I felt as if I were in His full armor, equipped for the many battles I would keep facing daily. The following is a transcription (with edits) of my speech that beautiful morning, following a massive downpour from heaven. I hope you can appreciate my realness and raw emotions!

> *First off—so we can get to laughing a little bit—I apologize that I'm wearing jeans to my daughter's funeral. Do you know why? I didn't shave my legs, so I had to put the pants on. You know how it is—I could probably braid the hair on*

my legs, but I thought it was worth spending more time with my daughter than shaving my legs. You get it.

I have changed what I was going to say probably five times this morning alone. Since the day I had the [celebration of life] dream, I knew my daughter would not be here long. I knew I was going to speak [at her service]. I dreamt about it—God ordained the people you see on stage today. They were in my dream, and now we're turning that dream into reality.

You asked me, how do I have it together? It's not me. I'm on a super drug called God. And let me tell you, no drug can touch this considering what I'm feeling right now. I am so proud to know every single one of you. I know you have lifted us up in prayer repeatedly, and we can never repay you for what you've done for us. I mean this sincerely and so does Lily. She has gone through so much, so much. So bear with me. My daughter lived a hundred and three days. We may be here a few hours. I promise I'll try not to talk that long.

But for you to understand exactly how Big my God is, I've gotta tell you the story. Okay? Now, not everything will be in this story. I'm going to write a book. It may not be that good, but I'll pray that I step aside and allow God to inspire that project. I'll let you know when it is written, and you can have a copy if you want.

I do have a disclaimer. I didn't get to write anything out. I thought I could get through it. Then I thought, I'm not going to make it through this. It's going to be really hard.

I have cried more tears in the last hundred and three days than I have or ever will in my entire life. They were happy tears—some very sad tears. You've seen pictures on Facebook. I've shared every picture known to man. I am a picture queen now. My daughter in some of the pictures is going, "Seriously, one more picture? Like, what are you doing to me?" I just needed to. I knew we had to live it up—every minute, every second; because we didn't know how long we were going to have [with her].

Now, let's go back before I get to another point. Six years ago, I married a man who I hardly knew. I was like, What in the heck am I doing? I'm standing next to him thinking, Is this really who I am supposed to marry, God?

Because I don't know. He does not have it together. Sorry, hun, I should have apologized before I shared this.

But I will tell you this. When our eyes met on that stage, all dressed up, I knew God brought us together. That day I married the man that would get me through this hard but amazing experience.

I have scars on my stomach from this pregnancy and scars on my heart. God has mended some of them. I have peace about it because we've done it right. I may not always have the right attitude. I may have thrown a chair, and it broke some stuff [by making a hole in the wall]. I tried to pay for it, but they wouldn't let me. They said, "We didn't see anything." I was like, "I just threw it! Did you not hear me? I was screaming bloody murder."

And dang it, they repaired that wall. And I was so mad that someone simply fixed it. But I heard God say, "If that wall is fixable, it's just as easy for Me to fix Lilian. It may not be how you want, but I'm going to heal her." I had to trust Him.

So six years ago, I looked into my husband's eyes. He wasn't my husband then, but I knew he was the man I was going to marry. I saw the man he was becoming. I thought, Wow, this is crazy! I hadn't met a man like him. And let me tell you, it took six years and a lot of tears, but he is exactly the man God showed me that day we got married. I praise God for bringing us together every day.

Michael and I weren't on the pregnancy page together in the beginning. I wanted to try the night we got married. I was like, Bring it on. I want to have a baby! I'm supposed to be fertile myrtle, right? I think God was like, "Yeah, you might be fertile myrtle, but we're going to go on a bumpy ride first. You need some equipment that will help you climb a mountain up ahead. I won't let you take on that mountain without you having what you need."

To rewind back even further to the day I was born, I gave my mom seventy-two hours of labor. Apparently, I was stubborn then [as I am now]. And my daughter—thank God she got it. Because that's why she lived here for as long as she did. I knew I wasn't a normal child [nor was Lilian], because who would do that to their mother?

Though I have survived difficult circumstances, I remember being mad and upset at times. I went through two miscarriages—one was terrible. My doctor at the time did not believe in anything but natural release. It took two weeks. We went on a trip with some family. We walked for probably four hours to wear my body out. In those four hours, I was like, God, please, I am done with this. I wasn't happy. When I released and saw my child in my hands, I lost it. I was not a good example of what or who God would be proud of. I fought through blood, sweat, and tears for two years.

Kim Arnold, who I worked with [at OSU Extension], can tell you. I was in her office, and she heard my stories a million times. She must be sick of me because I just can't get it together. I gained weight. I gained thirty-something pounds. We helped keep PF Chang's alive here. We ate there a lot, and our bank accounts showed for it. Michael was wondering what all the charges on the credit card could be—that would be PF Chang's. That's my medicine.

After I finally realized there was a problem, we went and got fertility treatments. We tried three different treatments. Here's another funny one: the economy is down (did anyone notice that?), and a fertility clinic actually sat us down and told us they were sorry, but they could no longer take our money. "It's not going to happen for you." The economy is down. Can you not just lie to me, take my money, and let me feel like I'm going to one day have a baby? That's all I wanted! She told us we had a 0.45 percent chance [of getting pregnant together]. So they were saying I don't even have a half-percent chance of getting pregnant? If God wants me to have a kid, then I'm going to have one.

I struggled through that in June of last year. It was hard news to hear. God worked on me over the summer to release what I had been so angry about for two years, including the miscarriage. I ended up finally accepting it all. I came to terms with a mistake I made a long time ago [a promise I made to God before I got married and then broke]. And I wondered if I was going through this because of that. You know what? God doesn't punish us.

Things happen to us because of what we do, but God doesn't punish us. I had to come to terms with that truth. My husband is the only one I've ever been with. Yet still, I broke a promise and thought that's why I couldn't have a kid. I came to terms with it by deciding to tell God that whatever He wants, I'm going to roll with it. I'm going to

THE FIGHT 251

trust Him now. I promise! It's hard to believe I have followed through with it, but the way He has worked in my life day to day has enabled me to rest in Him.

Shortly after, a family approached us about another family member who was pregnant. There might be an opportunity to adopt. Michael was totally against it at first. But then he said, "You know what? If this is what we are supposed to do, then yes." I remember telling God that this is in His hands, whatever He wants.

On top of that, one morning my mom called and told me my grandpa was in the hospital and might be dying. Then, we get a call from Robin, Michael's mom, that Michael's uncle is in the hospital, and he's going to die.

But the next phone call that day was too much. It was about the baby we were planning to adopt. The person on the line said, "Chrissy, the parents have taken the baby without medical release. We don't know where they are." You wanna know what my first response was? God, there's no way I can get through all that. But that was the first time I really experienced what it was like to give it all to Him and let Him lead me.

Later that night, I went to tan. My chest hurt, and I thought, I'm either pregnant or it's breast cancer. I didn't know what to think, but I debated whether or not to go to Walmart to get a pregnancy test. Michael is going to kill me [for buying another test]. I have purchased so many. We should have bought stock in a pregnancy test company!

He would be like, "Is that another pregnancy box, Chrissy, seriously?" Now, I'm going to get a little personal so I apologize, but that month Michael and I used protection every night, except one. I share that so you know how miraculous God is. I couldn't handle waiting until the end of the month to take a pregnancy test. So for the first time in six years, I decide we need protection every night for one month, except the night we conceived our miracle. How crazy is that? There's no question that was God. He is Bigger than any of us can imagine. And we try to put Him in a box!

I found out that night that I was pregnant. After tanning and going to the store to buy the test, I was home on the phone with my sister. I feel for her because I peed on a stick while we were talking. And there was no hiding it once I saw I was pregnant.

And I bought the good one that says pregnant or not pregnant this time! Forget purple, blue, stripes, no stripes, plus signs, negative signs (you name it, I have used them all). I wanted to be sure, so I went high price and bought a good one. It was a risk, but I needed a solid answer. I imagined Michael seeing the negative test later and saying, "Man, why did you spend twenty dollars? Come on!"

When I saw the word pregnant on that stick, I lost it. It probably sounded like I began talking in tongues. I don't even believe in that unless someone is there to translate, but I was all over the place. I dropped to my knees. I was screaming. I was shouting and praising God, and celebrating in every way possible, all while singing. I was pregnant! My sister thought, "What is going on? Is someone robbing her or trying to kill her? What just happened?" She said, "Stop. Stop freakin' out!" I'm like, "I can't. I can't breathe!" It was amazing!

I remember calling Michael who was out hunting (forgetting I had told him his uncle was in the hospital) and leaving him a message: "Please come home. I have something I need to tell you." He came home, and of course, I did something crazy. You know I'm out of my mind at that point because I'm pregnant, by golly! I had put these little stuffed toys on the couch with two positive pregnancy tests and covered them with a towel. He comes in, and I'm like, "Pull the towel up." He said, "Okay." He pulls it up and looks at me like, *She has lost it. Dear Lord, why are these toys on the couch? This is another level of nuts.*

He looks at me, and I say, "So what do you think?" And he's like, "Uh, is it mine?" I answered, "Is it yours?!" Like I had time as a 4-H extension educator to find someone else, let alone have the energy to do something with them. No, I don't have time. I barely have time for you. Well, let's see, I could have gone to the bank, withdrawn our savings, and hired a donor. But no, it's your child. I promise you, when she or he comes, you will know.

Lilian is a perfect mix of both of us. I see both of us in her. Sorry, I know this is long, but let's pretend you're at a seminar. This feels good being up here. Matt, I know why you like to have a mic and talk. Bear with me. We are getting there.

THE FIGHT 253

So Michael and I are scared out of our minds. When you've had miscarriages before, you don't know what to expect. It's a very scary ride. You think, It's never going to happen. And then it does, but you wonder, what will the next nine months bring? We've been through so much, but hopefully those things have prepared us. I don't think you are ever fully prepared to be a parent.

It's an emotional ride when you have this big desire to be a mother and nothing happens. Oh, that yearning! It's a period of drought. It's hard. It's lonely. All you care about is your hurting heart and wanting to be a momma but not getting to be a momma. I know some of you out there are dealing with this right now. Trust God because He will give you exactly what you need. When I finally got that, I stepped out of the way and let Him work. And now I'm doing what I was meant to do.

My yearning for a baby drove my husband nuts. I drove him nuts! All I could think about was babies—babies this and babies that. I was buying stuff and hiding it in the closet because I didn't want him to know I was buying stuff. Then he would get into the closet and ask me what I was doing. I couldn't resist. It was the coolest stuffed animal ever! It's going to help them, you know? He finally accepted the fact that he was along for the ride up to Crazyville or with me on the "crazy train" as we call it. There are two kinds of crazy—good and bad.

But moving on, it was a rough pregnancy. It was probably the hardest pregnancy I'm aware of, compared to others I know. I kept thinking of all those mommas who were happy while pregnant. Well, you lied, and I cannot like you. If you say you enjoyed pregnancy, you suck. I was mad. I thought, This can't be worth it. What the heck? Someone forgot to add something to the manual because I'm missing some information. I was sick the whole time.

Lily and I ran a marathon together in Greece when I was eight weeks pregnant. I did not want to be there. Every smell made me nauseous. I threw up everywhere we went. The surrounding people probably thought, Wow, this woman is bulimic or has a real problem. I was so sick. It was bad.

In January, we found out a cyst was growing in my right ovary. It was nineteen centimeters wide. Who does that? I do! We found out on a Friday, and I had emergency surgery a week later. They cut me all the way down my abdomen, which was my first scar from the pregnancy. It hurt. As if all that weren't enough, I caught C. diff (Clostridium difficile). I'll spare you details about C. diff, but imagine wishing you simply had diarrhea. It would come in a second. It's the worst thing I've ever gone through besides losing my daughter. I dropped over thirty pounds.

I could see my daughter molded within my tummy. I knew exactly where she was, every single part. It was the craziest thing. I thought, How is she going to make it through this? There's no way! I couldn't eat. I tried forcing myself, but it made me sick. I lost more weight.

But God provided. And in a bigger way than when we conceived at 0.45 percent chance. We made it through because God provided the tools I needed for that leg of our hike up the mountain. We thought, We've come this far. Let's keep going.

Then we found out about Lily's heart problems—six defects. Her doctor was amazing. She predicted each issue, and all of them came to be. She said it was probably going to be a chromosome problem, but they couldn't pencil her in. I'm like, Believe it or not, I know that feeling. It took ten years to figure out I had a bad gallbladder. Of course, we will not put our daughter in a box.

Since she ended up having heart problems, we started seeing another specialist. We went twice a week. Every appointment was scary. I was like, Twice a week, who does this? Each appointment brought more bad news. We were getting punched right and left. We couldn't catch a breath. Speaking of such, we were told her first breath would also be her last. I thought, Well, we can only keep moving forward in whatever God is going to do.

Dr. Donnelly, my first OBGYN, told me this is the worst pregnancy she's ever seen. And she has been practicing for some time. She couldn't see how I was doing it. Yeah, I know. I picked up this terrible luck somewhere and wish I could throw it back. I really don't like it. I need better luck. Where can I buy some or get some good luck? I don't know—I'm just doing it. Again, it's about God! I'm trusting that He has a plan.

Thinking about it all, I tried to be positive. Okay, I got pregnant, made it through surgery, and now I'm going to lose my child. However, before I got pregnant, I wondered *what it would feel like to have a child moving in my stomach, and I imagined hearing her heartbeat. No one can give me that. Somebody can give me a kid, but they can't give me that. So I was excited and got on board with that positive mindset. Okay, I'll just do this and get to adopt a child later. I'll get the full experience at some point.*

Lily came early. The day we went to the hospital, I was scared out of my mind because I was not ready to know if her first breath was going to be her last. But yet again, God is Big! He's been Big this whole time.

They prepped me for emergency surgery. Only three or four people were there. The anesthesiologist had an assistant. That's all! I thought we were supposed to have eight doctors there because of her heart condition. I was freaking out. It was the wildest ride of our lives. We were scared out of our minds. I shook badly and couldn't stop. I'm like, God, I'm not impressing You, but I'm trusting You! You're making it a little hard, though, so can You help me?

She came into the world and guess what? Her first breath wasn't her last. Praise God! Of course, a parent always wants more. But I decided, You know what? I'm going to stay on this ride as long as I can. I know it won't be long. She's now also fighting the preemie fight. She was two months early. And add two more weeks to that because she was two weeks behind on growth (there were issues with my placenta).

On day sixteen we found out she had trisomy 18, an extra set of the eighteenth chromosome. It's five times worse than Down's syndrome. Wow, we really know how to do it big in this family. God will use this to change people. We're going to step aside and let Him do what He needs to do. I've always wanted to be a missionary or a youth pastor. I've been a youth pastor at two different churches. Now I'm a missionary alongside my daughter. I love it. It's been hard but also awesome.

There have been unhappy moments and hurt feelings between me and some of my loved ones. I try not to dwell on it, but I'm guilty of that. There were also fun moments I look back on and laugh about. God has a tremendous sense of humor, and I've seen it through comical situations.

They told us that even though Lily made it past fifteen days, she probably wouldn't make it another week. Each week they kept telling us our daughter would not make it. She was going to die—she was on borrowed time. I want you to know how Big God really is. My daughter died in my arms once [before her final departure]. It was in the middle of the night. She turned gray three times. I couldn't do it anymore. I told the nurses to please just give her to me. Nurse Rita, I see you. She was there.

Had Lily died that first time, it would have been a crappy ending. You know what? God is so Big, because He knew that. We took everything off of her. She was in my arms as I sang every church song known to man. This is where God prepares you. The songs I sang for national conference are the songs I sang to my baby girl. Worship music I hadn't sung in a long time came back to me. We cried a lot. It was heartbreaking.

She choked on herself as she was going through the natural dying stage. I was like, I'm going to get through this, God, because You are here with me—I know! Disregarding what we did, God and Lily had another plan. Suddenly, my baby girl started crying and crying loud. I asked the nurses to put everything back on because she wasn't ready to go. Thank You, God, because I wouldn't have made it.

I wouldn't be standing here right now talking to you guys, being silly, or able to laugh. I cried and cried and cried that night and many days after. Thank you all for praying for peace because it's getting me through this. We survived that night, and it still wasn't the end. We got to go out with our daughter into the real world. The company that helped us transition home made it really cool as we left the hospital. I got to ride in a wheelchair with my baby like other mommas do when they leave the hospital for new beginnings.

We had some dear people come into our life who made sure we had special moments with Lily. I took tons of pictures, of course. We had three weeks with her at home, but it was nerve-racking. Honestly, I did not want to go home. I wanted my NICU staff. All twenty of them. In the hospital, it was like having a slumber party every night. They are good people. They are also hard core. Why can't I have them forever? My only problem was food. They could have fed me three times a day like they do the other floors [with breastfeeding moms]. But I'm not complaining. I was good.

When I left the hospital, I was like, Oh, my God, I don't think I am meant for this. I can't do this. I have to do all this stuff and see my daughter go through it all. We had to have her on a feeding pump and oxygen. There were wires and all the things. It was nuts, but we managed. I appreciate everyone who celebrated her monthly birthdays with us. My hope is that on the twenty-fifth of every month you will think of her and pray for all the babies in the world. There are so many babies out there in need of prayer. I've seen a sad side of the world that I didn't know about—mothers and fathers suffering with their babies.

It's also hard for the nurses, respiratory techs, doctors, and cleaning people (called environmental specialists. I think that's the full name). They made our environment wonderful. They have to see it day in and day out. Pray for them on the twenty-fifth too—they need it. They go through some hard core stuff.

To wrap up, I pray you know how Big God has been during this trial. We made it through those three weeks at home before she started getting sick again. She had some problems with reflux and then got a bacterial infection. This was the beginning of the end. Back at the hospital, I didn't want to leave whenever they were pushing us out. I reminded them I had surgery on Tuesday. It's my third surgery of the year. I have a huge hernia. Yes, I made it big. I cannot do this at home. I need you to keep her. They didn't listen. We had to go back home. We were home for another week until Lily's condition worsened. She was really sick. Michael and I both knew this was it.

We needed to make the most of our time with her. It was a rough week. Wednesday, she gave me a hug. She patted me on the back (a three-month-old who was two months behind). She knew that this was it. I was like, Oh, this is our goodbye. I'm not ready, but I'm never going to be ready.

I'm jealous of God. He gets to hold her and sing to her. She has a new body. He gets to walk with her and see her without all the crap on her. I'm excited because someday I'm going to be there, and I hope all of you are too. All you have to do is ask Jesus into your heart. That's all you have to do. He paid it all for us and died on the cross like we're worthy enough. He loves us that much, even though we waste time and focus on stupid things. I do it. I even take blessings for granted.

I am a better mother because of Lily. If I'm blessed with more children, those kids are going to have it good. I told Michael that we're packing up for vacation on day two of their life. Come on, let's just go! Get in the car and go, because it's going to be awesome. I can't wait.

To finish my story, on Wednesday when she said goodbye to me, she started declining pretty fast. We had to make a choice again. There were so many decisions throughout the whole thing. We had a wonderful time praying with our pastor and his wife. It was incredible. We always prayed through those hard moments. They came at the perfect time when it was hard. For our family, we could only handle it a certain way because we couldn't bear to watch their hearts break. It was too much. I can handle myself, but I can't watch other people go through it. It's really frustrating for me because I can't fix it, and I'm a fixer.

When we went down to the PICU and they intubated her, it was her one last shot. I thought, You know, we took her off everything before, she came back, and it wasn't time. This time we're going to give her one more chance. The viral infection that she was fighting took over everything. It really did. She was done. She coded twice in the night.

I just lay there praying, God, give me peace, because I know it's time. You have given us a hundred and three days (almost) of pure bliss wrapped around some pretty crappy things, but You've revealed the good in all of it.

On Thursday, she coded one more time. We were doing things to her instead of for her. That's when Michael and I went home, gathered some of her things, traveled back [to the hospital], and made the last decision—to let her go. She wasn't there anymore. The machine was doing everything for her.

I got to hold her as she left this earth. How many people get to do that for someone? I loved it. I sang the song you just heard earlier, "I Am with Thee." It was one I sang for competition. I'm going to try to sing one now that I sang to her. [The lyrics aren't included due to copyright.] I sang two songs a cappella, "I Will Never Be the Same

Again" and *"Jesus Loves Me."* I sang another song that I don't remember to Lily, but she was gone by that time. It was a precious moment. I just held her.

Now I Lay Me Down to Sleep is one of the coolest organizations I've ever worked with. They came and helped me take pictures of my baby without all the wires and nasal cannula. We got to dress her up in clothes she hadn't worn yet. Now, you tell me that God isn't Big. He's incredible, but you have to step aside and let Him work. If you don't, you'll miss out.

I'm here to tell you I'm not getting off this drug. God is amazing. And my relationship with Him is the coolest thing I will ever experience in my life. And, yes, I will weep again when it's time to weep. But when it's time to be happy, I will be happy. The setting for this service today is rain—God has blessed us with a cleansing downpour that makes me imagine heaven is rejoicing.

I came to church today and was here on stage, jumping around, trying to get in the mood to be here, trying to get fired up, because I know this is what I'm supposed to be doing. At thirty-two years old, it's time for me to be brave and let Him speak to you through me.

When the rain fell (the hardest rainfall I've ever heard in my life), I looked at Michael and said, "She's home. The angels are rejoicing and happy. She had to go through a lot, but she's there now." I was like, Oh, God, you are good. I felt grateful. The rain had a calming effect on me. How cool is that?

He has been here the whole time. I'm going to write every author who I connect with while reading their book when it's obvious they wrote that message for me [including devotionals]. Another example—I bought one of my girlfriends a card, and this is what it said on the back: "so that Christ may dwell in your hearts through faith. And I pray that you, being rooted and established in love, may have power, together with all the saints, to grasp how wide and long and high and deep is the love of Christ, and to know this love that surpasses knowledge, that you may be filled to the measure of all the fullness of God." Because a woman put that Scripture on the back of her greeting card, I felt encouraged and knew God was speaking to me about my current circumstance.

I hope Lily's life influenced you somehow. Some of you got to meet her. I wish you all could have met her and held her. She was our little missionary through the Caring-Bridge posts, the pictures you saw, even the emotions and tears she evoked. Let her life inspire you to live boldly! She was our Warrior Princess. She lived her life in a big way, and she lived it out loud.

Lily lived 103 days, three-and-a-half months, 2,472 hours, 148,320 minutes, and 8,899,200 seconds. How do you measure a year in your life? How about by love? Measure it in love because relationships matter the most. There will be seasons. Some are hard, like a long winter. But then spring, summer, and fall follow, and they bring new beauty, fresh air, and fun.

Keep in mind whatever you are going through right now is preparing you for the next season. I'm really hoping that God will let me take a little sabbatical so I can take a break from climbing. Maybe even an early retirement? I mean, I could run farther if He wants. I could do that because I've run some marathons, but I'm tired.

I won't lie though—Michael and I are exhausted. You can see it in our pictures. God and Lily knew. We climbed until our energy was spent. It was time—time for it to be done. I know you've heard this, but God doesn't give you more than you can handle. When the time was right, He let Lily come home to Him.

I don't know how the T18 moms do it. I've lived some of it, but I can't imagine doing this for ten years. I feel for them. I pray for them because they battle through a hard life. They love on their special babies every single day not being able to communicate with them like they want. They have to do a lot for them. The children have to be on multiple medicines. It takes so much just to care for these kids. Let's lift them up in prayer because they have the toughest job I've ever seen. Motherhood is tough anyway. It is the hardest job any woman will ever have in her life. It's the worst job sometimes. But it's also the most amazing and rewarding job you will ever have. Pray to God that your blessings outweigh the bad because the bad can give the enemy an opportunity to tempt you.

Mothers, I encourage you to hang on! Love your babies. Do the stuff. Let your babies sleep in bed with you. Hold them. Love them. Teach them. When they do something *really stupid, help them understand why it was stupid. Don't just say, "Don't do that."*

I would tell Lily, "Okay, honey, listen up. I know you're not much of a multitasker, but I need you to breathe. I need you to pump your heart. I need you to relax and let your bowel movement release so we don't have constipation." I had to tell her all the time, "This is why you need to do that. Because it's going to help you live." I had to teach her.

I went through the checklist when she cried. Okay, girl, I hear you! Diaper check—changed it. Food—your feeding tube is now full. Okay, we're good there. I don't know what's wrong. Did I say something? Do we need to move you to a different area? Do you hate your outfit? I can change it, but I need to know why. Mothers, you can relate.

Fathers, love your wives. A mother's heart—it's hard for us. We go through so many emotions. We have to consider hormones, people. Hormones suck because you just never know what you're going to be feeling when all the things are happening. Your babies are growing, and you just want to keep this little baby a baby! One day, you give their little hiney a pinch. The next, you want to spank their butt because they are being a butt. They grow up too fast.

Fathers and mothers, if you do not have God in the middle of your relationship, you will not make it. My husband and I have proven this truth. Michael thought I was going to have to go to Laureate [Psychiatric Clinic and Hospital in Tulsa], and I thought he was going to leave us. I really did when this first started. I thought, There is no way he's staying. He probably thought, Is she going to "stay" with me [mentally]?

I will say, though, you have to latch on to each other. You have to spend time together. Partners that spend too much time apart won't make it. I don't care who you are. And if you shut God out, you are shooting yourself in the foot. If we had tried going through this without God, I would not be standing here today.

I've watched mothers lose their children. I'll never forget a situation I witnessed in grade school. I think I was in grade school. Right, Mom? Kenny and Charlene Wood—I watched them go through losing their child, who was in college. Watching her mother go through that troubled me. It was hard, especially because it happened so suddenly, without warning.

I did get a warning, time and time again. I'm thankful for that. I also watched a cousin of mine, Lisa and Mike, go through losing their sweet baby girl. She had Down's syndrome. Beautiful, beautiful little girl. Faith was here for three days. I watched Lisa go through it. We didn't see everything there. Lisa kept to herself and did her thing. She survived, though, because they had God. Now she has two beautiful baby boys, and they are amazing. How cool is that?

God may never give me another child. I'm okay with that now. I won't beg. I won't plead. I will not ask Michael to do anything and everything to make it happen. We will not borrow millions of dollars to try to get one. I am a mother. I will always be a mother. When I do leave this earth and go home, I'll see my baby girl. I'll talk to her. I'll finally know what she was trying to tell me, instead of guessing.

Take all of this to heart because you were meant to hear this. I know I have rambled on. Thank you for being patient, because it needed to be said. My sister sent me a poem by Edward Estlin Cummings, "I Carry Your Heart with Me." [I read the poem, but it cannot be included in this book due to copyright.]

Now on to Facebook. I have not read all your messages, but I will get to them. I appreciate it. It's really cool. I know Lily touched a lot of people because I've seen hundreds of friends commenting, letting us know how much they care and love us. It's helped carry us through. Because you prayed, I'm able to speak today and not fall apart.

Last night, I was sitting there in the seats where you are, bawling my eyes out and going, "God, I know I had a dream [about speaking today], but was that really meant for me? Because I'm not feeling it right now. I don't know if I can keep it together." When I cry, I'm crying, people. It's not forced. I can't make myself cry. (I tried whenever I really wanted to cry, and it didn't work.) God knows when to release our hearts. When there's too much pressure in there, He lets it out through our tears.

Coy? Where's Coy? Can I read what you put on Facebook? He wrote a really cool comment. "For three months and twelve days heaven waited for the most precious baby to have ever lived. Every breath was a miracle. Every moment was a gift. Every second God proved how Big He is.

What doctors said could not happen, Lily proved could be done. What most parents would have given up on, Michael and Chrissy held on to [through] Jesus. I wish I could have seen Jesus' face when Lily made it home. That's right, my God Be Big."

Now, do you see how Big He really is? God is huge, and I love Him with all my heart. I praise Him for giving me the second greatest miracle that ever walked this earth. Like I said before, Jesus is the first and my daughter is the second [for me]. And I thank Him for it! If I had to do this all over again, I would do it in a heartbeat—even knowing the outcome and knowing what it would take. Why? Because God gave me what I needed to climb this mountain, and He knows my limit.

I love you guys. I love you with all my heart. I pray that you remember the lessons I have learned. Michael and I have finished this race, and I'm excited about what God has planned for Lily's platform, my mission, and the projects He has given me. To God be the glory!

264 Chrissy L. Whitten

In Loving Memory Of
Lilian Grace Whitten

Shared In Our Lives
April 25, 2010 — August 5, 2010
Tulsa, Oklahoma   Tulsa, Oklahoma

Celebration of Life
10:00 AM, Saturday, August 7, 2010
Cornerstone Church
Sand Springs, Oklahoma

Officiant
Matt Blair

Speaker
Chrissy Whitten

Musical Selections
"I Am With Thee" "I'll Fly Away"
"God Of The City"

Musicians
Angie Greer Pat Matherly
Patti Matherly Chuck Burton Shad Foley
Brooke Hunter Rachel Foley

Ephesians 3:17-19
So that Christ may dwell in your hearts through faith. And I pray that you, being rooted and established in love, may have power, together with all the saints, to grasp how wide and long and high and deep is the love of Christ, and to know this love that surpasses knowledge—that you may be filled to the measure of all the fullness of God.

AUGUST 10, 2010

87 › An Angel Earns Her Wings

My heart is smiling because God continues to take care of us. I've heard the saying, "God will not give you more than you can handle." Every time I heard this statement, I wondered what it meant. I would usually say something like, "Well, I think He's pushing it," or "Does He really stop when I've had enough?" I would even tell Him we needed to define what I can handle because this or that was really hard or You might have me confused with someone else!

Oh, how my Father decided to help me learn hands on what He can do for me and you. He taught me He will always be there to carry my burdens. He loves to show up and show me just what He can do through my weaknesses.

I look back at this journey and realize it took almost thirty-two years to prepare. Every heartache and every joy were meant to give me the tools to climb the highest mountain in life. On Wednesday, August 4, 2010, Lilian Grace, Michael, and I were almost to the top of this mountain. Lilian Grace looked the best she had in a long time. I took pictures of her and texted them to her daddy, grandparents, aunts, and uncles. I knew this was the calm before the storm.

I went to eat with Michael. When I came back, Lily looked at me, and I knew we were heading into the last storm together. Not long after we exchanged a look, Lily started declining. Her breathing problems increased, and her heart rate soared while we tried a "flow by" technique involving an oxygen/tubal delivery system resting right next to Lilian's face to give her nostrils a break from the irritating nose cannula. It worked for a little bit. Even with her nose cannula, we couldn't keep her oxygen level up.

We had to decide whether to intubate or not. I prayed so hard. I needed someone to tell me what to do. A couple of doctors said intubating would give her a chance to fight the virus, and even our pastor, who is against assistance, agreed. I knew this would help us know we had tried everything to give her a chance to fight.

That night after being intubated, Lily crashed a couple of times. It was hard, which I have already posted about. I knew at three in the morning or so this would be the end. I didn't know how much longer we had, but I could tell this part of the journey was almost over. No more rope. No more candle to burn.

When Lily coded three times and the doctors did chest compressions, my heart sank. Had it really come to this? Well, I thought, I didn't want them to go to that extreme, but I'm glad they did because it gave Michael a chance to get back to us before Lily earned her wings.

The doctor told us Lily's options, and all of them led to death. We picked the best option; it was the hardest thing we've faced. We pulled her off life support. The doctor told us we were doing things to her instead of for her.

Michael and I drove home, taking a load of her stuff back. We rode in silence. I knew this was for the best, but my heart was breaking. When Lilian Grace hugged me the day before and patted me on the back, it felt like this was it for our journey together.

When we got back to the hospital, we brought lots of clothes. We waited for the NILMDTS photographer, Kelli, so she could take our pictures as a family. I'm so glad we waited. The pictures we've seen so far are phenomenal. God has been so Big in all this. He gave me extra special moments and miracles with our baby girl, who really is our Warrior Princess. She is God's missionary, sent to kick our butts and get us moving in the right direction.

When the doctors unplugged Lilian Grace, she was in my arms first, then Michael's. I sang to our sweet baby girl as she left this earth, earned her wings, and flew. It's hard to describe the many emotions that overcame me, but the incredible thing is God healed our baby girl. He gave her what she needed, and He will continue to do so for us.

Taking pictures with her was breathtaking! Dressing her in gorgeous clothes without wires, cords, and nose cannula was perfect. I know she has a new body, and I can't wait till the day we join her and our heavenly Father. Lilian had an amazing send off. I miss her and still feel her on my chest, but I'm happy God stepped in and gave us His strength for this journey. His promises have rung loud and clear. Lilian Grace and God continue to make us smile.

A family handmade with love from above

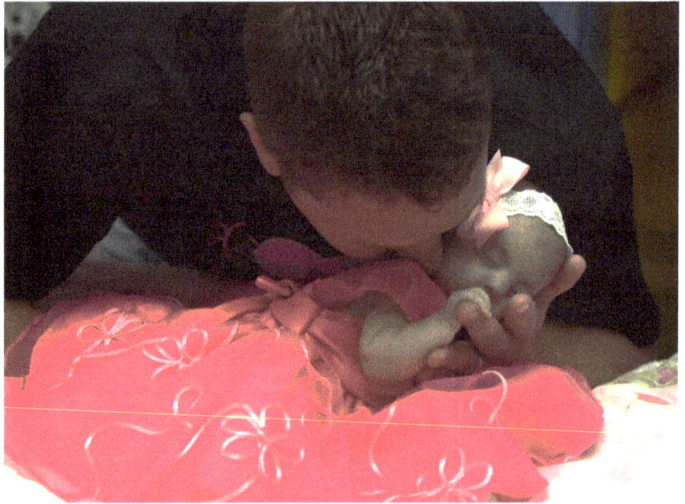

Sweet kisses for his baby girl

When I walked her through the hallways and down the elevator to place her in the funeral home van, I rejoiced at not having to carry three machines. I just carried my baby girl. She will always be in our hearts and will continue to change lives as I share her story with as many as I can.

When we planned her celebration of life, we shared a dream God gave me. Oh, how beautiful and glorious it turned out. God has made sure we know what our next chapter will be. He is taking care of us. May we all step aside and let God be Big. I love you all!

AUGUST 11, 2010

88 › Grief Begins

Ever feel nothing? That's me today. I realize nothing is what I feel until the flood gates open again, and then I cry and cry. Even though I understand why Lilian Grace is not here with us, I still miss her dearly. I don't think this yearning goes away ever. I just hope it hurts a little less in time. I'm still so in love with God, and I know He has a plan. He never left me while taking care of my baby girl!

A few people have asked me if we'll start trying again for another child. Deep breath! If God were to bless us with another child, I hope it's a girl and she looks just like Lilian Grace. How awesome would that be? Would I love to be a mother to another child? Yes! Will it consume me? No! I'm leaving it in God's hands. I will not be trying.

Right now, I just miss her. I miss hearing her. I miss holding her. I miss taking care of her. I miss changing her diaper, feeding her, giving her medicine, bathing her, singing to her, reading to her, and just being with her.

I've been sick for a few days, and this illness reminds me of how I used to be in college. I'd work my butt off until finals week ended, then I'd rest. Come to find out, every break, I'd get sick. I feel like I was in finals week for three-and-a-half months, and now I'm on break.

Deeper breathing as more tears roll down my face. I'm still smiling because I got to experience a miracle—an angel here on earth. I keep waiting to see if I'm going to snap and just lose it. I can't believe tomorrow at 6:19 p.m. will mark exactly one week since Lilian Grace earned her wings. One week already. Time sure does speed past us. I've decided I will keep posting now and then until I feel like moving to another outlet. I know I'm not the only one grieving.

Grieving. That's such a strange word to me. I tend to look at it in a negative way. We watched our daughter earn her wings. Knowing she will not be here on this earth will be a continuous grieving process.

I bought a book called *What the Bible Says About Grieving* when we first learned Lilian's prognosis. This book reminds me that there are five stages to grieving and that I won't necessarily go through them in order. I hope I can let myself cry whenever needed. I try to talk out loud when I feel down. I don't think I'm magically going to be okay with her not being here because I am human. I want my baby girl here with me. To look at this in a positive way, I remember that God holds me in His hands. If you need to, jump in His arms and let Him love on you. He's doing that for us right now.

Matthew 19:13–14, Luke 18:16, Psalm 139:13–14, Psalm 39:7, and Psalm 119:76 are suggested verses from the book to help when grieving the loss of a child. He knows our beginnings and endings. I didn't want to get in the way of God's plan. May God be with us as we trust Him to get us through. I wish I had my baby girl here, but I know she lived her purpose out loud, and He needed her back with Him. I hope to join her one day, but I'm not rushing it. I will rest in His comforting love. May we not waste this life He has given us nor neglect our relationship with Him and our purpose. Love you!

AUGUST 12, 2010

89 › Positive Perception

Michael and I spent some quality time with friends today. I just love my peeps, related and unrelated. God sweeps me away time and again by surrounding me with the best people in the world. I don't think someone could pay enough to have it as good as we do.

I'm looking forward to a future with endless possibilities for us. I am so stinkin' excited I could jump out of my skin. I feel different. Today, I've been trying to figure out why I'm handling things better than I thought I ever would. How funny is that? I'm confused that life isn't stopping, that I'm still breathing and trusting God, and that I'm not in a padded room. That, my friends, is my God being Big! I have a feeling there will be a million emotions we will go through, but my favorite is the one where I trust God. It feels more amazing than anything else. I see a future with God doing big things.

As I posted on Facebook, I am super excited about what the future holds. Writing a book, getting the Warrior Princess Foundation and Trail Run underway, working for the church, guest speaking, training to run 103 miles (this will take some time), scrapbooking all the mega pictures, possibly working part-time with one of my favorite buddies...the list goes on and on. Thanks to my God and my Warrior Princess for pushing me.

God is Big! I feel like I could conquer the world today. I'm crying happy tears because God sent her to wake us all up. Through Lilian Grace, He has given me a better life than I could have ever given myself. I hope you take a look at your life and open your eyes and ears to what God has planned for you. When you are in His will, oh, it will take your breath away and give you the greatest high in life.

I don't know how I will feel in an hour, a day, a week, a month, or a year. I do know how I feel right now. How do you feel? Are you where God wants you to be? I can say I've traveled the road called my plan, and it ended up the same in heartbreak, unhappiness, and disappointment. I hope to travel down the road called God's plan and have the greatest adventure ever! Whose plan are you following right now?

Michael and I are leaving early in the morning for an adventure for two. A vacation...a celebration...a time of renewing. I will not post regular updates while I am gone. When I get back, I'll continue to write until it's time to move on. While we are gone, we'd love for you to post something in the CaringBridge guest book for us to print later. Here's what we'd love for you to write if you are willing—tell us how God helped you through our adventure with you all. We'd love to hear how He has changed your life.

We love you all very much. Please pray for us to have a safe trip. Michael wants to play a fun game of *Where Are the Whittens*? Whoever guesses the closest to where we really are gets dinner on us. We will post clues throughout the vacation. You don't have to participate, but we thought it would be fun. Talk to you when we get back!

Where Are the Whittens clues include the following:

🌐 We're headed toward water.

💤 Naps are wonderful while traveling.

⛱️ We learned new dance moves. I finally got that tan I needed. Lizards and crabs roamed the land. We spent a day in our swimsuits with an NBA player.

🌅 A Martha Stewart photo shoot was happening. Fish were plenty. The sunsets were gorgeous, yet it rained a lot. We got to be like monkeys in a forest and climbed a huge waterfall.

🍍 The skies got us there. We enjoyed fresh pineapples and wore swimsuits a major portion of our trip. Parrots were pets where we stayed. We had entertainment every night, with the most amazing singers. Playmakers made it fun.

🤙 Where we were, there were no problems, only situations.

The Whittens were in...drumroll please...Montego Bay, Jamaica, at the Sandals Resort! It was a blast getting to refresh and reconnect with my hubby while soaking up the sun and taking adventures in the jungle and waterfall. Chuck Burton was our winner for a free dinner on us.

AUGUST 24, 2010

90 › Phantom Feelings in Healing

Lilian would have been four months old at 8:44 a.m., Wednesday, August 25, 2010. We were set to wear our "God Be Big" shirts. If you didn't purchase one, we'd encourage you to wear pink, black, white, or purple, or a combination of those colors. We're still moving forward with the idea. Please take pics and send them to me. I'm working on a picture book of all the birthday celebrations we had with her and now without her. I bought a black and pink purse along with a stuffed puppy for the event. I will gather all my stuff and wear it proudly.

God has been Big and will continue to be Big for all of us. God is good in making sure I can't turn back by giving me things to accomplish that will take forever. I'm in scary waters, but I know it's where I am supposed to be.

Even though Michael and I are not bitter, we find ourselves unable to escape the grieving process. No matter how positive I am, I still miss her. I long to hold her, kiss her cheeks, and press her against my chest. Tears of both happiness and sadness come and go these days.

Man, there are no pills, words, or techniques to deal with this fully. I told Michael that on days when we don't have it together, we may have to fake it till we make it. I'm not very good at this. If you see me smiling, then I'm happy. If you see me tearing up, then I'm sad.

The phantom feelings have kicked in, reminding me of how intense our memories are. The first time it happened, I could swear I had Lilian Grace on my chest, resting perfectly like many times before. I sat up, bawling. What in the world? Our brains are extremely complicated to recreate that kind of intense memory. Well, I cried because I was happy to know my chest and brain hadn't forgotten what she felt like. That she really had been here and wasn't a dream. She was real, and I got to be a mommy. A mommy. Oh, how my heart giggles.

Tears overtake me in moments like these, and I can't stop them. By the grace and mercy of God, my scarred heart will mend. Healing is never easy, no matter how positive we are. Healing is hard, and there's not a quick fix. My heart feels like it has a thousand rips in it.

I hope you enjoy time with your family and friends. We're not guaranteed any amount of time with them. Call someone you haven't spoken to in a long time, tell someone how special they are to you, write a letter, or do something unusual and sincere. God knows every hair on our heads and when we will take our last breath. Make sure to love and care for one another while you have the chance.

I know this much—the devil is not going to stay down. He's continuously trying to fight back. He picked the wrong warrior to mess with because God is my sword. God will step on the devil again and again. May we all have the strength and ability to step aside and let God knock evil down because we cannot do it on our own.

My heart pours out the pain of losing a child even as it rejoices in God's plan. Walking forward into the next chapter scares me, but I stand tall, knowing God's plan is better than mine.

I met with church leadership today, and I am super excited about what God has planned. I'll continue posting on here since I can't seem to stop. Hope you enjoy what this crazy woman types. Love you all.

A Letter to My Precious Warrior Princess

Lilian Grace,

You have made your mommy and daddy so very proud. You turned our world upside down as you followed through with God's will for your life on a daily basis. You rarely cried or complained. You took one blow after another, but you smiled through it all.

Oh, how I loved to sing, read, stare, hold, and kiss you, my dear child. You made me the happiest mommy ever. I can never thank you enough for fighting through 103 days and allowing us to experience everything you had to offer. You gave me memories I will always cherish. Chest-to-chest with you was my favorite place. I remember your sweet smell and gorgeous blue tear-drop pupil eyes.

You helped me see the beauty in our story by living out a plan I never thought I'd survive. Even with forewarning, I still would have struggled to believe it. It was too grand of a plan.

I remain shocked God chose me to be your mommy. Who was I to be worthy of such a miraculous gift? I know how I was worthy! God deemed me to be, which takes my breath away. I will never be the same, my sweet pea. There is no going back. God and you made it impossible for me to get out of what lies before me. Yes, I am really scared of this walk, but I keep saying over and over, "I trust You, God. I trust You, God. I trust You, God."

Tears stream down my face, and my heart aches for you to be here. I know you are completely healed by the grace of God.

He needed you back home. I get it, but a mother struggles to let go even if she knows deep inside it was time.

You have accomplished something many wish they could do. Baby girl, you soared high and taught so many to pray and trust God. Wow! How incredible! I can't even measure it all.

Thank you for loving me and fighting the good fight, even when you wanted to give up. I appreciate that you came back after trying to leave the first time. You gave me the greatest gift by waiting for me and Daddy before you earned your wings and departed from our arms. I look at your NILMDTS pictures and (sorry, the tears are falling even more) you looked so peaceful, which affirmed your need to depart. Thank you, thank you, thank you for letting us be your mommy and daddy.

You have touched endless lives and changed us forever. Thank you for showing us that no matter your circumstances, you can still do God's will. You can still reach people through the not-so-fun parts of life.

One last thing, Lilian Grace. I can't wait for the day I get to run, pick you up, swing you around, and kiss your face. I'll tell God, in person, how amazed I am by Him through you. Oh, to walk the streets of gold with you. Hmm, that's a picture worth keeping in my heart. I love you with all my heart, Tiger Lily. You are my sunshine. You are my catalyst to start a new chapter I've avoided for so long.

Love,
Your Mommy

AUGUST 30, 2010

91 › Triggers

Twenty-five days. Has it really been twenty-five days since my Lilian Grace earned her wings? Time moves swiftly as we grieve. I never know when grief will hit me. Triggers are everywhere. Hearing a song we danced to with Lily at the grocery store, over the car radio, or in an elevator. Seeing a stuffed animal that's measurable to her size. Smelling baby lotion. Hearing a baby with similar squeaks. Passing by the hospital and not getting to visit. These moments intensify my grief and bring it to the surface. I find myself staying busy, which is what I need at this time.

I've started volunteering as an administrative assistant for twenty hours a week at the church. I'm not looking for a paid job while my heart heals from all the rips and tears. To open our Warrior Princess Foundation account, I need to meet with our volunteer accountant to complete our official 501(c)(3) paperwork. Thank you to everyone who sent donations to give us a great start of $2,000! For those who mentioned giving on a monthly basis, I'm creating an official website and PayPal accounts.

I'm teaming up with RunnersWorld of Tulsa to organize a fundraising race set for April 25, 2011. Hopefully, in a couple months, people can start spreading the word. Meanwhile, I'm in scary territory starting my book project. I will be getting with everyone who said they'd help.

I couldn't be more excited about getting to meet some of the T18 and T13 families soon. My father-in-law and I are driving to Houston this weekend for a quick trip to meet some of the dear friends I've met through this journey. My milk is going to another T18 little girl. Lilian, just keep on giving! There are more opportunities to come. I can't wait to share, but I must run. Love you all.

AUGUST 31, 2010

92 › Proof She Existed

In a million years, I never realized how hard it'd be to see her death certificate. After Michael got it, I opened the envelope and paused. It didn't feel real. At times, I convince myself I'm just taking a break. I catch myself trying to drive back to the hospital to see her smiling face. I realize quickly she's not there anymore or anywhere else on earth. Tears stream down my face as grief overtakes me again.

Time! I'm hoping time mends my broken heart. My happiness and motivation are mixed with sadness. Michael said something that has stuck in my mind today. Other people's babies are not our baby. This is true, but oh, how I love to share in everyone else's happiness for their babies. Every single child is one of God's miraculous creations, bringing me joy as I hold them. No one, not even another of my own, will ever replace Lilian Grace as her existence is embedded in my brain and body memory.

When I finally read the death certificate, I cried a little. I wanted to wait until right now to really let myself feel. Reading your child's name on a death certificate hurts like nothing else I've ever felt aside from actually losing her. My breathing is shallow, and I feel a weight on my chest. There is no handbook to help me through this except the Bible. It gives me comfort and hope for eternity. I wish we could bypass the hurt, yet there is not a way. I know I will forever miss Lilian Grace while I am on this earth.

The death certificate is a piece of paper confirming our goodbye came too soon. Thinking positively, it's a piece of paper proving my daughter existed, but now she gets to be in a better place. I long for that place, my home, yet there are greater things to be done here.

    I am far from perfect and catch myself talking too much. I definitely have opinions. I hope I keep stepping aside so that God's kingdom can expand. There will be a day when my heavenly Father will remove my sorrow and pain. This gives me goosebumps. I share this moment only to show you how life comes at us quickly. We never know when things will change. I am trusting God to guide and help me through this crazy new chapter. May He do the same for you.

SEPTEMBER 3, 2010

93 › A Letter to My Younger Self

I finally sifted through the phone messages, emails, and Facebook comments, and I am comforted by your words. I'm going back to the beginning, Lilian's birth, and am reading and listening to your messages. It doesn't seem like four-and-a-half months have passed. It's been twenty-nine days since she earned her wings. Really? A month?

I've filled my time every day, perhaps too much on some days. Please be patient with me as I wish I could get to everybody as I catch up, spend time, or simply respond. Thank you for your love and giving me time as I heal.

I went to Stillwater today with two of my girlfriends. We had a blast remembering the past. Something came up about wanting to start our college days over. I giggle thinking about who I was then—a young girl trying to figure out who I was. I longed to have a boy love me and want to marry me. Let's just say I had a lot of boys break my heart a little, and I broke some hearts as well. Oh, the days of trying to figure out it all. If I could go back to myself in 1997, I'd tell myself this:

Chrissy, sweet girl, whenever you make a choice, be aware that your hormones and emotions will get the best of you. You can't change people. You can only educate and give them opportunities to see things from a different point of view. When you feel desperate or alone, know God is always here with you. There's no need to rush through life, always wanting something else. Enjoy the present. Accept and be content with what you have instead of wishing for something else. It's good to dream and plan and experience what's going on around you. Don't miss out. And you can't make someone love you. When you accept, trust, and love yourself, then you will be able to do that with others. If you get that weird feeling in the pit of your stomach, listen to it. That's the Holy Spirit trying to help you out!

There is so much more I'd tell myself. Most importantly, I would emphasize trusting God in my Christian walk while knowing He will always provide exactly what I need. I may not like it, but I know His way is more extravagant than anything else.

This weekend, I'll take my milk and donate it to a T18 family. I can't wait to share what happens. What started out as a milk delivery has flourished into a first-time gathering of T18/T13 families in the Houston area. I am tickled to see God making things happen. He is so Big! I will give you all the details after I get back from Houston. Pray for safety and perfect health to allow all our kiddos to be present. My eyes are open, Lord, as I praise You for showing me Your strength, will, and love! I am excited to buckle up and step aside, hoping we all can do the same during this miraculous ride. Amen!

SEPTEMBER 8, 2010

94 › Divine Direction to Houston

As part of Lilian Grace's celebration of life video, a special mother sent the song "Little Dreamer" to me. I play it a lot, closing my eyes and picturing Lily right here with me. It's good to listen to when I'm missing her more than usual. She will always be with me no matter where we both land. There're nights I close my eyes, fall into a deep sleep, and experience a radiant light shining bright as it pierces the darkness. I'd like to think she's taking a quick peek from heaven to check on us.

    I'm finding I can't handle watching people abuse or take their children for granted. I can't stand watching people waste time being angry or upset about something that just doesn't matter. We all struggle with a child not doing what we want, acting out in a way we wish we could change. Sometimes, we even try to fix something for them, but we can't. We feel useless. These are hard things to go through, yet I'd rather struggle with these than deal with Lilian Grace not being here. I'd rather argue with her and not like what she is doing than never hold her or wipe away her tears.

    God reminds me of His grace and mercy as I remember we all have a walk to walk. I don't want to judge. I need to come to terms with how hard it is to see. I may have been like the ones I don't like watching if it weren't for Lilian Grace. Thanks, God, for giving me a gift, and may I never forget with my future children or those around me right now. With that said, I'd like to tell you something that happened this past weekend. God's plan is better than mine could ever be, and He blew me into another galaxy by His love and grace.

When trying to figure out what to do with my breast milk, all I could think about was not throwing it away. I couldn't bear to throw out all those hours of pain and sorrow of being hooked up to that pump six to eight times a day. I knew Lilian Grace needed my milk almost as much as she needed the oxygen to breathe. I was so hard on myself because I knew there was nothing else I could physically do to help her. For 103 days, I pumped like crazy, making sure she'd have enough liquid gold. Praise God, He made me like a milk cow, blessed with an abundance of milk. I would have pumped until she turned fourteen months as recommended.

Hours of pumping

The milk was definitely one of the reasons she lived as long as she did. Praise God, my milk was enriched more than normal breast milk. When tested, breast milk is normally twenty to twenty-two calories. Mine was twenty-seven calories! Make no mistake, God had His loving hands on it. Lilian ate less at one time, so we were very blessed to have the increased enrichment in a smaller quantity. One of my friends called my milk Liquid Gold Warrior Food (LGWF). Love that name!

When Lilian Grace earned her wings, it took me twenty-five pain-filled days to dry up. If someone local could have used the milk, I probably would have kept pumping. I know now God was good to make sure I finally dried up. Being on the pump brought back memories, both good and bad. At home, Lilian lay next to me as I pumped. It seemed Lily's alarms would go off every time I pumped, and I learned to hold both cups while getting Lily to breathe or slow her heart rate. I smile just thinking about what I looked like trying to balance it all. A wild hyena trying to sit long enough for a tea party would best describe it. Michael and I got a really good laugh about it though.

Anyway, I wondered who the best person would be to receive my milk. I didn't know if it would creep people out or not since breast milk is very personal. I did offer it to a couple of people near here before realizing God wanted it to go to a precious mother, Denise Williams, for her daughter, Trishtan (T18), in Houston, Texas. So began our adventure this past weekend.

I had too much milk to ship, and I knew God wanted my father-in-law, Monty Whitten, to take me and the freezer full of breast milk on the 1,070-mile round-trip trek. I was not taking a chance on the milk going bad because Trishtan would hopefully benefit beyond anything else they could give her. I knew some of my grieving family members might not understand why they weren't asked to drive me, but I felt my father-in-law was the right choice. Sorry if you felt robbed of an experience, but God knows the best way to comfort you.

Why didn't Michael go? My husband wasn't ready to do something like this. I'm learning men grieve differently from women. A good man reminded me people usually think about the mother grieving the hardest. They tend to think men are tough and strong, when in truth they hurt just as much or more. Men are fixers, and in grief, there is nothing they can do to fix it, causing men to feel helpless.

Lilian Grace really did a number on her daddy. She opened up emotional doors in him I didn't even know existed. He is more loving and emotional, which I find very sexy! I just love that he was willing to give his new deep freeze up to hold my breast milk for this family. It wouldn't have been his first choice, but he knew it's what was meant to be.

Michelle Anderson, a T18 mommy who lost her little boy, Rhyder, last year, has become a very dear friend of mine. We spent many days and nights on the phone. She was so helpful in finding resources and connecting me to the wonderful world of T18/13. I spoke with her today and asked how in the world we originally connected since I couldn't remember. She told me she gets google search emails for T18, and my blog came up one day. Thank God she did because she is the reason I found Denise Williams. I'm forever grateful. This crazy lady (Michelle) got an idea to get us on the news. Little did she know that we'd end up having ABC, CBS, NBC, and the *Donor Milk: The Documentary* team all there to experience this event with us.

As we approached our destination, I almost backed out. I just kept saying over and over that I'm not ready for this. My father-in-law told me I was. I'm not good on film or ready to do all the things I'm trying to cram into my life right now. What's great about it all? I don't think anyone in the Bible was ready either. I think we just have to be willing to take the leap while God does the rest.

When I got out of the truck at Denise's place, I met Michelle for the first time. Emotions of gratefulness, indebtedness, and overwhelming love flooded my heart and soul. It was amazing to finally get to hug the neck of the women who helped me through the last few months. We have a bond like no other bond I've had before, sharing our journey with heavenly angels who fought the good fight here on earth. Their lives were short, yet they continue to impact others as we tell their stories.

Next, Denise walked toward me carrying little Trishtan. I wasn't prepared for the rush of emotions, ranging from owning my loss of Lilian to the pure joy of meeting this precious gift for the first time. Deep down, I had thought that meeting another T18 baby girl who resembled Lilian in a lot of ways might just take away the pain of missing her and fill the hole. I knew better, as nothing or no one can replace my lil' girl. Denise placed Trishtan in my arms, and I immediately knew...she wasn't Lilian Grace.

Lily is imprinted on my heart and soul, and no one can replace her, not even another one of my own children. They each leave their own fingerprints on us. I could feel another rip in my heart start to heal. I wouldn't wonder anymore if something would come close to filling that hole. God is so good in the healing process. I have many more rips to heal, but it's a start.

When talking with the girls and the news people, I was blown away by God's plan. He really is magnificent at making things work for the good. ABC actually put our story on the Houston news. I know Denise is so appreciative that I gave her my milk, and we got to share the goodness with the rest of Houston and beyond to those who watched the segment.

Holding another miracle

Behind the scenes of *Donor Milk: The Documentary*

I've even had many people send messages telling me how great I am. All I can say is I am appreciative of Denise. I would have been miserable if she hadn't accepted my milk because I would have had to throw it away. I'm the one who should be thanking a million people instead of getting all the thank you's and uplifting words. It feels good to give on behalf of my daughter, knowing she gets to keep blessing others even after her death. I'm the luckiest and most blessed woman and mother. By the way, I want to thank you all for being so encouraging with your words. I feel blessed to call you my friends.

The weekend didn't stop there. I had the privilege of meeting the Ramos family (daughter Darcy, earned her wings, T18), Freeman family (son Christopher, thirteen years old, T13), Nana Nancy March (granddaughter Addison, earned her wings, T18), Anderson family (son Rhyder, earned his wings, T18), Denise Williams (daughter Trishtan, five months, T18), and Don and Birdie (granddaughter Trishtan). I'm amazed by these incredible families, and I'm happy to be part of the Houston Trisomy 18/13 Circle of Friends first-ever meeting. Thanks, Lilian! You and Rhyder made this possible!

Quick note: Tracy Ramos has written a book called *Letters to Darcy*. It's on my list of things to read. I'm truly blessed by our meeting and look forward to another visit in the future with them and the other families. My world became a little less lonely.

As I looked around the room with all our families together, I could feel God smiling down on us as He works in our lives. It's incredible to be a part of it. It's natural to want to curl up and die when something tragic happens. Loss has many identities for us all. It's not just in death where loss lives. It breathes through shattered dreams, divorce, life choices of family members, job loss, and many other things.

God has reminded me that you don't have to lose a child to know what I'm going through. When you lose your hopes and dreams, you have a taste of what it's like to lose a child. Anything in life where you were moving forward one day and then not the next gives you a connection. Loss is not fun and will try to control, numb, and paralyze you if given a chance.

There are going to be bad days. Even after having such a phenomenal weekend, I still went through rough patches today. Many amazing moments this weekend kept me from letting the bad control, numb, and paralyze me. I'll keep marching forward because God has a plan!

SEPTEMBER 9, 2010

95 › A Prayer for Trishtan

My heart is breaking as memories flood my spirit, almost drowning me. All my prayer warriors, baby Trishtan needs prayer right now. Her mom, Denise Williams, sent me a text stating Trishtan's oxygen levels have dropped, and she's got lots of mucus. They are headed to Texas Children's Hospital. The wounds are very fresh from my Lilian Grace's experiences. The pain and sorrow are great when your child suffers. There's nothing to do except lift them up in prayer and repeat as I have a thousand times: I trust You, God! I trust You, God! I trust You, God!

Just a few minutes ago, I hugged Michael tightly through my tears and told him I didn't even know how to pray for them. He prayed for God's grace to be with them. Now that I am more put together, I can add to our prayer.

Heavenly Father...Daddy...You are magnificent beyond words. I come to You tonight and ask for Your grace and mercy. May Your will be done for Denise and baby Trishtan as You bring peace and comfort to both of them along with the doctors, nurses, and other hospital staff. You have not brought them this far to leave them now. Hold them tightly and carry them through this trial. Keep them safe from this storm that has shown up out of the blue. I love You, Lord, with all I could ever be and more. May evil have no place as You draw up Your sword and defeat it. Let nothing harm them while You guide and direct everyone involved. You are the almighty provider. Thank You. In Your glorious name, Jesus. Amen.

Tears...breathe, Chrissy. I trust You, God! I trust You,

God! I trust You, God! Peace. Contentment. One more wound starts to heal. Oh, the memories that turn from dark to light. Lord, be with the Williams and pour Your love over them tonight as You know what is best. More tears stream down. I'm breathing now. This hits really close to home. Oh, Lord, I love You. I love them. I trust You!

SEPTEMBER 12, 2010

96 › Compassion for Parents

God caught me off guard today by blessing me with so many messages from you all. Thank you to everyone who sent me a message recently. You stepped aside so He could fill me up again. I seem to be going full force these days, and today was my day to stop, reflect, and redirect my thoughts. I was running almost on empty, which is easy to do if you don't fill up.

I'm so excited about what God has in store for me, yet I still have moments where it all feels like too much. There's a mixture of sadness and pain as well that sometimes overshadows my excitement. I pray I won't go so fast that I miss the journey the way I see many others doing. Distractions galore keep us from God's will. I googled "God's will" and found a song with that title by Martina McBride.

This song reminded me of Michael's and my visit to Orange Leaf on Friday when we saw a mother with her disabled son. He was in a wheelchair with a strap wrapped around his head and attached to the chair. He stared into space, not able to talk or walk or barely move. My heart broke, and I cried inside as I thought about my precious Lilian Grace. She was a prize in every way, but I knew she would have needed assistance with almost everything. I humbly come to you tonight to say it would have broken my heart to watch her year after year in this state. I would have taken the journey and made it a blast along the way, but it would have been hard.

I see kid after kid with different challenges. I think about how much stronger their parents are than I could ever be. They are my heroes as they live every day, come what may, with their special babies. I can't even imagine what those families go through as they juggle various disabilities, but I see a mother's heart and mind seeking the positive while giving her child as normal a life as possible.

These parents teach me that life is what you make it. Day after day, they fight for normalcy, for whatever normal is in this world and theirs. It has to be exhausting, yet they do it with such grace and love. They don't miss a beat. Wow! God definitely gives these special babies to warriors. Please join me in praying for a special touch for the children who fight for their lives and want to be accepted. Also, remember their families and caretakers who need all the filling up they can get.

If you know anyone with a special needs child (or any child for that matter), give them some help. Being a parent is hard, and no one should do it alone. My life is blessed more than I can fathom, and I don't want to take it for granted. God is a giant among giants. He makes me smile every day even through my tears.

Continue to lift up my trisomy 18/13 families whose babies are struggling. I've grown close to these families and know their hearts are heavy right now. Pray someone is there to wipe away their tears and just love on them. May their babies get extra special care. May they be healed. May their purpose be fulfilled letting God's light shine bright and expanding His kingdom.

SEPTEMBER 13, 2010

97 › Lily's Platform

One of my dearest friends thought of me today and sent me the song "Whatever You're Doing (Something Heavenly)" by Sanctus Real. How amazing that it describes my life to a T right now. Moving on is never easy, and it doesn't mean I'm forgetting about all the goodness. I'm just not going to be stuck in the sorrow and sadness. I can't escape all the emotions, but I can feel them when they arise and release their hold on me. I look forward to what He's going to do with my brokenness and weakness. I want to live in the joy of all things.

Yesterday's Grandparents Day was tough for me. I always call my own grandparents, but I couldn't, and I feel horrible about it. I just can't seem to call. I'm not ready. I've decided I will pick a day coming up to make it special. Right now, I need to process that I had plans for both Michael and my parents for this special day that didn't get to happen. I was going to proceed with the plans until I was stopped by my own grief. I can't fully explain it, but I decided it was time to deal with things just like the song says. There will be a time I need to clean some things out, but I'm not ready for that step yet, and I'm okay with that.

Also, we are going to be featured in the *Tulsa World*. People we have never met will learn about our unique and miraculous adventure. Matt Gleason, *Tulsa World* feature writer, and I spent somewhere between one to two hours on a phone interview. Even though I've shared Lily's story many times, I still got emotional and shed more tears while talking to him.

God is so good. Matt asked the right questions. I loved sharing Lilian Grace's stories and our adventures together; there just wasn't enough time to tell it all. Referring back to the song, God provides peace even as I continue to struggle with the chaos inside. Life doesn't always make sense, but I acknowledge God is still in control because there's no way I have it this together on my own.

When I hear other mothers talking about babies and pregnancies, I smile and laugh with the thought of my experience. I really had the worst pregnancy ever, but I had the most amazing child to make up for it. Some memories hurt, but I know they have been made for good. I pray I live out God's plans. I'll keep you updated on all the projects. It's crazy how fast life is moving, but I love being in God's will.

God's making so many cool things happen by helping me step aside and start to follow up on things. The devil came up in conversation tonight, and I'm telling you that the devil picked the wrong momma to mess with, and I'm not stopping! It's a scary place yet very empowering at the same time. I've talked about Job previously in regard to our kindred spirits. I know exactly how he survived the worst of the worst. He had no other way but to look up and trust God to get him through things.

SEPTEMBER 14, 2010

98 › Between the Bumpers

Why have I been staying up so late? Well, last night I got my answer. For the first time since we've been back from our trip, I actually went to bed early. The harder I tried to close my eyes and drift to sleep, the more I pictured the day Lilian Grace earned her wings. While in the moment, that day was a blessed one, reliving it isn't as grand. Each time I see her leave us over and over, my heart breaks a little more. Viewing the past is more of a nightmare than a blessing. I cried silently while Michael was in the other room with no idea what was happening to me.

It was really hard, and I didn't know what to do with myself. I only want to remember that day as a precious moment where I sent my daughter to the arms of Jesus. I don't want to continuously feel the loss, but it may be this way for a long time. I will persevere and trust God, hoping to close my eyes tonight and see only light and happiness and Lilian Grace in my dreams.

Now that would be nice—to see her in my dreams playing, running, and growing up. Ah, I'm thinking about her beauty and His magnificent ways, and I'd love to see her and Jesus living it up. I love imagination and could visualize them all day and night. On another note...

Today, I had to do another hard task as I was honored with the Impact 4-H Club appreciation luncheon invite. This luncheon is held annually for the 4-H staff. It was so good to see those who had supported us through prayer and thoughts. It was bittersweet for me because I miss the kids and parents I connected with on a deeper level.

I want to thank the families from Impact 4-H Club for including me in such an amazing appreciation dinner. I no longer work at the 4-H office, but you made me feel like I'm still part of the family. You have no idea how this has touched my heart, but it meant everything to me.

After talking to one of my dearest friends, God confirmed I'm headed in the direction He set forth for me. Though at times I may wonder what in the world is happening and why it's happening all at once, I know He's omnipotent, providing a way and a million blessings.

I see God making things happen in my life in order to keep me moving forward in His plan. There are moments I wish I could go back and do things the way I used to do them. I told a few moms today that it's like my life is a bowling game. God's got the bumper rails up so I can't go off the lane or in the gutter. Thinking about life this way makes me smile that He's answering my prayers and loving me so much. Someone later said if I went back to how things were, it would be like having no bumper rails, meaning I wouldn't be where He wants me to be.

I know I am far from having it together. God puts a mirror in front of me all the time so I can see those things I don't want to deal with. I'm not always ready to work on them at the time, but I know I will have to at one time or another.

Hopefully, my rambling gives you something to think about right now. Just know when you stay in God's will, He provides what you need. He even gave me a refund check and a personal donation, which will cover both of my tickets for upcoming trips to New York and Arizona. Praise God for providing! I'm tickled to see just how this adventure goes, hoping the not-so-fun stuff will be at a minimum. I looked up Bible verses about God's provision to remind me what He says. A big theme is that God alone is my strength. I need to make cards and memorize the following verses:

Memory Verses 18-23

⚔ *"Look to the LORD and his strength; seek his face always" (1 Chronicles 16:11).*

⚔ *"...Do not grieve, for the joy of the LORD is your strength" (Nehemiah 8:10).*

⚔ *"The Lord is my light and my salvation—whom shall I fear? The Lord is the stronghold of my life—of whom shall I be afraid?" (Psalm 27:1).*

⚔ *"The Sovereign LORD is my strength; he makes my feet like the feet of a deer, he enables me to go on the heights" (Habakkuk 3:19).*

⚔ *"But the Lord stood at my side and gave me strength, so that through me the message might be fully proclaimed and all the Gentiles might hear it" (2 Timothy 4:17).*

⚔ *"If anyone speaks, he should do it as one who speaks the very words of God. If anyone serves, they should do so with the strength God provides, so that in all things God may be praised through Jesus Christ. To him be the glory and the power for ever and ever. Amen" (1 Peter 4:11).*

I'm praying God will reveal Himself and His will to you. Jump on board! Beware! The ride goes all over, but if you stay on the track, you'll be blessed. I love you all!

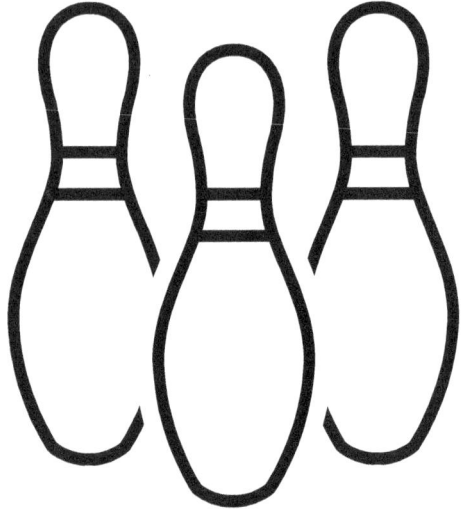

SEPTEMBER 17, 2010

99 › Tears Fall in New York City

What I'm about to write may seem strange to you, but I'm going to put it on here anyway. I still carry a little bit of Lilian Grace's cremains with me. It's only a tiny bit that looks like white sand. The rest of her cremains are still at the funeral home because I haven't been able to go get them.

I'm not sure why we haven't picked her up yet. I know when I get back from my NYC trip with my brother, we have no choice. It doesn't matter anymore if we are ready or not because Michael and I will be out of state when our sixty days is up. Yes, we have only sixty days to find enough strength to return to the funeral home and gather her cremains. Guess it makes it more real that she isn't here anymore. "Out of sight, out of mind" really is true. Perhaps this is why we haven't picked her up yet. Anyway, please lift Michael and me up in prayer to have peace about finally making it happen. It's going to be a tough day.

Back to carrying Lilian with me. Today, I did two things I wish I could have done with Lilian Grace—I went to Central Park and the FAO Schwarz toy store. Walking through Central Park, I thought about how wonderful it would have been to watch Lilian Grace play on all the fabulous playgrounds. I watched the kids play hard—laughing, jumping, pushing, grabbing, hopping, smiling. I know Lilian's laugh would have been sweeter than honey! Oh, how this brought tears to my eyes!

Going into the toy store may not have been my smartest move. Still, I felt as if Lilian were with me. I actually caught myself talking to her off and on as I glanced at the oversized stuffed giraffes, elephants, monkeys, and others in their animal kingdom display and wall of Muppets at the Muppet Whatnot Workshop station. I thought I might be losing it finally, but I think I handled myself well. My brother and I went to the basement where all the baby stuff was displayed. My heart caught in my chest as I stared at all the baby toys while he went to the bathroom. Tears rolled down my cheeks, both then and now, but no one noticed as I wiped them away. I managed to gather myself before my brother returned using some yoga breaths and reminding myself that God is with me. He asked if I was okay. His thoughtfulness touched me, and I told him I was better now.

Going through those two places wasn't as hard as it could have been. I think that's the hardest part about all this—not knowing when I will react. No one ever tells you it can happen in a second. Grief comes in waves at any given moment. It's okay to cry. It's okay to talk to yourself. It's okay to think about them. It's okay! I say that to remind myself. There's no guidebook to prepare for this.

I remember on day seventeen when a nurse handed me a folder with pamphlets about grief, planning a funeral, trying again, and more. I wondered if this were really happening. Was my daughter really going to die? Could they be wrong? Could I be in a nightmare? Who died and made them God? Thankfully, I did not need that material until 103 days later. I took all that information into perspective and decided to live life out loud until it was over.

Being in NYC with my daughter's cremains does not bring her back, yet it reminds me that I can think about what life would be like if she'd lived. I know one day God will call me home, too, and what a day that will be. Oh, what a day that will be! Until then, I will keep living life to the fullest because we are not guaranteed one more second, hour, or day. Love and prayers to everyone.

Memory Verse 24

🗡 *"He will wipe every tear from their eyes. There will be no death or mourning or crying or pain, for the old order of things has passed away" (Revelation 21:4).*

SEPTEMBER 20, 2010

100 › Reflecting on Balance

After I get home, I want to tell you all about the two Broadway shows I watched yesterday. Right now, I want to share a lesson I learned when I was hurt by something and found myself in the hotel stairwell weeping last night.

Don't spend your life sacrificing your time and family for anything. Make sure you get your priorities straight. People will use you until they can't use you anymore. I feel like the time I gave wasn't wasted, but I also feel like I became non-existent in a heartbeat to something I gave so much of myself to. This can happen to anybody at any time for anything in your life.

I guess I've been hit in the face with the reality of staying balanced. I've known how amazing and patient my husband has been when it comes to my commitments. I've put so many things in front of him, but he's always there when things come crashing down around me. I wouldn't change anything I've committed to, but I need to make sure I reach a balance. There's no need to let those commitments take over my life.

Feeling non-existent hurts, but I also miss Lilian Grace even more than before. When you are finally forced to slow down and face unwanted feelings, things get more real. There's never a good time to face reality.

Today, two special T18 babies celebrated their heavenly birthdays. My heart aches for their mommies and their families. I thank God He gave me the vision for Lilian's race no matter if she lived or not. I know organizing the Warrior

Princess Challenge for April 25, 2011, will help me survive that day. I figure her birthday, her heavenly birthday, the fifth of every month, and the twenty-fifth of every month will be my tougher days for an X amount of time.

To relieve some of the pain, I've decided to plan something for these special days. Lilian Grace, a true miracle from above, deserves to see her mommy and daddy celebrating her life instead of being sad and lonely. Though this sadness is inescapable, I will do my best to have a positive outlook and do things instead of curling up and shutting others out. Let me just say, shutting people out would be easier to do.

Last night, I told God I wanted out of it all. I was done! It would be so much easier just to forget it all. Well, God heard me, and He won't let me check out. He filled me up with words of encouragement from special people who wrote to me this morning. He is so Big and so good to me. I just love Him and praise Him on high. I will keep moving forward even when I want to quit because He will never leave me behind or let me wander into the wilderness of no return. Love you all!

SEPTEMBER 22, 2010

101 › Crown of Beauty

For forty-eight days since my baby girl earned her wings, I've feared and dreaded the day I must pick up the remainder of her ashes at the funeral home. We've wanted to go many times, but we were frozen. Michael made it to the parking lot at least three times, but he couldn't make himself get out of the car. There were so many days I wanted to go get her, but I just couldn't find the strength to do it.

I know the closer we've gotten to this day, the harder it's been emotionally for the both of us. I was afraid I might finally lose it. I thought I might not make it out of the funeral home myself. I thought I wouldn't have the strength—this makes it more real. Reality bites, or so I thought.

When Michael and I drove to Broken Arrow tonight, I carried a bundle of emotions with me: loneliness, separation, anxiety, death, reality, tears, stress, anger, and more. I wasn't mad at anyone. I was just angry I couldn't get it together until now. Why in the world would I leave Lily's ashes for forty-eight days when all I wanted was for her to be with me forever?

I understand why more now. She's not here anymore. She's in a better place. I know this, but it doesn't make all my feelings, emotions, and desires fade away. Until tonight. Our funeral guy graciously helped us prepare for her celebration service while he was on vacation. Tonight, we ended up with another lady who was just as wonderful. While waiting for my daughter's cremains, I cried. Memories from her life rushed over me—my pregnancy, her life, her death, the grieving process.

I grabbed one Kleenex after another, overwhelmed with emotion. I'd dreaded closing the door on this day so another one would open. But we weren't alone! I know deep down Lilian Grace and Jesus were there in spirit, comforting us and giving us strength.

While I went into the other room to pick out the urn and the jewelry pieces for her ashes, Michael stayed in the small waiting room. He wept like I hadn't seen before. I love him so much. She really was a daddy's girl. He loved her more than anything. And oh, how she looked at him. It was phenomenal to watch a daddy connect in a deeper way with his little girl. My tears flow now as I remember the moment.

I cried all the way into the other room. I apologized to the lady. Why? I'm not sure. I guess I thought I shouldn't be crying anymore after forty-eight days. Shouldn't the crying stop? No, I don't think so. The lady reminded me of something I usually tell people. She said, "Honey, don't apologize for crying. It's God's way of letting you get it out. This is not easy."

She was right. I remembered reading about people trying to comfort those who have lost someone. They either say the wrong things or don't say anything at all because they're afraid. Well, if anyone wonders what to say, the best thing is just to let them know you are thinking about them. You don't have to say everything. Just something to help them know you love or care for them. It's that easy.

Anyway, she asked me how Michael was doing. I told her that he's broken as am I. You don't go through something like this without it leaving a mark. You bear a new look. You feel different, and you are never the same after something like this. For better or worse, you are changed, and there's no going back. Now you know more than you ever wanted to know about life, death, and the grieving process.

After picking out the urn (a beautiful blue-green) and two pieces of jewelry, we waited while Lilian Grace's ashes were moved into her resting places. There wasn't very much. When the pieces were placed into our hands, I felt relief, as if I had feared the wrong things. This wasn't a bad thing. It was just one more part of the journey where we needed to release the things being held in.

As Michael and I walked out together, we saw a family grieving for a young girl who had passed. The grieving period was just starting for them. I pray they hold tightly to God because it's tough. When we walked out, small raindrops fell on us. We just looked at each other, smiled, and then looked up. Lilian Grace was there with us just like she was during her celebration service.

God provides and provides and provides. Praise His name to the highest mountain and beyond! It was a beautiful moment. We drove to the little waterfall and put out the jewelry, urn, travel bag, and rose (provided by the funeral home) and took pictures. I have one with the urn and waterfall that's as gorgeous as can be.

Through it all, I found a deeper peace. I don't know what tomorrow will be like, but picking her up was wonderful in every way. I love God's timing, even if I don't agree all the time. He knows exactly what we can handle, and He gives us His strength when we can't handle it. It's so cool how He works. We find strength in the following verses:

Memory Verses 25-29

"For I am the LORD your GOD who takes hold of your right hand and says to you, Do not fear; I will help you" (Isaiah 41:13).

⚔ *"Be strong and courageous. Do not be afraid or terrified because of them, for the Lord your God goes with you; he will never leave you nor forsake you"* (Deuteronomy 31:6).

⚔ *"Have I not commanded you? Be strong and courageous. Do not be afraid; do not be discouraged, for the LORD your GOD will be with you wherever you go"* (Joshua 1:9).

♛ *"And provide for those who grieve in Zion—to bestow on them a **crown** of beauty instead of ashes, the oil of joy instead of mourning, and a garment of praise instead of a spirit of despair. They will be called oaks of righteousness, a planting of the LORD for the display of his splendor"* (Isaiah 61:3, boldface added by author).

⚔ *"Come to me, all you who are weary and burdened, and I will give you rest"* (Matthew 11:28).

Whatever your journey is right now, know He has your back. He's holding your hand, and you can let those tears loose one drop at a time, clearing out the damage inside. Be courageous in Him and know you can do all things through Him.

I love you all! Thank you for paying attention and continuing to read what this mother has to say. I know God is not done with me yet. There are greater things to come.

Rest in Peace

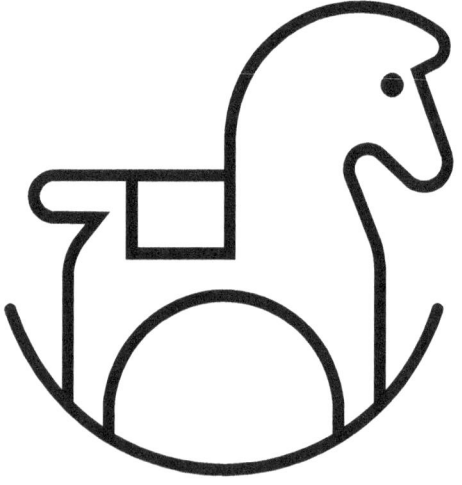

SEPTEMBER 25, 2010

102 › Missing My Cowgirl

Though Lilian Grace, my precious little angel, is no longer here, I can't help but think about what today, her five-month birthday, would have been like for her. The theme was going to be OSU all the way with orange, black, and white. Since it's football season, we wanted to celebrate in style. She was our Cowgirl!

I had set aside OSU blankets, outfits, burp rags, shoes, a specialty hat, and a book in preparation. At least we had the chance to take her picture with most of it after she earned her wings. I stare at her picture and wish she could be here to celebrate today. Man, this sucks no matter which way you look at it.

I had to figure out how to keep it together today while taking a certification test. Before the test, we went over the cardiovascular and respiratory systems. I put on my fake smile so the tears and pain wouldn't show. All I could picture was Lilian's poor little heart from the echoes, ultrasound pictures, and heart diagrams that explained how much of a struggle my squeaker faced. Plus, I can't forget the breathing problems she had even with oxygen.

I did make it through and passed the test. I pictured my Warrior Princess fighting the heart and respiratory conditions, surviving, and living out God's purpose for her life as she went through the deepest valley. If she did it, then I need to keep trying.

When I got home, Michael and I went to Walmart. I'd like to say, if our grocery list could talk, it'd probably tell you today has been more stressful than we've let on. This list includes A & W Root Beer, Sausalito milk chocolate macadamia cookies, Cocoa Pebbles, tortillas, milk, Cinnamon Toast Crunch, blueberry muffin top Pop Tarts, Velveeta cheese, Hershey's bar with almonds, strawberry banana yogurt, and trash bags.

Hello, comfort food! The problem with junk food is that it leaves you with a horrible tummy ache and feeling worse. Only God can make me feel better. Amen! We also enjoyed a good one, two, three scream-at-the-top-of-your-lungs in the car about five times. So where are you? Count to three, then scream-as-loud-as-you-can. Ready...one, two, three...AHHHH! This is great for the soul. Repeat as many times as needed to reduce stress and/or pain!

I wish I could have a five-month picture of Lilian Grace, but I have to settle for my NILMDTS photo after she passed. She's still as beautiful as can be, forever in our minds as a precious little baby. Please join me in prayer:

Dear Heavenly Father, we come to You today in awe of You and Your miraculous ways. Thank You for always providing for us even when we get distracted in our everyday lives. You make getting out of bed worth it. Today would have been a very special accomplishment for Lilian Grace, but You decided she would make the grandest accomplishment of all when she left this earth fifty-two days ago.

Thank You for making her exit so beautiful and breathtaking. You made her life more magnificent than most I've known. You let the most amazing Warrior Princess join our family exactly five months ago. You turned the worst thing that could ever happen to us into the most miraculous adventure any of us has ever taken. You made her life for good by teaching us how You provide and comfort every day.

We lift up all the children, families, medical staff, and

anyone else who needs it. We lift them all up in prayer for You to pour Your love all over them. May You continue to bring people into their lives who show Your love, comfort, guidance, and whatever else they need. Everyone deserves to be surrounded by a team who battles against the evil, the pain, and the sorrow and who shares the joy and the breathtaking moments.

Father, thank You for helping us each start to heal where wounds run deep. The Lilian Grace adventure was one battle after another, but it was worth it all. Every single wound was worth it. We love You with every part of ourselves. Please give strength, comfort, and peace to everyone who is hurting and healing. In Your most precious and glorious name. Amen!

You may be battling your own hardships. Hold tightly to God because there will be good days and really bad days. He knows exactly what's going on even when we have no words, no clue how to answer when asked how you are doing, no idea how deep the hurt runs. Thank God, He knows! We must be willing to let go of the hurt and release what has been done. He is the One who is going to make it all better.

I will be the first to say that I don't get my words right with people. I harbor things I shouldn't. I have many hurts I need to let go of and let God take care of. I'm not ready for some of it, but I'm going to slowly start releasing them one at a time. There are many layers to my grieving. Time will keep marching as I do my best to get through each of the layers. One of my dearest friends reminded me that I have to walk through, not around, the hard times...through the grief. I don't get to skip that part. Facing each layer will not be fun, but God gave me one, two, three scream-as-loud-as-you-can for release.

My dear friend. Yes, you! You don't have to do everything in one night. Just start walking forward. Here are some really good verses I found at https://www.whatchristianswanttoknow.com/20-bible-verses-to-comfort-the-hurting/ about comforting the hurting. May God walk you through your journey. I love you!

Memory Verses 30-33

🗡 *"You have kept count of my tossings; put my tears in your bottle. Are they not in your book?" (Psalm 56:8 ESV).*

🗡 *"But the Helper, the Holy Spirit, whom the Father will send in my name, he will teach you all things and bring to your remembrance all that I have said to you. Peace I leave with you; my peace I give to you. Not as the world gives do I give to you. Let not your hearts be troubled, neither let them be afraid" (John 14:26–27 ESV).*

🗡 *"Cast your burden on the LORD, and he will sustain you; he will never permit the righteous to be moved" (Psalm 55:22 ESV).*

🗡 *"The LORD is a stronghold for the oppressed, a stronghold in times of trouble" (Psalm 9:9 ESV).*

Before I forget, I need to share this photo of my daughter dressed in her Cowgirl gear after she earned her wings. Happy five-month birthday, Lilian Grace!

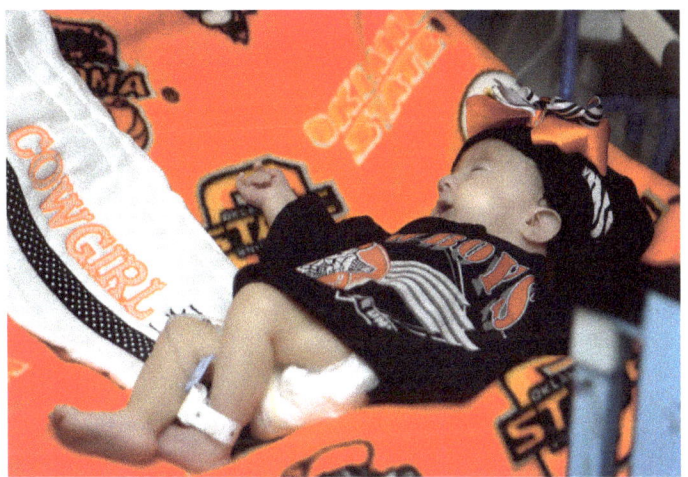

Loyal and True Wherever I Find You!

Baby girl,

I hope you are living it up with Jesus. I wish I could be there with you. I will be one day when He calls me home. Until then, I will think of you often. I may shed a tear here and there but know it's just because I love you so. You make me so proud. The more I think about your time here, the more blown away I am. Even though you were little, you taught me to live life out loud while doing God's will.

Oh, little squeaker, I hope you remember to say hello to your siblings. I hadn't thought of them as much before now, but I know they are there with you. I hope you all are giggling and playing to your heart's content. Someday, we will be together as a family for eternity. I love you, birthday girl!

P.S. Your daddy thinks about you all the time. You filled his heart up to the fullest mark. He has been so good through your departure, but I know he aches to be with you. I promise, we will continue to do the best we can. God has a plan, and we will step aside so He can do it. Love you to the moon and back and for all eternity.

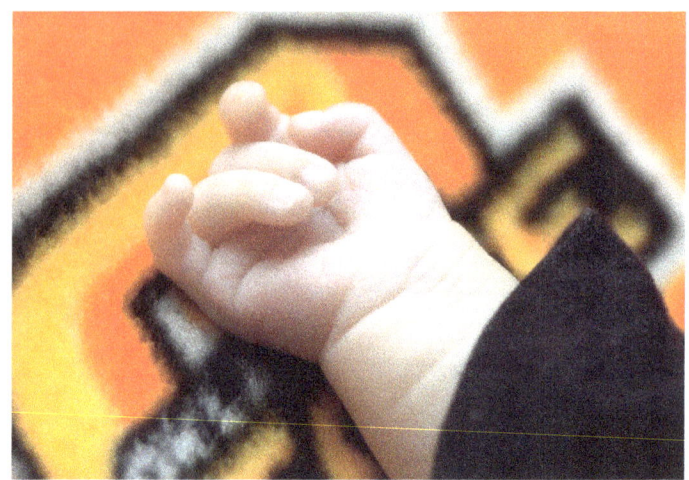

I love you!

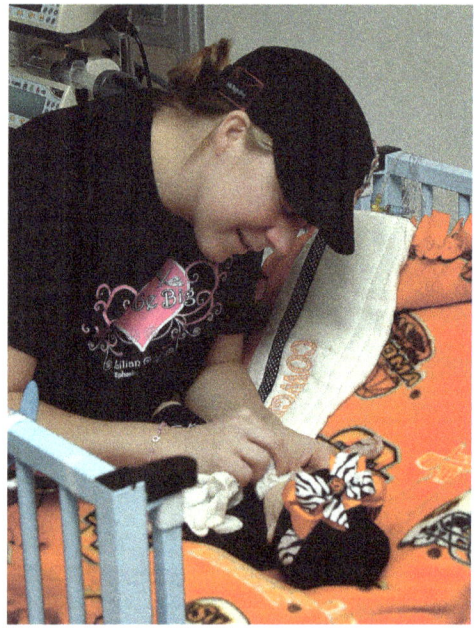

My baby you will always be.

SEPTEMBER 29, 2010

103 › Dust Off and Rise

Things keep coming at me a million miles per hour. Just when I think I'm getting through and gonna be okay—BAM! I get hit again and find myself on the ground. Life seems to be full of trials and tribulations, no matter who we are. I've felt so much pain and witnessed others going through the same pain or deeper. All I can say to anyone going through difficult times is that God will give you the strength you need to get through it.

People, including me, will fail one another. People will promise things and not follow through. People will hurt you even when you have no clue why they could do such a thing. I look back at my time with Lilian Grace, and I smile because I continue to learn from the experience. God used this horrible situation to teach me and many others how to keep going and how to live. He's such an amazing Father who pays attention to details. He's the only one I know who can turn something so bad into something gorgeous and breathtaking.

The Yolanda Adams song "Still I Rise" reminds us we can still rise through the ashes, tears, or wounds. Just when I think I'm rising smoothly, I experience turbulence and fall, finding my butt on the ground once again and my soul wounded.

I picture my heavenly Father reaching down and pulling me up time after time. After rising one more time, I dust myself off. There will be a day when I won't have to get up anymore. Oh, Lord, I cannot wait.

Lilian Grace wasn't able to get up and down physically, but her spirit kept falling down and getting up. She got hit with one trial after another, but she rose to the challenge time after time. I daydream about her struggling and finding enough strength to keep going. If she could have walked, I would have witnessed my Warrior Princess slowly rising after a blow and dusting herself off with a huge smile on her face. She'd march straight toward whatever her trial would be, almost running, to conquer any obstacle by meeting it eye to eye. Her theme song playing in the background would be "We Fall Down" sung by Bob Carlisle.

Whatever is knocking you down right now, let God help you up. Dust yourself off and march forward. People, things, and experiences will try to keep you down. Don't let them win. I know I can't control any one person or situation. I can only control how I respond to my trials or to people who try to hurt me. I have the power not to let them affect me.

I may shed some tears and talk it out, but they will not win. I will fall, get up, dust off, and rise. God Almighty is my strength, and no one can break Him. When I let Him be in control, then I'm able to face whatever comes my way. Are you down, or are you rising up? I pray God gives you the strength, hope, and faith to keep getting up no matter what you face. Love you all!

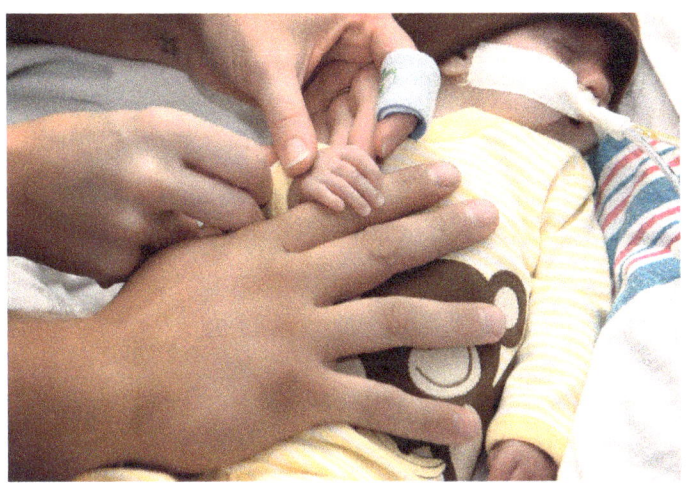
God strengthened our family for the fight.

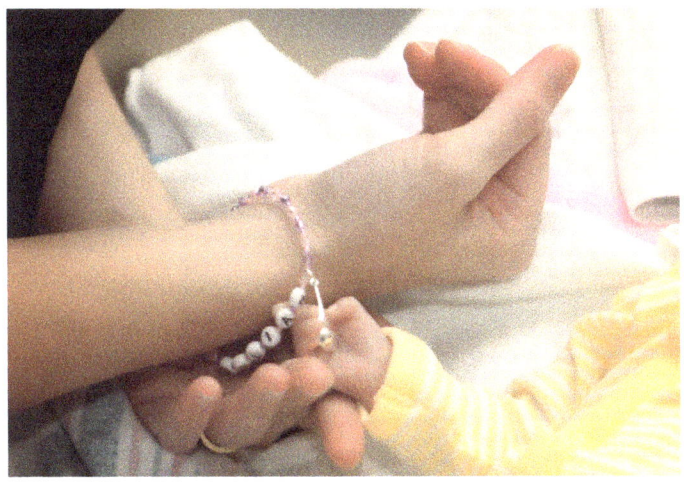
Hold on—this isn't the end. Eternity awaits!

A NOTE FROM THE AUTHOR

Thank you for reading my story. I published this book for parents who are fighting similar battles, for individuals who need encouragement because their dreams have shattered, and to offer my perspective as a warrior angel's mother from the battlefield. My intention is to equip and encourage you for your fight and to remind you to trust God through your journey.

If you found *The Fight* helpful or healing, please recommend it by leaving a review on Amazon, Goodreads, or wherever you browse for books online. Who do you know who might relate to my battles or loss? Lend or gift a copy to them, or donate one to your local hospital or medical office. It's a great resource to include in a care package.

This momma's heart is happy you were able to trek this far with me. I pray my journals help you rise up and fight another day. Hopes and dreams shatter, but know God's grace and strength are sufficient when you rest in Him. You are never alone, and your story's not over yet. You have a purpose to attend to. Let that purpose catapult you from the battlefield forward.

Love and prayers,

Chrissy

BOOK COVER LEGEND

Circle Window

God knows our future. He created each of us in His image. There is a beginning and ending to our story which brings us full circle. Though not a smooth round circle, the curves represent the bumps, turns, and twists on the path along our journey.

› **Conch Shell:** We were awakened to appreciate the present and overcome adversities. The shell is a sign of victory over suffering while prospering in our journey.
› **Colors (gold and iron metal):** These precious metals promote confidence, strength, beautification, purity, growth, protection, healing, and resilience.
› **Lily Flower:** Her name along with the vibrant orange and yellow mix of colors are associated with key words and phrases: innocence, purity, return of happiness, sweetness, humility, love's good fortune, and Christ's second coming.
› **Lily's Heart with Pulse:** Lily's Vitals were often reported in the journal entries. It's the perfect symbol to remember she had a heartbeat and made a difference during a short stint on earth. This icon is throughout the book.
› **Red Cardinal:** The little cardinal is Lily visiting after she earned her wings. There's a legend behind these beautiful birds being visitors from heaven. It seems as if they always show up at the appropriate time.
› **Red Garnet Stones:** The garnet is known as a symbol for love, light, and vitality. Lily's heart beat against all odds. She was a life source telling us to take advantage of the

present and let God guide us. Her inner fire of God's love and energy glowed for others to experience. The six stones are divided in half between the radiant lily to represent the six years and three-and-half months it took to get Lilian here from our wedding date to her birth!

- **Tree of Life:** Michael and I keep our feet rooted in Christ like a tree rooted deep in the ground. He is our source of essentials for survival, and we grow stronger as our relationship with Him matures. Our family trees bear warriors and fighters throughout time with lineage in the Cherokee and Chickasaw tribes. This tree is a symbol of our roots and our intent to keep moving forward with God's strength. We are His warriors, battling whatever confronts us physically or spiritually. Our church and family have been the hands and feet of Jesus reaching out like branches from a tree. They rejuvenate us (at the hospital, at home, and at church) and encourage us to press on each day toward triumph.
- **Boxing Gloves (hanging):** We kept getting punched with one bad news report after another. God gave us boxing gloves (strength) to keep fighting, moving forward, and defeating whatever came against us.
- **Tree Branch Heart:** Love helps things grow and heal. We all need to love and be loved. God's love motivates us to venture on through life. We must provide space for love to exist, grow, and thrive in our lives.
- **Writing on the Tree:** Lilian Grace Whitten will never be forgotten. Her name, birthday (April 25, 2010), and angelversary (August 5, 2010) are carved along the right side of the tree starting from the trunk.

THE FIGHT 329

Door Background

God opens and closes doors while helping us fulfill our purposes in life.

› **Dark Wood Color:** The dark wood color represents the unknowns we face about who, what, where, why, and how throughout our journey. Walking blindly through uncertain times can be a fight in itself.

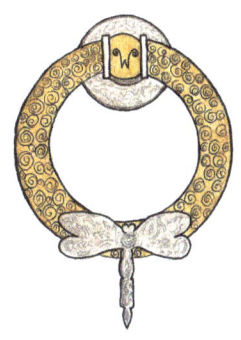
Door Knocker

God loves us unconditionally and wants to give us good gifts. In Mathew 7:7, Jesus reminds us to ask, seek, and find the door that we are meant to go through in His wisdom and timing.

› **Arrows (within wings and body of dragonfly):** Continue moving forward. Allow God to lead you. It may seem like a dance of two steps forward and five steps back, but His timing is perfect. He will open doors when the time is right.
› **Circle Ring:** In life, we sometimes circle back to where we began, but we are wiser and changed for the better.
› **Dragonfly:** Jesus carries us toward our purpose. Never stop trusting Him, because He knows our future.
› **Swirls:** The twists and turns along our journey can be a whirlwind of confusion and distraction. We must be persistent in seeking God's will.
› **W:** This letter represents the weariness of trudging through hard times. God's will is not an easy path, yet He

opens doors when we knock.

Dragonflies symbolize change. Change is inevitable. Without change, we can't evolve into the person God created us to be. To change is to level up in the game of life and grow wiser because of our experiences.

Dragonfly

› **Boxing Gloves:** The gloves on the wing tips point to God in praise for giving us His strength and enabling us to persevere in the daily fight.
› **Colors (gold, purple, red, teal, and yellow):** The overall color scheme communicates love, success, compassion, strength, courage, wisdom, passion, serenity, growth, loyalty, joy, remembrance, and clarity.
› **Flying Position:** When a dragonfly's wings are open in flight, it creates a cross. This reminds me of Jesus, who paid the price for us as He hung on the cross. He carries us through hard times just as He carried His own cross.
› **Gold Heart:** Though Lilian was a baby, she had a heart of gold and a beautiful spirit that radiated from within.
› **Purple Lilies:** Just like our Lilian, purple lilies are known to be rare and exclusive. Many of us were in awe of God for her abilities and accomplishments in the face of adversity.
› **Red Circles:** The three circles represent the Trinity: God the Father, God the Son (Jesus Christ), and God the Holy Spirit. Each provide protection, strength, wisdom, and comfort in their own way.
› **Swirls:** The whirlwind of storms we faced before, during, and after Lilian Grace arrived is illustrated by the swirls in the tail of the dragonfly. We were tossed and thrown all

over the place.

› **Upside-Down Teardrop:** Lilian's pupils were the shape of upside-down teardrops. We cried more tears than we ever thought possible during our short time with her. It also reminds me of how we compared the crazy upside-down circumstances to our normal.

› **W:** The letter W on the gold heart represents our weaknesses. "Three times I pleaded with the Lord to take it away from me. But he said to me, 'My grace is sufficient for you, for my power is made perfect in weakness'" (2 Corinthians 12:8–9). A wonderful reassurance that when we are weak, He is strong.

This keyhole represents transitions in life. Sometimes, we hesitate to enter a new stage, but God graciously leads us through doors by reminding us to trust Him. Considering God's eternal perspective propels us forward and helps us adapt to new normals.

Keyhole Plate

› **Butterflies:** Eleven years later, we now have three daughters. To unite and represent our girls, we designed a butterfly for each.

🦋 **Lilian (top right of keyhole):** The pink, yellow, and purple butterfly fits the firstborn of our family. She is tender, loving, compassionate, comforting, kind, and joyful. She proved to be a light from above while inspiring us to look to God in all things. She was His little missionary.

🦋 **Piper (top left of keyhole):** The teal and lime green butterfly mirrors our middle daughter. She is graceful, sincere, compassionate, empathetic, and calm. She has proven to be a wonderful rainbow baby who is full of harmony and hope as she influences our interpretations, expresses her creativity, and opens her heart to those around her.

🦋 **Daphne (right of keyhole):** The pink, teal, lime green, and dark purple butterfly portrays our baby girl. These colors parade her personality! She is independent, bold, courageous, sympathetic, playful, intuitive, and ambitious. She has proven to be a fabulous completion to our family with her ability to help us learn and grow through patience, understanding, and persistence.

› **Letter L (above red heart):** Lilian's first initial and Mom's middle initial (Larie´)

› **Red Heart:** Love never fails!

› **Swirls:** The whirlwind of storms we faced before, during, and after Lilian Grace arrived is illustrated by the swirls on the top and bottom of the keyhole plate. We were tossed and thrown all over the place.

› **Two Hearts (bottom of the plate):** Dad and Mom united to make Lily, a branch of our family.

› **Vines:** God is our vine, our source of strength and nourishment to live and bear fruit.

God provides what we need to open doors. These keys enable us to fulfill our purposes and are the tools that help us succeed in bringing God glory.

Skeleton Key

› **Blooming Lily (middle of stem):** Against all odds, Lilian prospered and let her light shine as she bloomed into her purpose. The orange color is a blaze of emotional strength on our part as we tried to remain positive and optimistic.

› **Butterflies:** The metamorphosis from caterpillar to butterfly exemplifies new beginnings. Michael, Lilian, and I each had our own flight pattern through this experience, but we will be reunited one day in heaven.

🦋 **Michael (lower left):** The blue and lime green butterfly stands for the leader of our family. He is loyal, generous, confident, responsible, and trustworthy. He has proven to be a man we can count on as he supports our family and keeps us balanced through good times and bad.

🦋 **Chrissy (top right):** The purple and teal butterfly characterizes the caregiver of our family. She is compassionate, spiritual, supportive, imaginative, and intentional. She encourages spiritual growth and renewal during hardships and is passionate about making beautiful memories.

🦋 **Lilian (center):** The pink, yellow, and purple butterfly fits the firstborn of our family. She is tender, loving, compassionate, comforting, kind, and joyful. She proved to be a light from above while inspiring us to look to God in all things. She was His little missionary.

› **Cross (in the key ward):** Christ died in our place, sacrificing His life for us. With Him, all things are possible. His grace and mercy cover our shortcomings and power our successes.

› **Iron Metal (color):** Iron is one of the most human metals because it's found in our bodies and promotes growth, confidence, courage, strength, stamina, and resilience. We learned how human we are while Lily depended on our family and team for care.

› **Red Garnet Stone (bottom of bow):** Lilian's first month birthday color was red. It represents God's love, Lily's heart, and her favorite book, *The Secret of the Red Shoes*. The illustrator of our book had the honor of reading it to her first. The single stone represents meeting our first living child.

› **Twenty-Five (rotate key 90° to the right):** Lilian's birthday, April 25, 2010, is represented within the key ward. The twenty-fifth of each month reminds us to pray for others as they work through their challenges and purpose.

› **Vines:** God is our vine, our source of strength and nourishment to live and bear fruit.

› **W (top of stem):** W is for Whitten, our family name. Lily will forever be part of the Whitten five—Michael, Chrissy, Lilian, Piper, and Daphne—as we thrive with Jesus by our side.

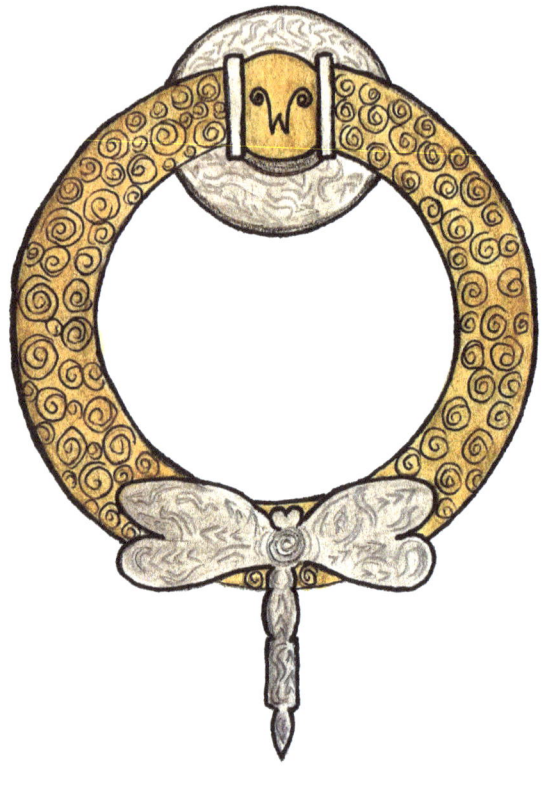

MEMORY VERSES

🗡 *"And I pray that you, being rooted and established in love, may have power, together with all the Lord's holy people, to grasp how wide and long and high and deep is the love of Christ, and to know this love that surpasses knowledge—that you may be filled to the measure of all the fullness of God" (Ephesians 3:17–19).*

🗡 *"And the God of all grace, who called you to His eternal glory in Christ, after you have suffered a little while, will himself restore you and make you strong, firm and steadfast" (1 Peter 5:10).*

🗡 *"The secret things belong to the LORD our God, but the things revealed belong to us and to our children forever, that we may follow all the words of this law" (Deuteronomy 29:29).*

🗡 *"The Lord will guide you always; he will satisfy your needs in a sun-scorched land and will strengthen your frame. You will be like a well-watered garden, like a spring whose waters never fail" (Isaiah 58:11).*

🗡 *"But he gives us more grace. That is why Scripture says: 'God opposes the proud but gives grace to the humble'" (James 4:6).*

🗡 *"Therefore, since we have been justified through faith, we have peace with God through our Lord Jesus Christ, through whom we have gained access by faith into this grace in which we now stand. And we rejoice in the hope of the glory of God.*

🗡 Not only so, but we also glory in our sufferings, because we know that suffering produces perseverance; perseverance, character; and character, hope" (Romans 5:1–4).

🗡 "For you, God, tested us; you refined us like silver. You brought us into prison and laid burdens on our backs. You let people ride over our heads; we went through fire and water, but you brought us to a place of abundance" (Psalm 66:10–12).

🗡 "Come to me, all you who are weary and burdened, and I will give you rest. Take my yoke upon you and learn of me, for I am gentle and humble in heart, and you will find rest for your souls. For my yoke is easy and my burden is light" (Matthew 11:28–30).

🗡 "So that CHRIST may dwell in your hearts through FAITH. And I pray that you, being rooted and established in LOVE, may have power, together with all the Lord's holy people, to grasp how wide and long and high and deep is the love of Christ, and to know this love that surpasses knowledge—that you may be filled to the measure of all the FULLNESS OF GOD" (Ephesians 3:17–19, all caps added by author).

🗡 "Then Jesus declared, 'I am the bread of life. Whoever comes to me will never go hungry, and whoever believes in me will never be thirsty'" (John 6:35).

🗡 "Peace I leave with you; my peace I give you. I do not give to you as the world gives. Do not let your hearts be troubled and do not be afraid" (John 14:27).

🗡 "In peace I will lie down and sleep, for you alone, Lord,

make me dwell in safety" (Psalm 4:8).

⚔ "Even though I walk through the darkest valley, I will fear no evil, for you are with me; your rod and your staff, they comfort me" (Psalm 23:4).

⚔ "For the Spirit God gave us does not make us timid, but gives us power, love and self-discipline" (2 Timothy 1:7).

⚔ "Come to me, all you who are weary and burdened, and I will give you rest. Take my yoke upon you and learn from me, for I am gentle and humble in heart, and you will find rest for your souls. For my yoke is easy and my burden is light" (Matthew 11:28–30).

⚔ "Search me, God, and know my heart; test me and know my anxious thoughts. See if there is any offensive way in me, and lead me in the way everlasting" (Psalm 139:23–24).

⚔ "The God of peace will soon crush Satan under your feet. The grace of our Lord Jesus be with you" (Romans 16:20).

⚔ "Look to the LORD and his strength; seek his face always" (1 Chronicles 16:11).

⚔ "...Do not grieve, for the joy of the LORD is your strength" (Nehemiah 8:10).

⚔ "The Lord is my light and my salvation—whom shall I fear? The Lord is the stronghold of my life—of whom shall I be afraid?" (Psalm 27:1).

🗡 "The Sovereign LORD is my strength; he makes my feet like the feet of a deer, he enables me to go on the heights" (Habakkuk 3:19).

🗡 "But the Lord stood at my side and gave me strength, so that through me the message might be fully proclaimed and all the Gentiles might hear it" (2 Timothy 4:17).

🗡 "If anyone speaks, he should do it as one who speaks the very words of God. If anyone serves, they should do so with the strength God provides, so that in all things God may be praised through Jesus Christ. To him be the glory and the power for ever and ever. Amen" (1 Peter 4:11).

🗡 "He will wipe every tear from their eyes. There will be no death or mourning or crying or pain, for the old order of things has passed away" (Revelation 21:4).

🗡 "For I am the LORD your GOD who takes hold of your right hand and says to you, Do not fear; I will help you" (Isaiah 41:13).

🗡 "Be strong and courageous. Do not be afraid or terrified because of them, for the Lord your God goes with you; he will never leave you nor forsake you" (Deuteronomy 31:6).

🗡 "Have I not commanded you? Be strong and courageous. Do not be afraid; do not be discouraged, for the LORD your GOD will be with you wherever you go" (Joshua 1:9).

👑 "And provide for those who grieve in Zion—to bestow on them a **crown** of beauty instead of ashes, the oil of joy instead of mourning, and a garment of praise instead of a spirit of despair. They will be called oaks of righteousness, a planting of the LORD for the display of his splendor" (Isaiah 61:3, boldface added by author).

⚔ "Come to me, all you who are weary and burdened, and I will give you rest" (Matthew 11:28).

⚔ "You have kept count of my tossings; put my tears in your bottle. Are they not in your book?" (Psalm 56:8 ESV).

⚔ "But the Helper, the Holy Spirit, whom the Father will send in my name, he will teach you all things and bring to your remembrance all that I have said to you. Peace I leave with you; my peace I give to you. Not as the world gives do I give to you. Let not your hearts be troubled, neither let them be afraid" (John 14:26–27 ESV).

⚔ "Cast your burden on the LORD, and he will sustain you; he will never permit the righteous to be moved" (Psalm 55:22 ESV).

⚔ "The LORD is a stronghold for the oppressed, a stronghold in times of trouble" (Psalm 9:9 ESV).

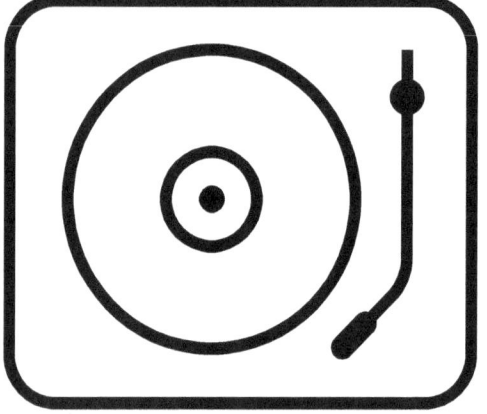

PLAYLIST

- ♪ "Peace" by Watermark
- ♪ "The Motions" by Matthew West
- ♪ "Bring on the Rain" by Jo Dee Messina and Tim McGraw
- ♪ "Lean on Me" by Bill Withers
- ♪ "Happy Birthday" by Patty Hill, Mildred J. Hill, Warren Jones, Martin Katz
- ♪ "Your Grace Is Enough" by Chris Tomlin
- ♪ "Oh, What a Beautiful Mornin'" from *Oklahoma!*
- ♪ "Sweep Me Away" by Kari Jobe
- ♪ "God Bless the U.S.A." by Lee Greenwood
- ♪ "Praise You in This Storm" by Casting Crowns
- ♪ "Untitled Hymn (Come to Jesus)" by Chris Rice
- ♪ "You Are for Me" by Kari Jobe
- ♪ "Come unto Me" by The Bishops
- ♪ "The Family of God" by Bill Gaither
- ♪ "You Are My Sunshine" by Mississippi John Hurt
- ♪ "Go Light Your World" by Kathy Troccoli
- ♪ "One More Round" by BarlowGirl
- ♪ "In Christ Alone" by Michael English
- ♪ "It's My Party" by Lesley Gore
- ♪ "Who Am I" by Point of Grace
- ♪ "Prepare the Way – Live" by Passion and Charlie Hall
- ♪ "Healer" by Kari Jobe
- ♪ "He's Got the Whole World in His Hands" by St. John's Children's Choir
- ♪ "Little Dreamer" by Christina Aguilera

♪ "God's Will" by Martina McBride
♪ "Whatever You're Doing (Something Heavenly)" by Sanctus Real
♪ "Still I Rise" by Yolanda Adams
♪ "We Fall Down" by Bob Carlisle

https://open.spotify.com/playlist/0m5jszKtvcesvGL5n2y81m?si=aab622828c544a19

ACKNOWLEDGEMENTS

To my beautiful Warrior Princesses, Lilian Grace, Piper Allegra, and Daphne Mae: You are forever my sunshine no matter the day. One's in heaven and two are on earth, and no matter where I may find you, I will always love my girls. You bring me such joy and pride in getting to be your mother. I was given a tiny percentage of a chance to become a mother, and God let me meet the three of you. You each are unique, gifted, and talented, and God has great plans for you. You have to trust Him and know He will provide along the way and lead you to His perfect plan.

To my handsome Warrior King, Michael Whitten: Our journey has given us so many reasons to give up. I thank God every day that we haven't quit! I'd do it all over again as long as I knew you'd be by my side leading us into battle. God will always provide. I love you to the moon and back and for all eternity! Thank you for believing in me and making sure I kept a promise I made to God! We are not perfect, but we are getting there with forward motion.

To all our family, friends, and supporters over the decades: I can never thank you enough for your prayers, time, help, calls, messages, participation, friendship, care, concerns, and beyond. This life is not meant to be lived alone. We have an amazing tribe full of believers, and every person fits perfectly on our journey. We have had some hard storms/seasons in a row, but you've been there for us one way or another. I appreciate your thoughtfulness and follow through when it came time for you to step up and share your gifts.

To my team who got me to this finish line: I know you met numerous disruptions and adversities, yet you kept dusting yourselves off and moving forward with me. Thank you for putting up with me when I wasn't willing to let go of certain ideas. I appreciate your willingness to share your incredible, god-given gifts with me and the world. You were chosen and created by Him. I praise Him for getting us together. I think we are a fabulous tribe of believers. I'm very proud of how He shaped this project with each of you helping. I had a long, hard road to get my final team. Each of you were worth all the struggles and disappointments over the last decade that I had to experience to get to you. May God bless you extravagantly on your journeys. He's not done with us yet. We have more books to work on, polish, and share. Buckle up, the ride is waiting!

May God bless you abundantly! Keep being the hands and feet of Jesus. Always show kindness and unconditional love. Do things expecting nothing in return. We have endless possibilities to help make this world better, starting with ourselves and in our homes. You have each proven to us what it's like to have one of our needs filled. We wouldn't be where we are without you. Love you all!

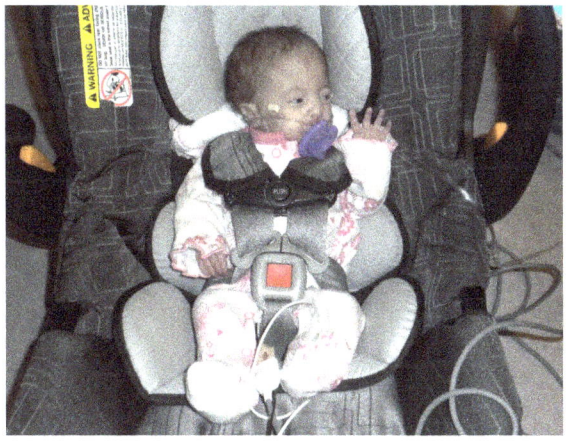

See you again soon!

ABOUT THE AUTHOR

Chrissy L. Whitten holds a bachelor of science in leisure service management and a master of interdisciplinary studies in educational psychology, REMS, and leisure service management from Oklahoma State University (OSU). She has over thirty years' experience working in youth programming and teaching fitness. She grew up in the Cushing and Stillwater, Oklahoma, communities before marrying her husband, Michael, in December 2003.

They lived in Sand Springs, Oklahoma, for fourteen years, where Chrissy was the Tulsa County 4-H extension educator for five years and Juntos 4-H educator for over a year and a half. She founded the Warrior Princess Foundation after Lilian passed away and ran it for five years to raise money for trisomy 13 and 18 children. She organized seven races with Ken TZ Childress. Many donors and volunteers helped with fundraising efforts. It was a healing experience.

Michael's work moved them to Tuttle, Oklahoma, with

their two children (on earth), Piper and Daphne. She enjoys going on adventures around the world with her family, discovering and exploring together. She loves getting involved with her church and volunteering for her girls' schools and extracurricular activities where needed.

She enjoys challenging herself by running ultras—50Ks, fifty milers, seventy milers, hundred milers, and anything in between. She has quite a buckle collection for completing hundreds of miles. Her most recent race, Aravaipa Running's Merry Vertmas, was a virtual treadmill run where she completed 402.7 miles and 318,146 feet at a fifteen percent incline from December 1–25, 2020, in forty-one runs.

Chrissy facilitates Calm Waters Grief student support groups in schools in Blanchard, Bridge Creek, Mustang, Newcastle, Tuttle, Yukon, Oklahoma City Metro, and virtually throughout the state of Oklahoma. She teaches local fitness classes—barre, Pilates, PiYo, kickboxing, yoga, and a fitness mix at Steppin Out Dance Studio. She's excited to get book one of four out into the world despite the countless distractions, adversities, and detours along the journey.

MORE FROM CHRISSY L. WHITTEN

The Fight Reflection Journal

The Fight Reflection Journal is a transformative guide designed to help you navigate life's challenges with faith and resilience. Drawing from each chapter in *The Fight*, this companion journal is filled with reflective prompts and creative activities on topics like loss, relationships, stress, a positive mindset, God's provision, setting goals, and hope for the future. Jump into your own journey of self-discovery and spiritual growth and let *The Fight Reflection Journal* be your key to a fulfilling and purposeful life.

The Fall to the Climb (Book Two)

How does a mother get through the days and months following the loss of her child? In *The Fall to the Climb*, Chrissy continues to chronicle her journey through a valley of loss and grief in 2010 before beginning the climb to a higher hope-filled perspective in 2011. The year after *The Fight* is a whole new wilderness. Chrissy describes how emotions, depression, nighttime, holidays, relational strains, and new endeavors loomed large after losing her baby girl.

If you've experienced loss of any kind, reading Chrissy's CaringBridge posts feels like finding a friend who understands. You'll see how she processed her grief and healed incrementally over the course of that first year.

The Fall to the Climb (book two) is available on Kindle or in paperback. Illustrations by artist Tammy Edwards and photos of the Whitten family are printed in color in the Collector's Edition.

Rainbows and Brainstorms (Book Three)

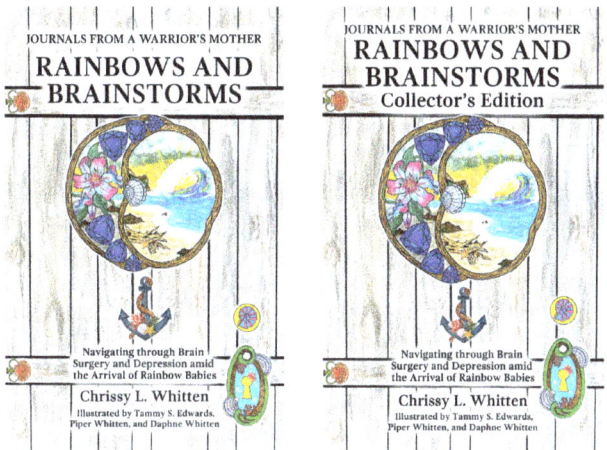

How do you mentally prepare for a surgery you might not survive? Is it possible to be at peace in the face of impending death? Are you battling depression that stems from a heartbreaking loss or a physical affliction? In *Rainbows and Brainstorms*, Chrissy Whitten journals her way through all of it on top of having two rainbow babies.

She describes the difficulty of being torn between the spiritual world (after losing her firstborn daughter) and being present with her second baby, how her faith in Jesus helped her face a life-or-death brain surgery, and how she navigated through headaches and clinical depression following the operation.

With video messages, memory verses, symbolic art, and music included, *Rainbows and Brainstorms* is a rich resource for anyone in need of a lighthouse. Readers will receive wind in their sails and hope for the future.

REVIEW REQUEST

Thank you for purchasing *The Fight*! I hope it encourages and equips you for your fight. I would love to know your thoughts. What did you enjoy? How can you relate? Please take a moment now to leave an honest review on Amazon and Goodreads. Doing so will help others discover the Journals from a Warrior's Mother series.

MORE TO COME

The Fall to the Climb Reflection Journal
Rainbows and Brainstorms Reflection Journal
Triumph over an Aching Heart (Book Four)
Triumph over an Aching Heart Refection Journal

CONNECT

I would love to connect!
You can find me on Facebook and Instagram @chrissylwhitten and at chrissylwhitten.com.
Speaking engagement requests may be sent to chrissylwhitten@gmail.com.

www.ingramcontent.com/pod-product-compliance
Lightning Source LLC
Chambersburg PA
CBHW040422100526
44589CB00022B/2801